D0706716

RETREAT FROM REFORM

RETREAT FROM REFORM

The Prohibition Movement in the United States 1890-1913

JACK S. BLOCKER Jr.

Contributions in American History, Number 51

GREENWOOD PRESS
Westport, Connecticut • London, England

Library of Congress Cataloging in Publication Data
Blocker, Jack S.
   Retreat from reform.

   (Contributions in American history; no. 51)
   Bibliography: p.
   Includes index.
   1. Prohibition--United States--History. 2. Prohibition Party. 3. Anti-
Saloon League of America. 4. Populism--United States--History. I. Title.
HV5089.B63   322.4'4'0973   76-5325
ISBN 0-8371-8899-7

Library of Congress Catalog Card Number: 76-5325
ISBN: 0-8371-8899-7

First published in 1976

Greenwood Press, a division of Williamhouse-Regency Inc.
51 Riverside Avenue, Westport, Connecticut 06880

Manufactured in the United States of America

To the Memory of Three Friends

Vince (1963-1974)
Pebble (1970-1974)
and
Travelin' Shoes (1970-1975)

Oh, what are you going to do, brother,
    The morning of youth is past;
The vigor and strength of manhood,
    My brother, are yours at last:
You are rising in worldly prospects,
    And prosper'd in worldly things;
A duty to those less favored,
    The smile of your fortune brings.
Go prove that your heart is grateful—
    The Lord has a work for you!
Then what are you going to do, brother?
    Say, what are you going to do?

The White Ribbon Hymnal, 1892.

Contents

Tables

Acknowledgments

My thanks go to all those who have provided advice, encouragement, criticism, and support during the preparation of this manuscript, both before and after its presentation as a dissertation. I owe a special debt to Merle Curti, who, beyond his supervision of the early stages of the dissertation, has provided an example of humane learning and engaged scholarship. His generosity needs no testimony from me. Paul W. Glad's patient criticism was invaluable in completing the dissertation. Robert A. Hohner read the entire manuscript before revision; whatever value it may have owes much to his comments and encouragement. I am indebted to the members of the American historians' seminar at the University of Western Ontario, who read chapters 1 and 2, and especially to Craig M. Simpson, friend and scholar. Richard S. Alcorn and Fred W. Burd introduced me to the computer. My former wife Renny knows well the costs of scholarship.

The staffs of numerous libraries provided essential support: the University of Wisconsin Memorial Library; the State Historical Society of Wisconsin; Silcox Memorial Library, Huron College; D. B. Weldon Library, University of Western Ontario; the Library of Congress; Kansas State Historical Society; the Women's Christian Temperance Union Archives; and the Temperance Education Foundation. Special thanks are owed to the staff of the Michigan Historical Collections and particularly to its Field Representative, Kenneth P. Scheffel: together they have assembled a collection of temperance materials whose scope extends far beyond the borders of Michigan. The University of Wisconsin provided a dissertation fellowship, and grants from the Canada Council and the Huron College Faculty helped to support further research, revision, and typing. Mrs. G. B. McCall typed the entire manuscript three times. A portion of chapter 2 first appeared in a slightly different form in *The Historian* and is reprinted here by permission of Phi Alpha Theta. Errors of fact or interpretation are of course my responsibility alone.

RETREAT FROM REFORM

Introduction

As if to gird themselves for the approaching new century, many Americans made fundamental political decisions during the 1890s. The choices I find most interesting were made by middle-rank Americans who had benefited from the economic expansion of the previous thirty years. These people had also helped to pay the costs of that expansion, but for them the charges had been intangible: the nostalgia evoked by transformation of familiar places or the pain incurred by frequent breaking of ties to friends, family, and community. What gave them greater cause for worry was the fact that their gains came at the price of someone else's loss. Wriggle as they might, they could not escape it. Their self-help literature bloomed with hope for justice in this world; at the same time, popular romantic writing found happy endings in nearly every setting but the present one. Middle-class flight to the suburbs put the losers out of sight but not out of mind. The ties of blood, of place, of sentiment, and of interest which had held together an earlier America were eroding, and middle-class mobility showed it; in fact, success in a mobile, competitive, increasingly impersonal society seemed to depend upon the breaking of such ties.

What was to be done? One solution, the revolutionary redistribution of the benefits of industrialization, appeared to them through the blood and smoke of the Paris Commune of 1871, but it had little popular support in the United States. Yet many Americans thought they could discern its outlines in the railroad strike of 1877, the Haymarket bombing of 1886, the Homestead and Pullman strikes, the Commonweal Army, and the People's party. This perception caused them to subordinate their uneasy consciences to their longing for security and to choose a second solution. It consisted of placing power more firmly in the hands of stand-pat politicians and businessmen, and then withdrawing from public affairs into a quietist isolation which paralleled their increasing physical and cultural insulation from the losers in the competitive struggle.

There was also a middle way. It began with a more realistic perception of the protests of the Gilded Age, for the various strikers, Commonwealers, and Populists in fact wanted no more than a larger share in the benefits of industrialization. From there, the middle way proceeded to a recognition that the institutions of Gilded-Age society functioned not to satisfy but to deny that need. Finally, it ended in a determination to change the institutions so as to satisfy the real needs of those who so far had failed to benefit. Social cohesion would be achieved through social justice.

The story of the Populist and Progressive periods is the story of the interpenetration of the middle way and the reactionary solution. The two approaches, which seemed at first to be contradictory, turned out to be complementary. Drop the quietism (though not the isolation) of the reactionary approach and the middle way's determination to achieve social justice, and you have Progressivism: reform which changes nothing, but satisfies the middle way's need for the appearance of change while retaining power in the same hands. Looked at in isolation, as a distinct "period," Progressivism seems to represent something unique: a time when Americans sought to humanize their economy. Seen, however, as the child of the 1890s and the parent of the 1920s, Progressivism takes on a different aspect. In fact, the view is reversed, and Progressivism appears as a device to avoid humanizing the economy. For many erstwhile followers of the middle way, the device worked. What follows is the story of one such group.

Interest in the prohibition movement has passed through two phases since repeal of the Eighteenth Amendment in 1933. During the first phase, which might be considered an ex post facto attempt to justify repeal, prohibitionists were studied because of their freakiness, their differences from "ordinary" people. Artifacts of this phase include the three biographies of Carry Nation (while there are few biographies of first-rank leaders of the Prohibition party or Anti-

Saloon League), and its capstone was Andrew Sinclair's *Era of Excess*, which pictured prohibitionists as rural fanatics and their crusade as a social aberration, a manifestation of extremism provoking extremism in return.[1] The second phase has been characterized by a determination to understand the passage of the Eighteenth Amendment rather than to justify the Twenty-first. It began with James H. Timberlake's *Prohibition and the Progressive Movement* and Joseph R. Gusfield's *Symbolic Crusade: Status Politics and the American Temperance Movement,* both published in 1963. These works and their successors were based on the assumption that the movement is important because of the ways in which prohibitionists were like other Americans, not because of the ways in which they were different. In demonstrating the likenesses between prohibitionists and other Americans, they have demolished Sinclair's picture of rural fanatics and have shown instead that the prohibition crusade was firmly rooted within the native middle class.[2]

I propose to carry the inquiry one step further. Accepting the claim that prohibitionists acted on behalf of their middle-class compatriots, we now need to know why American society during the Populist and Progressive years produced the particular prohibition movement which it did rather than some other. Brian Harrison's superb study of the nineteenth-century English temperance movement has shown that English prohibitionists had a stronger base within the working class and more catholic reforming interests than the American movement in the twentieth century ever developed.[3] Ross Paulson's comparative analysis of prohibition and woman suffrage has revealed a closer relationship in the Scandinavian countries between prohibition and broader movements for social change than existed in the United States.[4] Paulson has also reminded us of the close links between the antislavery and prohibition movements in America during the antebellum years.[5] From a comparative perspective, then, the middle-class base and the narrow approach of the American prohibitionists in their time of triumph stand out. Why?

One prerequisite to an answer is to explain the development of the movement. In order to do so, we must examine the years preceding prohibition's time of triumph, and in particular look closely at the tumultuous decade of the 1890s. At first glance, this seems to be a strange time during which to explore the peculiar qualities of the prohibition movement in the light of wider changes in American society. It was a period of failure for prohibitionists, an interlude of frustration between the second wave of successes in the 1880s (the first wave came during the 1850s) and the third and final wave which began in 1907 and ended with the ratification of the Eighteenth Amendment in 1919. My reason for focusing upon this quarter-century of frustration is that the movement underwent a significant reorientation during that time: the movement which reached fruition in 1919 was not the same movement which had achieved limited and temporary success during the 1880s.[6]

If middle-class Americans, by voting for prohibition after 1907, were in effect validating the changes which had taken place in the prohibition movement, then by the same token they were telling prohibitionists during the 1890s what kind of prohibition movement they did not want. The prohibitionists' response to this message thus becomes an important matter for study in order to understand both the reorientation of the movement and the stimuli which produced it.

To sum up: Between 1890 and 1913 the prohibition movement underwent a fundamental change, a change which reveals a great deal about what it meant to be a middle-class American in the nineteenth century and what it means to be a middle-class American in the twentieth. Superficially, the change was merely a shift from a failed institution, the Prohibition party, to a new organization, the Anti-Saloon League, which promised and delivered tangible results. But this shift is only a key to the real change, a transformation of social outlook so profound that it can be understood only in the context of a cataclysmic era—the 1890s.

NOTES

1. Andrew Sinclair, *Era of Excess,* Harper Colophon ed. (New York, 1964).

2. Two excellent state studies confirm Timberlake's view of the movement and the issue: Norman H. Clark, *The Dry Years: Prohibition and Social Change in Washington* (Seattle, 1965); and Larry D. Engelmann, "O Whiskey: The History of Prohibition in Michigan" (Ph.D. dissertation, University of Michigan, 1971).

For a summary of recent findings on the composition of the prohibition movement, see Robert A. Hohner, "The Prohibitionists:
Who Were They?" *South Atlantic Quarterly* 68 (Autumn 1969):
491–505.

3. Brian Harrison, *Drink and the Victorians: The Temperance
Question in England, 1815-1872* (London, 1971), pp. 25-28,
173-178, 226.

4. Ross Paulson, *Women's Suffrage and Prohibition: A Comparative Study of Equality and Social Control* (Glenview, Ill., 1973),
pp. 75-78, 109, 148.

5. Ibid., pp. 69-70.

6. James R. Turner, "The American Prohibition Movement,
1865-1897" (Ph.D. dissertation, University of Wisconsin, 1972), p. ii.

1

"The revolt of decent citizens"

*F*ew prohibitionists suffered from alcoholism. Unlike Washing-tonians of the early nineteenth century and crusaders against poli-tical corruption or trusts in their own time, temperance reformers of the late nineteenth and early twentieth centuries could not make credible complaint that the institution they attacked had damaged them personally. *The Voice,* unofficial national organ of the Pro-hibition party, once acknowledged this fact: "the Prohibitionists have been seeking for legislation, not in behalf of themselves, but in behalf of the nation—legislation for which they *least of all men* feel any personal need or from which they would receive personal advantage."[1]

Although this ideal of disinterested benevolence had great appeal for nineteenth-century reformers, it is not wholly satisfactory in explaining participation in the prohibition movement. The self-justifications of reformers should be taken at face value no more readily than those of their opponents. The thesis that prohibition-ism spread with a "rural-evangelical virus"[2] is even less satisfactory. Recent historical research has shown that the prohibition issue at-tracted considerable urban support, and the men and women who formed "the backbone of the dry cause," to use Andrew Sinclair's phrase, were anything but the disgruntled, bypassed rural isolates of Sinclair's conception.[3] The career lines of 641 leaders of the Prohibition party and Anti-Saloon League, active between 1890 and 1913, make clear that these men and women swam with the main-stream of American development in their time.[4]

TABLE 1: BIRTHPLACE AND RESIDENCE OF PROHIBITIONIST LEADERS BY REGION
IN PERCENTAGES

	Birthplace (n=607)	Residence (n=610)
NEW ENGLAND (Maine, Vermont, N.H., Mass., Conn., R.I.)	11.9	8.4
MIDDLE ATLANTIC (New York, Pa., N.J.)	20.9	14.3
EAST NORTH CENTRAL (Mich., Ohio, Ind., Ill., Wis.)	34.3	38.9
SOUTH ATLANTIC (Del., Md., D.C., W.Va., Va., N.C., S.C., Ga., Fla.)	10.7	9.0
EAST SOUTH CENTRAL (Ky., Tenn., Ala., Miss.)	4.9	4.1
WEST SOUTH CENTRAL (Ark., La., Okla., Texas)	2.1	2.8
WEST NORTH CENTRAL (Minn., Iowa, Mo., Kan., Neb., S.D., N.D.)	4.9	11.6
MOUNTAIN WEST (Mont., Wyo., Colo., N.M., Ariz., Utah, Nevada, Idaho)	0.2	3.4
PACIFIC WEST (Wash., Oregon, Calif., Hawaii)	1.0	7.4
ENGLAND AND SCOTLAND	4.0	0.2
IRELAND	1.2	—
CANADA	3.1	—
OTHER FOREIGN	0.8	—
	100.0	100.0

Source: Study data (see Note 4).

Two-thirds of the prohibitionist leadership was born in the Northeast, an area which throughout the nineteenth century held an average of 53 percent of the nation's population.[5] Although three-fifths of them moved beyond the borders of their states of birth, nearly two-thirds came to rest in the Northeast, which by 1910 contained 49 percent of the total population, 68 percent of the urban population, 58 percent of the cities over 100,000, 62 percent of the manufacturing establishments, and 73 percent of the wage earners in manufacturing (Table 1).[6]

Prohibitionist leaders were more urban in origin and residence than the general population. One out of six Americans born between 1815 and 1890 came of parents living in an urban area (2,500+). One out of four future prohibitionist leaders did. Less than half of the American population lived in urban areas by 1910. Four-fifths of the prohibitionist leaders did, and nearly two-fifths of them lived in cities of more than 100,000, compared to less than one-quarter of the total population (Table 2).

Although a firm conclusion is impossible, the individuals who led the prohibition movement seem to have gained upward occupational mobility. While a majority of their fathers seem to have been farmers, most of them became clergymen, businessmen, or lawyers (Table 3). They were almost certainly better educated than the general population (Table 4).

Evangelical they were. Four-fifths belonged to evangelical denominations, distributed as follows: Methodists, 45.5 percent; Presbyterians, 15.8 percent; Congregational, 11.1 percent; Baptist, 8.3 percent.

Of those who reported Civil War service, three-quarters had fought on the winning side. Of those who claimed previous party affiliation, three-quarters had been members of the Republican party.[7]

Educated, mobile geographically and probably occupationally, winners in politics as in battle, living in close contact with the dominant social forces of the century —urbanization and industrialization—these men and women had every reason to feel at ease in the world which they had helped to create. Why then did they dissent?

To answer this question, we must examine the prohibitionists in their cultural, social, and political contexts. No historian would argue, I think, that Americans by 1900 shared a common culture. In the antebellum years, regional economic and social differences had produced regional cultures; and in the late nineteenth century, class and

TABLE 2: BIRTHPLACE AND RESIDENCE OF PROHIBITIONIST LEADERS BY POPULATION (COMPARED TO TOTAL U.S. POPULATION)
IN PERCENTAGES

Population	U.S. Births 1815-1890	Prohibitionist Leaders Births 1815-1890 (n=487)	Prohibitionist Leaders Residence (n=476)	U.S. Residence 1910
100,000 and over		4.7	37.8	22.1
25,000-99,999		2.7	16.2	9.0
10,000-24,999	16.4	4.7	12.4	6.1
5,000-9,999		5.1	7.6	4.7
2,500-4,999		6.8	8.2	4.5
Under 2,500	83.6	76.0	17.9	53.7
	100.0	100.0	100.0	100.0

Sources: U.S. birth percentages computed from Wilson H. Grabill, Clyde V. Kiser, and Pascal K. Whelpton, *The Fertility of American Women* (New York, 1958), pp. 17-18, and Ansley J. Coale and Melvin Zelnik, *New Estimates of Fertility and Population in the United States* (Princeton, 1963), p. 38, and adjusted from U.S. Bureau of the Census, *Historical Statistics of the United States: Colonial Times to 1957* (Washington, 1960), p. 14. U.S. residence for 1910 computed from Bureau of the Census, *Thirteenth Census of the U.S., 1910*, 1 (Washington, 1913), pp. 87-98. Percentages for prohibitionist leaders are from study data.

TABLE 3: OCCUPATIONS OF PROHIBITIONIST LEADERS
AND THEIR FATHERS
IN PERCENTAGES

Occupations	Probib. Leaders (n=616)	Fathers (n=131)
Farmer	3.7	53.4
Clergyman	37.2	26.7
Businessman	17.2	9.2
Lawyer	15.9	3.1
Temperance or Social Worker	8.6	0.8
Journalist	5.0	1.5
Teacher	4.4	2.3
Lecturer	3.7	——
Physician	1.5	1.5
Clerk or Salesman	2.3	——
Skilled Laborer	0.5	1.5
	100.0	100.0

Source: Study data.

ethnic differences emerged in the wake of industrialization, urbanization, and massive immigration. Urban middle-class men and women believed that growing differences existed between themselves and their inferiors and betters as profound as those which had separated northerners and southerners before the Civil War. Social distance became physical with the removal of middle-class dwellings from the central cities.[8] Their perception was stated most clearly in their best literature.[9] Ordinary people refused to speak in terms of class; they preferred the language of respectability. Thus, in middle-class circles, "decency" became a synonym for middling status. Its use

TABLE 4: EDUCATIONAL ATTAINMENT OF
PROHIBITIONIST LEADERS
IN PERCENTAGES

Highest Educational Attainment	Prohib. Leaders (n=496)	Cumulative
None	2.6	2.6
Grammar School	7.1	9.7
Secondary School	8.5	18.1*
Trade School	1.6	19.7
Academy	4.6	24.4*
Attended College	15.7	40.1
College Graduate	13.1	53.2
Attended Graduate School	13.7	66.9
Seminary	22.6	89.5
Law School	10.5	100.0

* Figures rounded.
Source: Study data.

reflected a hope that their class was as culturally unified as it was
physically separate.

That was only a hope, for the adult generation of the 1890s stood
at a hinge-point in American cultural styles generally and in the middle-
class life-style in particular. A society which had put self-restraint to
the service of production was giving way to one which could maintain
production only by encouraging consumption. The wealthy led the way,
and in 1899 Thorstein Veblen's satire of conspicuous consumption
merely recognized an established trait among those who could
best afford it. The saturnine Norwegian's distinction between socially
useful and socially wasteful production utilized a theme long established in prohibitionist literature; both reflected a conflict for cultural
hegemony within the middle class between competing norms of behavior.

To the reader of this book, aware of the outcome, the struggle

to enthrone restraint at the heart of the middle-class life-style must
seem chimerical. So too does the broader effort to create a middle-
class culture by political means. From the perspective of the 1890s the
struggle appears less strange. The middle-class activists of the late nineteenth century believed that, as American society had created the
wealth and status which they enjoyed, so too could it produce first
a middle-class, then a national culture which would legitimize their
achievement. Restraint had allowed production to reach volumes hither-
to unknown; now restraint by those who had profited would allow those
who had not to share in the bounty. Restraint would also make the
latter content with their share. Restraint and the values clustering
around it—industry, frugality, and sobriety—explained their own
personal achievement; now restraint—self-restraint if possible, social
control if necessary—was to cure industrial society of exploitation
and heal its resultant social divisions.

All this is a way of saying that prohibitionists were not unhappy
simply because other people drank too much. They were unhappy
for a broader reason which they never stated in so many words because
saying it would have destroyed the balance by which they maintained
a more or less satisfactory relationship to their environment. Their society
seemed to them to be socially and culturally divided and, because of
this, spiritually purposeless. They believed that it should have a transcendent purpose partly because of their evangelical heritage, but beyond
that they shared with other Americans a sense of mission which was
only heightened by their evangelicalism. Prohibitionists were only one
of the many groups attempting to define the American mission in their
own terms.

Thus, prohibition in the late nineteenth century functioned as a
political device to create a middle-class cultural consensus, to protect it
from penetration by competing norms of behavior, and to extend a
life-style embodying restraint as its cardinal feature to classes above and
below. A new ideal of social welfare would govern economic life, and
dedication to that ideal would unify the estranged classes. What began
as an attempt to create a middle-class culture would end by producing
social harmony and spiritual purpose for the nation.

To accomplish these ends, prohibitionists employed a value system
built on self-denial, an ideology emphasizing social control, and a
program of political action. None of these required that prohibitionism
be either conservative or radical in its approach to political action.

The choice depended upon prohibitionists' answers to open questions: self-denial by whom, social control by whom, and political action by whom and in whose behalf? The answers came from the prohibitionists' past and future—from the reform tradition which shaped their expectations on entering the movement, and from the events which fulfilled or defeated those expectations.

Nothing in the American reform tradition, as the prohibitionists saw it, predisposed them toward a conservative or defensive stance on public issues. At least until 1896, their model of a successful reform movement was abolitionism, and the Civil War its fulfillment.[10] They took from radical abolitionism a belief in the need for national renewal and a faith in individual regeneration. These corresponded neatly to their own experience: as individuals they had succeeded, but as a nation Americans had failed to measure up to their own ideals.

Contradictorily, they also adopted from conservative abolitionism a belief in the need for political action. It was a paradoxical program because political action involved coercion, which implied that some men would remain unreformed. Their only resolution was majoritarianism, which retained the radical faith in regeneration along with the conservative expectation that a minority could not be reformed. Prohibitionists expected, until the dark days of the 1890s, that their ultimate majority would be very large, for they defined their enemy not as a legitimate business venture but as the "liquor *traffic*," and saw its support coming from "popular passion and appetite."[11] Both would succumb eventually to sober conviction. In 1890, they could find confirmation for their optimism in federal statistics on liquor consumption: per capita consumption of absolute alcohol had dropped 20 percent from its peak thirty years before.[12] Prohibition, unlike abolition, would not require a civil war.

It would, however, require a rededication to the national ideal of progress through improvement of the general welfare. In the breadth of its platform as well as its longevity, the Prohibition party, as James C. Malin has pointed out, was the leading reform party of the postbellum years, the apparent legitimate descendant of abolitionism.[13] In the steady increase of its support, and particularly after the great leap from 10,000 votes in 1880 to 150,000 in 1884, prohibitionists saw the harbinger of a new dawn.

These patterns of motivation come into focus in the lives of individual prohibitionists. The chronicles of their lives have been

unjustly neglected, for they illustrate "in a small way," as Frances
E. Willard observed of her autobiography, "the result of American
institutions upon individual and family life."[14] In their autobiographies,
candid prohibitionists confessed their distaste for the economic standards
by which they measured their success, announced their dissatisfaction
with the political and religious institutions of their class, and celebrated
their allegiance to the prohibition movement as the panacea for their ills.

THE INSUFFICIENCY OF SUCCESS

A 1903 editorial from the Prohibition party's national organ
illustrates the class-based categories by which the prohibitionists distinguished themselves from their fellow men. Searching for the drinking elements in American society, the writer first eliminated "the whole
better class, that is to say, the 'middle' class, the working, paying,
thriving, home loving masses, whose lives are lived between and distinct
from the idle on the one hand and the vicious on the other." To
make clearer just whom this better class included, he went on to name
specific groups: Protestants and their ministers, "teachers and professional
men, skilled mechanics and railroad men, clerks, commercial men and
successful men generally." Lumping together moral, educational, and
economic criteria, he concluded: "Drunkenness and tippling belong
now to the very rich, the reckless, the ignorant, the vicious and the very
poor."[15]

"*Successful* men generally"! This reflex attribution of worldly
success as well as abstract virtue to their own segment of the middle
class pointed directly to the state of cultural warfare within that class.
A confident and secure group does not need to reassure itself constantly
of its exclusive possession of virtue. For the prohibitionist, the virtue
which he felt must lie in sobriety was demonstrated not merely by
conformity to the laws of God (although he ransacked sacred texts
and engaged in heated polemics over obscure differences in trans-
lation) but also by the unmistakable authority of worldly success.
Thus the Reverend A. E. Carhart, founder and Superintendent of the
South Dakota Anti-Saloon League, looked back in 1908 upon his boy-
hood: "Several of our boyish set are dead. Drink had something to
do with the death of more than one. Three or four of us are living
and have won success. These without exception have lived sober

lives." Thus Samuel Dickie, newly installed Chairman of the Prohibition party, told its convention in 1888 that God's Providence
was illustrated by the fact that all eight of the party's national candidates since 1872 were still living, while only four of their sixteen
major-party opponents survived.[16] Such self-congratulations are
best understood as cries for help, indicative of a "revolt of decent
citizens" against a world which distributed its rewards without
apparent regard for "decency."[17]

Their search for order took male prohibitionists to reference
points other than that of class. Some of them were careful in their
reminiscences to note the historic and ethnic backgrounds of their
families, while others sought to identify their heritage through the
moral value of temperance convictions.[18] Bishop James Cannon, Jr.,
pointed to the life-style underlying the middle-class value system
when he related that "I had learned to restrain and to repress any
public exhibition of my feelings, and reckless or even random speech
had never been characteristic of my home life."[19]

The uncertain courses of their careers induced, and the ambivalence of their retrospections upon them revealed, the prohibitionists' need to find meaning in their daily lives. William J. Demorest,
the party Prohibitionist who with his wife acted for a time as the
dictator of fashion for middle-class women, was drawn early in his
life from preparation for the ministry into the dry-goods business.
Demorest then felt it necessary to accompany his business success
with thirty years of Sunday-school teaching and to compensate
further for that success by devoting a large part of his fashion
magazine to reform movements, particularly temperance. James
Cannon, Jr., moved the other way, from college studies aimed
through law school ultimately toward the Supreme Court bench,
to a religious conversion entailing a self-imposed commitment to
the ministry. For James W. Bashford, who, like Cannon, later
became a Methodist bishop, the abandoned career was to have been
in politics rather than law and the school was the University of
Wisconsin instead of Randolph-Macon, but his decision and its
results were precisely the same as Cannon's. Charles M. Sheldon, who
moved from the obscurity of a Congregational pastorate in Topeka,
Kansas, into national literary and reform circles by writing the
immensely popular sermon-novel *In His Steps,* complained that
the scope of a minister's experience was normally much too small;

he felt that the minister should embrace "the entire compass of human
experience and human sin and human need and human regeneration."[20]
John Bascom, president of the University of Wisconsin (1874-1887),
was torn early in life, like Cannon, between the conflicting claims
of law and the ministry. Coming as he did from a long Puritan ancestry,
Bascom must have felt keenly the pressure generated by the need to
find his "calling." He avoided the problem by seizing a fortuitous
opportunity to become a teacher at Williams College and later
justified his decision in many ways, among them a concentration
upon the disciplines of philosophy and ethics and modification of
the concept of "calling" to "a willingness to walk in any open path
which seems to invite us."[21]

The male prohibitionists' attitudes toward business success and
the terms by which it was measured made a curious mixture. At
times they could denounce the economic system, as Sheldon was
moved to do in 1890 at the sight of its victims. They could equate
wealth and social success with greed and selfishness and join Cannon
in seeing John D. Rockefeller as the "representative of the greatest
evil in public life." But these things could be said only because
prohibitionists clung tightly to the values of work and self-discipline
which supposedly characterized the climb to the top. In the 1880s,
William J. Demorest could note that Jay Gould had "accumulated
a gigantic fortune by means not altogether creditable to his moral
sense" but at the same time balance the picture and restore confidence
in the potency of sound values by pointing out that "withal he is
a man without any small vices. He never uses intoxicating drinks
or tobacco, nor does he play cards. He has a large family, and his
domestic life is a happy one." The prohibitionist leaders went out
of their way to celebrate the moral value of hard work and frugality,
and when Bascom and Bashford became college presidents, they
freed their students from rigid supervision and sought instead to
teach self-regulation.[22] Clearly, they had assimilated the lesson,
taught by the Gilded Age, of the incongruity between virtue and
social mobility: the good did not always prosper, nor were the pros-
perous always, or even often, the good. But to apply that lesson to
themselves would have been unthinkable; it was, in fact, what they
most sought to avoid. The distressing perception of wealth attained
without virtue led prohibitionists directly to their contradictory
attempt to enforce self-control.

Thus seeking to bring moral order to the social order, prohibitionists turned to the churches not for divine sanction but rather in search of political support. Disappointed, some became agnostics, or spiritualists. Most, however, struggled all their lives within conventional Protestantism, belaboring the churches with charges of apathy, inertia, selfishness, ambition, sectarianism, and a lack of "genuine soul hunger." In strident tones that must have tried the patience of more than one minister, prohibitionists urged the churches to involve themselves more actively in the affairs of this world while at the same time they warned them to avoid the stain of its materialism.[23]

Many of the patterns of these men's lives appear in the life of James B. Cranfill, Prohibition party candidate for Vice-President in 1892, whose prohibition activity spanned the period from 1890 to 1913, and who recorded his reflections in autobiographies published in 1916 and 1937. Born in Parker County, Texas, in 1859, Cranfill moved from a farm to eventual residence in Dallas, a city which grew from 38,000 population in 1890 to 92,000 in 1910. Cranfill's awareness of his English and Scottish ancestry included the tradition that his ancestors had come to America before the Revolution as well as the belief that his American lineage was composed almost exclusively of Baptists.[24]

As the son of a Union-sympathizing Confederate soldier, Cranfill regarded the Civil War experience with ambivalence. On one hand, he believed in neither slavery, secession, nor Jefferson Davis and regarded the war as "the insanest struggle in which intelligent white men ever engaged"; on the other, he professed admiration for the patriotism of those who fought the war.[25] Thus he could justify respect for his father and rescue an ideal from a repulsive situation.

After the war, Cranfill's father became a peripatetic farmer and renewed his self-taught medical practice. Cranfill recalled both his father's thriftiness and his constant urge to move on, which became an insuperable obstacle in the family's path to prosperity. He also remembered from an early age the connection between property and social standing, illustrated when his father's purchase of a new "thimble-skein" wagon for $125.00 "elevated us very considerably in the scale of respectability."[26]

Cranfill's early training in temperance principles must have been traumatic. His father, in addition to his farming and doctoring, shared with several uncles the title of preacher in the Primitive, or Hardshell,

Baptist sect. "Reared in Hardshell Baptist atmosphere," Cranfill recalled, "I had been trained by my associates to the belief that whiskey,
temperately used, was not dangerous or deleterious. My sweet mother
had taught me from my childhood that there was nothing good in
whiskey from any standpoint whatsoever, but the Hardshell Baptist
brotherhood did not share her views. It was common for their ministers
to take their drinks. I have rarely known a Hardshell preacher who
was not an anti-prohibitionist."[27] At about ten years of age he fell
afoul of the inevitable book of moral lessons, called *Little Things,*
which taught, he said, that "little missteps, little falsehoods,little
evil practices grew into larger sins and, if not checked, led the rest-
less sinner into tragedies and destruction."[28] Reinforced as this lesson
was by blue-backed Webster spellers, dime novels which he read in
hiding from his father, and the omnipresent McGuffey's Readers,
Cranfill's education contributed to a cast of mind that was both
literal and moralistic, but not humorless.[29]

Despite the influence of *Little Things* and McGuffey, and perhaps
in reaction to the hated farm life, Cranfill enjoyed a youth which he was
later to call "dissipated" and which included card playing, dancing,
smoking, and fiddle playing.[30] This lasted until his eighteenth year,
when he was converted to the Hardshell Baptist faith. As he later
recalled, he had always intended to become a Christian and equated
religious commitment with a strict discipline extending to everyday
behavior.

> I felt . . . that a young man could not have a good time
> as a member of the church, and I was deliberately with-
> holding any active interest in religion until I should have
> married and settled down, my theory being that a married
> man who had gone through with all the dissipations and
> indulgences of youth, could consistently be a Christian,
> while it would be very difficult for a single man to walk
> the narrow way.

His plans were disrupted, however, when he attended a religious meeting at which the preacher triggered a response from the young man by
appealing to those who expected at some future time to become
Christians. As Cranfill went forward, he reported, "conviction seized
upon my soul as strong as the powers of the world to come," and he

allowed himself to be initiated into the faith, forswearing immediately such frivolities as fiddle playing and dancing, refusing even to continue on his way to a dance at which he had been scheduled to perform that very night. Connecting religious commitment with the ministry, he also announced his intention to become a preacher.[31]

About this time, however, Cranfill was married and set out on his own, trying successively to establish himself as a teacher, phrenology lecturer, doctor, and storekeeper. The last of these led him into journalism when he established a town paper to advertise his wares, and he found there a career that was to occupy him until 1907. Within two years after his conversion he had decided against preaching on the ground of personal unfitness and had entered as well into a reaction against the Hardshell Baptists. In 1882 he renewed his faith during a revival and offered himself to the Missionary Baptists, a group more amenable to prohibition, revivals, and evangelism than the Hardshell sect.[32]

In that year the various threads of Cranfill's life began to converge, as he moved to Gatesville, Texas, a town which tripled in size during the decade of the 1880s. Establishing the *Gatesville Advance,* Cranfill found a link between the mob violence endemic to rapidly growing western towns and Gatesville's ten saloons. As he later put it, "The saloons and the mobs went hand in hand."[33] Clearly the path to respectability in Gatesville lay in opposition to the disreputability and violence associated with the saloons and the "saloon crowd." Cranfill's distaste for "mobs" and saloons and his desire for respectability made up the negative and positive sides of his claim to middle-class status, a claim which he sought to validate by joining the local temperance movement. He plunged into the fight with gusto, adding to his duties as editor an assignment as county lecturer for the United Friends of Temperance. He had made a "decision to major on the prohibition issue."[34]

This decision led him into danger, when the "liquor element" threatened his life, and into politics, where he initially found success. For a rising young Texan in the 1880s, politics meant the Democratic party.

> In 1884 the temperance element in the county dominated the County Democratic Convention. As editor of the paper, I enjoyed quite a degree of prestige, and I had increased my clientele in a temperance way by making the acquaint-

ance in their own respective neighborhoods, of the leading
temperance workers of the county. The result was that I
was chosen as a delegate to the State Democratic Convention.[35]

The young editor soon discovered that the advocacy of temperance
principles which had accompanied his religious rededication and
brought him local social respectability and political success was less
than helpful in statewide Democratic politics. After unsuccessful
attempts to commit the state party to temperance, Cranfill was
defeated for a county delegate's seat in the 1886 Democratic convention. "That was my first rebuff in local politics. It woke me up
to the gravity of the liquor business as never before." Failing
once again to win support in the Democratic state convention
for a temperance plank, Cranfill "returned home with my mind
made up to lead in the organization of the National Prohibition
party in Texas. . . . The following week I published a call for the
meeting of a State Prohibition Party Convention."[36]

In his new party Cranfill found the leadership position which had
been denied him in the Democratic party and an expanded field
for his journalistic enterprise as well. "The election of 1886 changed
the course of my life. The Prohibitionists, many of whom I now
had met and personally knew, realizing the vast importance of
larger prohibition activities, urged me to move my publication to
Waco, and thus seek a larger clientele."[37] In 1887 he plunged his
Waco Advance into the thick of the unsuccessful fight in the statewide prohibition referendum and, during most of the campaign,
made money with his paper. His prominence in reform work led
to an appointment as financial secretary for Baylor University
in January 1889 and to the superintendency of Baptist mission
work in the entire state in October 1889.[38] Success led in turn to
his founding in 1892 of the Dallas *Baptist Standard*, which quickly
became an influential voice in the Southern Baptist church.
Meanwhile, his star had risen in political circles with his election
to the Prohibition party National Committee in 1888 and his nomination at the age of thirty-three for the Vice-Presidency.

Cranfill's thought sprang directly from his personal experience
and reflected with little distortion his rise into the middle class
and his need to defend the achievement. Having had little formal

education, he belittled those with more as "kid-gloved effeminates" and glorified "the degree of C.S.—Common Sense."[39] Because he had achieved success in a trade requiring proficiency in the use of language, however, he claimed the correct use of grammar to be a hereditary gift: "I didn't learn to spell, capitalize, or punctuate in school. I always knew. This quality of mind was doubtless inherited from my mother." This attitude in turn supported his view of his vocation. Despite, or perhaps because of, the fact that he had come to journalism after leaving farming and trying doctoring, lecturing, and storekeeping, he saw his trade as God-given: "Newspaper men are born. Like poets, they come into the world without any heralding and with instincts and intuitions that fit them for their chosen task. God makes them and in the highest sense equips them for their life estate."[40] The insecurity that underlay this attitude emerged clearly in the highly self-conscious use of puns and clichés in his 1916 autobiography, *Cranfill's Chronicle.* For example, on page 266 he wrote: "My work as a merchant increased by leaps and bounds. (If by any means you have ever before seen this expression, 'by leaps and bounds,' please notify me.)"[41] On one level, this seems to have been a self-conscious attempt to swim with the literary stream of southwestern humor, which by 1916 had obviously become polluted. On another, it constituted a heavy-handed effort simultaneously to show the reader that he had a down-to-earth sense of humor and to demonstrate that he possessed enough literary sophistication to recognize the bad taste evident in the use of puns and clichés.

Cranfill also used language to demonstrate the middle-class standing he had achieved, pausing at one point in his narrative to observe: "If I were writing a fictitious romance, I would say that she referred to her father and mother as 'Papa' and 'Mama,' but she didn't. It was plain Pa and Ma, as was the custom in the higher walks of country life. In the lower strata, parents were called by the cognomens[!] of 'Pap' and 'Mam.' "[42] Recognizing that he had achieved success in material terms, Cranfill at the age of fifty-seven nevertheless repudiated any satisfaction in such success. "If I could traverse life's way again I would have naught to do with mere temporalities or materialities . . . . A man's life consisteth not in the abundance of the multitudes of the material things which he accomplishes." He described businessmen as "slaves to their business and their money" and the

ability to make money as "a low and groveling talent at its best."
He claimed that "none of that has ever appealed to me, and my
connection with money-making has been an incident, and one in
which I took and take no pride." "Looking back upon my life as
I have lived it, I feel that every hour of my time spent in any line
of business, save that of religion, philanthropy and literature, has been
a wasted hour, and one for which I shall at life's end give a strict
account to God. . . . To me all mere business, whether successful
or not, has been dull and prosaic."[43]

Rejecting man-made law as well as business success as a proper
guide for life, Cranfill found his touchstone in Baptist orthodoxy.
Having changed his sectarian affiliation at a time of increasing personal success and prestige, he thereafter clung to his chosen sect with
a tenacity that resisted all the winds of theological change. His
creed was more personal than institutional, however, as he assumed
God's protection over his person and found sinfulness among Baptist
preachers. He made clear the equation of virtue, wisdom, and religious
belief in his account of a series of civil trials in 1898-1905 in which
he and other members of his Texas Baptist faction were successfully
sued by the leader of the opposing faction. His defeat, he wrote, was
due to the ignorance of the "Populist" members of the jury.[44]

Other orientations of Cranfill's mind depended largely upon the
ways in which events outside his career impinged upon his primary
interests. Although whites were in a minority in the Texas county
where he lived much of his early life, he tended to regard common
black people as nonpersons except when they joined the disreputable
classes by allowing themselves to be mobilized by the liquor interests
to vote against his side. He strongly disapproved of the murder of
an old white man who had tried to conduct a nearby black school
during Reconstruction, but seems to have been shocked more because
the murder had been committed next to a church than by the political reasons for the act. He served as a trustee of the black Bishop
College in Marshall, Texas, and claimed credit for the election of its
first black president. Cranfill's distaste for labor unions mirrored his
status as an employer, but he persisted in viewing the matter in
individual, moral terms, asserting that "the non-union men are as
good as the Union men. All of them were made out of the same clay,
and each man in his place, union or non-union, has a right under
God to earn bread for his family and to order his life according to
the dictates of his own conscience." In 1890 Cranfill supported the

participation of women in Texas Baptist missionary work, and at the
Prohibition party national convention of 1888 he opposed a women's
suffrage plank only, he said, because of southern resistance, claiming
that "my head has always been converted to woman suffrage."[45]

From Parker County to Dallas, from shiftlessness to respectability,
Cranfill's life moved in a way that may have been typical of the prohibitionist leadership and perhaps their followers as well. For Cranfill,
prohibitionism and Missionary Baptist orthodoxy, which had both
required conversion at a strategic point in his career, filled a need
for commitment to something beyond the business of everyday life.
Together with the middle-class status which they indicated, these
commitments provided Cranfill with a satisfactory meaning for his
existence as well as an acceptable social role in nineteenth-century
America.

BEYOND FEMININITY

Many male prohibitionists believed in woman suffrage and gave
the plank much more support than Cranfill ever did at the party's
national conventions. Indeed, the controversy over the woman suffrage
plank provided one of the more durable themes of those conventions.
John Bascom, one of the Prohibition party's senior theoreticians,
combined the prohibitionists' search for social purpose with their
attitude toward women when he wrote in 1900, "The womanly mind
has the free entry to life far more than the masculine mind: because
by virtue of the wisdom of the affections, it lays more direct hold on
substantial, spiritual possessions."[46]

Like Bascom, many male prohibitionists saw women in closer
rapport than men with spiritual verities and supported woman suffrage as both a functional and symbolic means of cleansing society.
On the other side, prohibitionist women looked with disgust upon
their role in society and wanted for themselves the more secure and
established roles which they believed that men occupied.[47] In addition to sharing in the general middle-class cultural conflict that
afflicted male prohibitionists, they were affected by the identity
crisis that preoccupied middle-class women during the late nineteenth
century.[48]

The women, for the most part lacking by themselves the usual
means of economic advancement, were preoccupied less than the men

by the problems of business success. They devoted less effort to
definition of a class standing already achieved by family or marriage
connections. While prohibitionist activity was sometimes for the men
a means of gaining entry into the middle class, for women it functioned more as a tool for identifying themselves within that class.
While the men raged at organized religion and politics for failing
to institutionalize their values, the women nursed the more concrete
grievance of an almost total lack of recognition from either church
or party. For men the problems of sex and personal relationships
were peripheral to their concern for a social identity; for women,
who started with a less satisfying social role, they were personally
vital. The male prohibitionists were concerned with defining themselves vis-à-vis other economic classes, while the women began with
the task of identifying themselves relative to men.

Thus, many of these middle-class women were able to make an
imaginative leap over class barriers and identify themselves with
the outcast and downtrodden of society, a leap difficult for the
men, who began by positing for themselves a firm position in
the economic order. Such a leap went beyond both the paternalism
endemic to the charitable activity of the Women's Christian Temperance Union (WCTU) and the validation of the middle-class life-
style pointed out by Gusfield.[49] It demonstrated more than anything
else their feeling of deprivation induced by the unacceptability of the
personal definition afforded them by middle-class society.[50] As Stow
Persons has noted, "It was inevitable that in the various victims of
discrimination and injustice women should recognize themselves."[51]
Anna Prosser, a WCTU worker in Buffalo, New York, observed:

> Naturally, I had all my life felt drawn towards the poor,
> oppressed and down-trodden ones, and, as a child, invari-
> ably chose for my playmate some plain, unattractive child
> from a vastly different station in life, someone unnoticed
> in school by the wealthy and "upper ten" girls, much to
> the disgust of my family who were full of aristocratic ideas.
> . . . Consequently, I fell in line very quickly with the noble
> women of the WCTU, and took my place in the ranks with
> keen delight.[52]

Carry Nation, herself poor for part of her life, always felt drawn to
tramps, Catholics, Jews, and prostitutes. Her support for a woman

accused of adultery led to her expulsion from the local Methodist church.[53] Nation's lectures in dance halls, beer gardens, and burlesque shows scandalized many temperance reformers. She characteristically counterattacked by predicting that "publicans and harlots" would enter the kingdom of heaven before hypocritical churchgoers, a charge that could also be found on occasion in the official prohibition press.[54] This association with the outcasts of society was remarkable in an organization like the WCTU, which, since the end of the Women's Crusade of 1873-1874, had operated on the most respectable flank of the feminist movement. It suggested that the WCTU slogan of "Purity" might describe a state sought for the reformer as well as the reformed.

One of the most prominent targets of their criticism was the conspicuous consumption by which the middle class aped the gaudy luxury of the rich. Carry Nation's repugnance toward the display of material possessions stemmed partially from hostility toward her mentally unbalanced mother, whose self-assumed role as Queen Victoria loaded the family with a heavy burden of ornamentation. Nation later stated:

> From the time my Christian experience began, I never
> wished to be associated with rich people or rather people
> that had wealth for display. I would feel uncomfortable in
> a house filled with furniture or bric-a-brac. . . . It mortified
> me to see a very well-dressed woman. I noticed that those
> so-called fashionable women really never had time or money
> to do charity. Of course there are exceptions. The display
> of wealth to me is an evidence of a depraved nature.[55]

Anna Prosser claimed to have been in early life a "heartless society coquette" whose "highest aim [was] that of being more exquisitely attired than my young lady companions and of having a greater number of suitors at my feet." Later in life she hooted, "What pitiable slaves the votaries of fashion are!"[56] Belle Kearney, a WCTU lecturer, recalled three years in the swirl of fashionable society in postbellum Mississippi and found in them little of permanent value and much that was potentially damaging to character. "After the last fierce struggle with the finer elements of my being, a definite determination was made to *abandon* the shallow, aimless life that had been entered upon." The experience lay behind her definition

of "radicalism" as "Christianity brought down into daily life" and
"conservatism" as "selfishness."[57]

American society refused women full participation in its life,
and women retaliated by rejecting the limited role allotted to
them and attacking its boundaries.[58] They directed a part of their
attack at the churches which accepted them as workers but not
as independent leaders. Carry Nation's conflicts with a series of
churches were legion, and she responded by creating her own unique
religious practice from elements of both Catholicism and Protestantism while acknowledging her indebtedness to both Jew and Greek. "All
the Christian work I ever did," she wrote, "seemed to meet with severe
opposition from church members. . . . There is no organization but the
church of Christ that persecutes its own followers." Rejected by and
rejecting the respectable denominations, she received support in her
prohibition work from the Free Methodists, a small holiness sect with
a history of abolitionist activity.[59] Ellen Curtis Demorest turned late
in life from the established denominations to Christian Science.[60]
Anna Prosser denounced the churches as apathetic and materialistic,
combined antimaterialism with a zeal for evangelism by organizing
bands of "Self-Denial Workers" who pledged to provide support for
foreign missions by denying themselves, and also found a home in the
holiness movement.[61]

The passivity that was women's assigned lot in the late nineteenth
century as well as their privileged middle-class position, however, largely
prevented these women from pushing to realization their critique of
middle-class society. Although Carry Nation raged at conspicuous
wealth, she concluded, "Still, 'tis well to get all the money in a good
way, that you can then use it in a good cause."[62] Ellen Demorest's sympathy with the cause of dress reform still could not lead the fashion-set-
ter to repudiate the corset rather than the bloomer, which she called "not
only too revolutionary, but [also] extremely inelegant and unwomanly in
appearance."[63] Jane Agnes Stewart, who wrote for the WCTU paper, the
Union Signal, in the 1890s, approved of the initial clearing of necklines,
shortening of skirts, flattening of heels, and disposal of garters and corsets,
but was shocked by further developments along these lines in the twentieth century.[64] The dictates of nineteenth-century fashion were anathema also to Frances Willard on both health and libertarian grounds, but
she herself never dared to adopt less restrictive styles.[65]

Instead, these women repressed their feelings of resentment and
resolved their personal dilemmas by commitment to the WCTU and

other prohibition organizations, seeking through institutions a satisfactory mode of social change. Carry Nation, thrown out of the Methodist church in Medicine Lodge, Kansas, turned her energies to organizing a local chapter of the WCTU.[66] For Belle Kearney, exposure to Frances Willard during the latter's southern lecture tour in 1889 crystallized her early abstinence training, her rejection of fashionable society, and the sense of personal destiny and special mission to which she had clung in compensation for the seeming aimlessness of her life; immediately thereafter she hastened to accept appointment as young people's organizer for the Mississippi WCTU, an organization with which she had been entirely unacquainted until then. She joined the Prohibition party when she joined the WCTU.[67] Anna Prosser, disenchanted with the materialism of the churches and fashionable society and tormented by the theological doubts and questions, found ease for her mind and balm for her conscience in the ceaseless activity of WCTU mission work in Buffalo.[68]

The elected leader of the WCTU from 1879 until her death in 1898, Frances Willard exemplified many of the problems and solutions characteristic of her co-workers and occasionally brought to bear enough wit and detachment to describe their situation incisively in the autobiography they forced her to write in 1889. Willard had a subtle and sometimes devious mind and an extraordinarily graceful pen, and consequently was able to make revelations and express opinions upon subjects which her more straightforward contemporaries dared not touch. Thus her autobiography, *Glimpses of Fifty Years,* remains an immensely valuable guide for exploration of the social history of late nineteenth-century America, and for this reason if for no other she deserves the place accorded her by her state of Illinois in the Capitol's Hall of Statuary.

Willard viewed her times as a "transition period" whose maladjustments had created an "anomalous position" for women. This ambiguity was most evident in women's confusion about their proper sexual and social roles. Here she noted the circumstances of her own early life: brought up on a remote Wisconsin farm, she was allowed for most of her youth to believe that her life would be much like that of the beloved older brother with whom she and her sister played. Eventually distinctions appeared, such as long dresses for the girls and a formal education and political activity for the boy. She asserted, "I always believed that if I had been let alone and allowed as a woman, what I had as a girl, a free life in the

country, where a human being might grow, body and soul, as a
tree grows, I would have been 'ten times more of a person,' [in] every
way." This was a protest not against restrictive city life but against
confining long skirts and hairpins. Frances, who liked to be called
"Frank" by her intimates, never relinquished her hopes for the
masculine role she felt had been denied her by social conventions.[69]
One of her classmates wrote that Frances, as a student at Evanston
Female College, "came to be something of a 'beau,' " and as a teacher
she attracted love letters from her girl students written in passionate
terms that hardly seem appropriate even for heterosexual corres-
pondence in that Victorian age.[70] Listen to a WCTU woman's
description of the greeting on her first day of work at national headquarters: "On my first day, seated in a small room (off the main
editorial reception room) bent over my desk, I suddenly heard
a sweet, clear voice, 'Where's the girl from Ohio?' Two soft arms
were pressed around my neck and a warm kiss was planted on my
rosy cheek. It was Frances E. Willard!"[71] Discussing the loves of
her life, Willard candidly confessed that most of them had been women.
She attributed her lack of success in establishing heterosexual romantic
relationships to her "forceful mind and imperious will" as well as
her inability to accept the conventional rule that women remain passive
in the development of such relationships. She claimed, like Carry
Nation, to have had a passionate nature whose possibilities were
never explored. Willard pointed to the widespread existence of "the
loves of women for each other," but refused to accept them as a
permanent part of her world. "The friendships of women are beautiful
and blessed; the loves of women ought not to be, and will not be,
when the sacred purposes of the temperance, the labor, and the woman
movements are wrought out into the customs of society and the laws
of the land."[72] Thus, Willard saw her WCTU work as an attempt
to move society out of its present undesirable "transition age."

Living in a transition age presented other problems to a sensitive
young woman. Willard detested the uselessness she felt as an unemployed
college graduate and accepted an early career as a teacher, one suspects,
largely to prove that she was in fact a useful and worthwhile person.
Sex was another problem. One did not really know how to deal with
it in the absence of instruction withheld by a reticent age. Apparently
neither Willard nor Carry Nation received any sex education from their
parents, for both devoted portions of their autobiographies (and in

Nation's case, her newspaper) to stern warnings for parents to provide
for their children the saving knowledge Willard and Nation had lacked.[73]
For Willard, sex was a trap laid for the unwary woman. In Mormon
polygamy she found the extreme of sexual oppression.[74] Forced by
her society to choose between passion and participation, she had chosen
the role best fitted to her nature, and she wanted for other women at
least the possibility of an informed choice. But at the same time she
felt that women should not have to choose.

The problems which Willard faced produced reactions similar to
those of other female prohibitionists. She resolved to narrow the
gap between her world and that of society's outcasts and was vociferous in her support of the American labor movement. She denounced
the love of money and could not submit to the urgings of her colleagues
to speak out against theosophy and Christian Science because "we
live in a strangely materialistic age" and "a philosophy that takes
immortality as its major premise must conduct toward a good life,
as opposed to the materialism that says, 'I was not—I lived and loved—
I am not'—the saddest epitaph ever penned."[75] Viewing religion as
a guide for good works, she joined the Methodist church at twenty-one
with some indifference, because

> I like its views of the doctrines taught in the Bible better
> than those of any other branch of God's church militant;
> because I have been reared in it, and for me to attach
> myself to any other would cause great sorrow and dis-
> satisfaction in quarters where I should most desire to avoid
> such consequences, other things being equal. I honestly
> believe that I regard all the churches, the branches rather
> of the one Church, with feelings of equal kindness and
> fellowship.[76]

She defended her Methodist orthodoxy, but claimed religious
eclecticism, and said that she did "not live upon theology."
She quit her precedent-setting work with Dwight Moody in
1877 because she viewed his evangelism as too narrow for the
needs of temperance work and woman's emancipation, and denounced Christians and their ministers in 1889 for supporting
high-license laws rather than prohibition.[77]

Despite her criticism of the status quo, Willard was a strangely restrained reformer. As she once stated, "To *re*form one must first one's self *con*form."[78] As President of Evanston Female College and later Dean of Women after the college's merger with Northwestern University, Willard's bitterest battle had been for what she called her system of "self-government" for her girls, which was actually a stricter form of the internalization of rules established by Bashford at Ohio Wesleyan and Bascom at Wisconsin. When she lost the battle to her former beau, President Charles Fowler of Northwestern, Willard entered WCTU work, which she saw as an opportunity to combine her temperance proclivities, identification with the outcast, and antimaterialistic feelings in deeds of "philanthropy." Recognizing the conservative nature of the WCTU membership, she slowly pulled them into a commitment to social change while at the same time she compromised her own position in the hope of achieving success for the movement. At the 1884 and 1888 Prohibition party national conventions she was instrumental in toning down the women's suffrage planks for which she was the recognized spokeswoman because she hoped thereby to attract southern support for the party.[79] Having pledged her fears and her hopes for escape from the "transition age" to the prohibition movement, she was now willing to allow the shape of the new age to be determined by the movement's success.

Such a choice of institutional means to solve personal problems, when made by thousands of middle-class Americans, created the prohibition movement. Thus they threw back in the face of American society the burdens which that society had placed upon their shoulders. For the reasons elucidated at the beginning of this chapter, they believed that prohibition would lead to significant change in their society. But their choice of prohibition did not exclude other reforms, nor did it necessarily mean that other classes would have to pay for resolving the spiritual problems of the middle class. The ultimate direction of prohibition as social change would be determined by the conduct of the middle class in the troublesome decade of the 1890s.

NOTES

1. *The Voice*, January 8, 1891. Italics in original. Citations of the periodical press include editorials, news articles, serials,

and letters to the editor. Publishing requirements preclude citation of individual items.

2. Richard Hofstadter, *The Age of Reform* (New York, 1955), p. 290; Andrew Sinclair, *The Era of Excess* (New York, 1964), pp. 23-35.

3. Robert A. Hohner, "The Prohibitionists: Who Were They?" *South Atlantic Quarterly* 68 (Autumn 1969): 495-496; Robert E. Wenger, "The Anti-Saloon League in Nebraska Politics, 1898-1910," *Nebraska History* 52 (Fall 1971): 272-273; Larry D. Engelmann, "O Whiskey: The History of Prohibition in Michigan" (Ph.D. dissertation, University of Michigan, 1971), pp. 119-124. The English temperance movement in the 19th century was predominantly urban. See Brian Harrison, *Drink and the Victorians: The Temperance Question in England, 1815-1872* (London, 1971), p. 31.

4. The following conclusions were derived from a computer-assisted analysis of biographical data pertaining to 370 leaders of the Prohibition party and 271 leaders of the Anti-Saloon League. The party group includes 16 candidates for national office, 122 gubernatorial candidates, 119 National Committee members, and 87 state chairmen, as well as lesser candidates and officials. The League group includes 29 paid national officials, 64 volunteer national officials, 102 state superintendents, and 103 volunteer state officials, as well as lesser officers. Sources included L. E. Van Norman, ed., *An Album of Representative Prohibitionists* (New York, 1895); E. H. Cherrington and W. E. Johnson, eds., *Standard Encyclopedia of the Alcohol Problem,* 6 vols. (Westerville, Ohio, 1924-1930); and the prohibitionist periodical press, 1890-1913. A more detailed analysis will be published separately.

5. Including the census divisions of New England, the Middle Atlantic, and East North Central.

6. Correlation of the state-by-state residence distribution for 362 Prohibition party leaders with the mean percentage of the Prohibition party vote by state, 1872-1912, resulted in a Pearson's r value of +.7882, with a probability value of 7^{-10}. The residences of the leadership thus seem to have been distributed in pretty much the same fashion as the party vote. No similar test was possible for the Anti-Saloon League leadership, as there is no comparable way to ascertain the distribution of League support.

7. Henry J. Silverman, "American Social Reformers in the Late Nineteenth and Early Twentieth Century" (Ph. D. dissertation, University of Pennsylvania, 1963), studies about 170 social reformers listed in *The New Encyclopedia of Social Reform,* ed. W.D.P. Bliss (New York, 1908), who were active from 1890 to 1908. Compared

with Silverman's group, a larger proportion of prohibitionist leaders were native Americans or English-speaking foreign born and rural, midwestern, and southern in origin; more midwestern and western in residence; and less well educated. See Silverman, "American Social Reformers," pp. 33-36, 40-41, 56. Compared with 260 leaders of the Progressive party studied by Alfred D. Chandler, Jr., more of the prohibitionist group were foreign in origin and fewer were Republican in politics; both groups were urban, Protestant, and middle-class. "The Origins of Progressive Leadership," in *The Letters of Theodore Roosevelt,* ed. Elting Morrison (Cambridge, 1954), vol. 8, p. 1462.

8. Sam B. Warner, Jr., *Streetcar Suburbs: The Process of Growth in Boston, 1870-1900* (Cambridge, 1962), pp. 2, 46. For evidence of similar disintegration of community life in midwestern small towns, see Lewis Atherton, *Main Street on the Middle Border* (Bloomington, Ind., 1954), pp. 216, 245-249, 285-295.

9. See, for example, the discussion of William Dean Howells in Stow Persons, *The Decline of American Gentility* (New York, 1973), pp. 113-129.

10. For typical expressions of this view, see: Samuel D. Hastings to Thomas C. Richmond, April 26, 1883, T. C. Richmond Papers, State Historical Society of Wisconsin (WHS); *The Voice,* June 1, 1893, August 2, 1894, August 22, 1895; *Northwestern Mail* (Madison, Wis.), April 1, 1897; Edna T. Frederickson, "John P. St. John, Father of Constitutional Prohibition" (Ph. D. dissertation, University of Kansas, 1930), pp. 226, 234, 300. Nineteen prohibitionist leaders claimed to have been abolitionists themselves, and thirteen more recalled their family's abolitionist commitment.

11. E. J. Wheeler, *Prohibition: The Principle, the Policy, the Party* (New York, 1889), p. 190.

12. Raymond G. McCarthy, ed., *Drinking and Intoxication: Selected Readings in Social Attitudes and Controls* (New Haven, 1959), p. 180.

13. James C. Malin, *A Concern for Humanity: Notes on Reform, 1872-1912, at the National and Kansas Levels of Thought* (Lawrence, Kansas, 1964). See also James R. Turner, "The American Prohibition Movement, 1865-1897" (Ph. D. dissertation, University of Wisconsin, 1972), p. ii.

14. Frances E. Willard, *Glimpses of Fifty Years: The Autobiography of an American Woman* (Chicago, 1889), p. 695. The remainder of this chapter rests upon an examination of fourteen autobiographies of thirteen prohibitionists and eleven biographies of nine prohibitionists, with representation from the Prohibition party (8), Anti-Saloon League (5), and the WCTU (6), and some duplication between the groups.

In all, twenty individuals are dealt with. Because of the small number involved, it was not feasible to distinguish among leaders of the three groups by organization. Although some socioeconomic differences existed between leaders of the Prohibition party and the Anti-Saloon League, it will be assumed that their expectations upon entering the movement were similar.

15. *New Voice*, February 19, 1903.

16. Albert Elijah Carhart, *A Partial Life Story, How Booze Was Beaten in a Mid-Western State* (n.p., 1931), p. 8; "Minutes of the National Committees, Conferences and Conventions of the Prohibition Party" (Michigan Historical Collections, Ann Arbor), vol. 1. p. 11.

17. The quoted phrase is from Frederick A. McKenzie, *"Pussyfoot" Johnson, Crusader—Reformer—A Man among Men* (New York, 1920), pp. 32-33. This interpretation owes much to Richard Weiss, *The American Myth of Success* (New York, 1969).

18. John Bascom, *Things Learned by Living* (New York and London, 1913), pp. 5-7; Charles M. Sheldon, *His Life Story* (New York, 1925), p. 23; Frederickson, "John P. St. John," p. 14; Carhart, *Partial Life Story*, p. 7; McKenzie, *"Pussyfoot" Johnson*, pp. 17, 19. Both before and after repeal, Ernest H. Cherrington, General Secretary of the Anti-Saloon League, busied himself constructing an American genealogy of his family. Cherrington to Mrs. Walter A. Funk, June 22, 1935, Cherrington Papers, Temperance Education Foundation, Westerville Ohio.

19. James Cannon, Jr., *Bishop Cannon's Own Story: Life as I Have Seen It,* ed. Richard L. Watson, Jr. (Durham, N.C., 1955), p. 25.

20. Ishbel Ross, *Crusades and Crinolines: The Life and Times of Ellen Curtis Demorest and William Jennings Demorest* (New York, 1963), pp. 9-10, 44, 243; Cannon, *Bishop Cannon's Own Story*, pp. 33, 108; George R. Grose, *James W. Bashford, Pastor, Educator, Bishop* (New York, 1922), pp. 29-35; Sheldon, *His Life Story*, pp. 79-80. For a perceptive analysis of Sheldon's *In His Steps*, which complements this chapter, see Paul S. Boyer, *"In His Steps:* A Reappraisal," *American Quarterly* 33 (Spring 1971): 60-78.

21. Bascom, *Things Learned*, pp. 52, 58, 60, 136-137.

22. Sheldon, *His Life Story*, pp. 26, 81-82; Virginius Dabney, *Dry Messiah: The Life of Bishop Cannon* (New York, 1949), p. 311; Cannon, *Bishop Cannon's Own Story*, p. 53; Ross, *Crusades and Crinolines*, pp. 69, 197; Justin Steuart, *Wayne Wheeler, Dry Boss* (New York, 1928), p. 18; Bascom, *Things Learned*, pp. 61-63, 87; Grose, *Bashford*, p. 96.

23. Jesse Yarnell to T. C. Richmond, May 30, 1895; J. L. Ingersoll to T. C. Richmond, July 27, 1891; J. N. Baker to T. C. Richmond, August 1, 1891, Richmond Papers; *New Voice*, August 18, 1904; *Chicago Record-Herald*, May 27, 1912; Frederickson, "John P. St. John," pp. 361-362; Grose, *Bashford*, pp. 64-65, 79, 126-127, 176-177, 180-181; Sheldon, *His Life Story*, pp. 60-61, 69-70, 79-80, 170, 274-275; Cannon, *Bishop Cannon's Own Story*, pp. 14, 68, 84, 344; John Sobieski, *The Life-Story and Personal Reminiscences of Col. John Sobieski* (Shelbyville, Ill., 1900), pp. 310-311; Dabney, *Dry Messiah*, p. 166; Bascom, *Things Learned*, pp. 126-127, 171, 182, 195-197, 208-209; Ross, *Crusades and Crinolines*, p. 245; Carhart, *Partial Life Story*, pp. 33-34.

24. James B. Cranfill, *Dr. J. B. Cranfill's Chronicle: A Story of Life in Texas* (New York, 1916), pp. 1, 6.

25. Cranfill, *Chronicle*, pp. 14, 17-18; Cranfill, *From Memory: Reminiscences, Recitals, and Gleanings from a Bustling and Busy Life* (Nashville, Tenn., 1937), p. 30.

26. Cranfill, *Chronicle*, pp. 19-20, 21, 25-26, 32, 94; *From Memory*, p. 60.

27. Cranfill, *Chronicle*, pp. 59, 284; *From Memory*, p. 18.

28. Cranfill, *From Memory*, p. 74.

29. Cranfill, *Chronicle*, pp. 27-28; *From Memory*, pp. 33-34.

30. Cranfill, *Chronicle*, pp. 46, 58; *From Memory*, pp. 43-44.

31. Cranfill, *Chronicle*, pp. 165-166, 179.

32. Ibid., pp. 185, 189, 240-241, 244, 246, 260, 266, 267, 269, 277-278, 463.

33. Cranfill, *From Memory*, pp. 28, 178; *Chronicle*, chs. 40 and 41.

34. Cranfill, *Chronicle*, p. 297; *From Memory*, p. 178.

35. Cranfill, *Chronicle*, p. 298.

36. Ibid., pp. 303-306. The Republican John P. St. John of Kansas similarly joined the Prohibitionists as their presidential candidate in 1884 after having been defeated for a third term as Governor of Kansas in 1882 by the defection of antiprohibition Republicans because of his support for the state's prohibition constitutional amendment. See Frederickson, "John P. St. John," pp. 238-239.

37. Cranfill, *Chronicle*, p. 307.

38. Ibid., pp. 363-373, 463; *From Memory*, p. 205.

39. Cranfill, *Chronicle*, p. 54. By 1937 this attitude had so calcified that Cranfill found "some of our so-called Christian schools . . . shot through with modernism, liberalism, agnosticism, and Communism." *From Memory*, pp. 40-42.

40. Cranfill, *From Memory*, pp. 33-34, 125; Cranfill, *Chronicle*, p. 27.

41. See also Cranfill, *Chronicle,* pp. 1-7.

42. Ibid., p. 85.

43. Ibid.; pp. 470, 494-495.

44. Ibid., pp. 20, 294, 400, 454-455; *From Memory,* pp. 40-42, 108, 128-129.

45. Cranfill, *Chronicle,* pp. 101, 132-133, 147, 303-305, 369, 395, 424; *From Memory,* pp. 82, 191-192.

46. Bascom, *Things Learned,* p. 29; see also pp. 28, 31, 55.

47. Carry Nation's adoration for her father and her unfeminine attacks upon saloons lend support to this interpretation, as do Frances Willard's well-known masculine proclivities. See Herbert Asbury, *Carry Nation* (New York, 1929), p. 6; Willard, *Glimpses,* pp. 25, 63, 69, 76, 100, 107, 193; Norton Mezvinsky, "The White-Ribbon Reform, 1874-1920" (Ph.D. dissertation, University of Wisconsin, 1959), pp. 193-195.

48. Christopher Lasch, *The New Radicalism in America, 1889-1963* (New York, 1967), ch. 2, seeks to limit the phenomenon to female intellectuals of the middle class. But even Lasch's evidence (see, for example, p. 58) suggests that his intellectual women saw their problem as one shared by the majority of middle-class women, not merely those of "intellectual ambitions."

49. Joseph R. Gusfield, *Symbolic Crusade: Status Politics and the American Temprance Movement* (Urbana, Ill., 1963), pp. 69-86. Middle-class men did not, however, find this imaginative leap impossible. See Boyer, *"In His Steps:* A Reappraisal," pp. 72-78.

50. Mezvinsky, "White-Ribbon Reform," p. 239.

51. Stow Persons, *Decline of American Gentility,* p. 91.

52. Anna Prosser, *From Death to Life,* 2nd ed. (Chicago, 1911), p. 46.

53. Carry A. Nation, *The Use and Need of the Life of Carry A. Nation* (Topeka, Kan., 1909), pp. 73-74, 102, 116, 124.

54. Carleton Beals, *Cyclone Carry: The Story of Carry Nation* (Philadelphia and New York, 1962), pp. 270, 274.

55. Nation, *Use and Need,* pp. 120-121.

56. Prosser, *Death to Life,* pp. 13-14; see also p. 62.

57. Belle Kearney, *A Slave-holder's Daughter* (New York, 1900), pp. 68-71, 189.

58. Jane Agnes Stewart, *I Have Recalled* (Toledo, 1938), pp. 19-20; Kearney, *A Slave-holder's Daughter,* pp. 40-41, 84.

59. Nation, *Use and Need,* pp. 116, 139, 228.

60. Ross, *Crusades and Crinolines,* p. 274.

61. Prosser, *Death to Life,* pp. 20-22, 67-68, 73, 141-148, 195-197, 205.

62. Nation, *Use and Need,* p. 121.

63. Ross, *Crusades and Crinolines,* pp. 32, 56.

64. Stewart, *I Have Recalled,* p. 25.

65. Mezvinsky, "White-Ribbon Reform," pp. 193-195.

66. Nation, *Use and Need,* p. 102.

67. Kearney, *A Slave-holder's Daughter,* pp. 133-154, 187.

68. Prosser, *Death to Life,* pp. 47-48, 77.

69. Willard, *Glimpses of Fifty Years,* pp. 69, 76, 193, 605.

70. Ibid., p. 100; quoted in Mary Earhart, *Frances Willard: From Prayers to Politics* (Chicago, 1944), pp. 77-80.

71. Stewart, *I Have Recalled,* p. 33.

72. Willard, *Glimpses of Fifty Years,* pp. 638-645.

73. Ibid, pp. 84, 124, 159, 165, 638; Nation, *Use and Need,* pp. 64, 325-327, 343; *The Hatchet* (Guthrie, Okla.), July 1, 1906. Carry's warnings to young boys against the dangers of masturbation brought her into federal court on a charge of sending obscene matter through the mails.

74. Willard, *Glimpses,* pp. 325-326, 328-329; Kearney, *A Slave-holder's Daughter,* p. 240.

75. Willard, *Glimpses,* pp. 128, 274, 636.

76. Ibid., p. 127.

77. Ibid., pp. 359-361, 453, 534, 627.

78. Ibid., p. 693.

79. Ibid., ch. 10, pp. 333, 342-344, 400-401, 441-442, 444, 445, 470-471.

2

The magnet of populism

THE NEW REPUBLICANS

On the eve of the presidential election of 1888, Prohibition party leaders firmly believed that they stood at the gates to the political Promised Land. A spectacular jump in the party's vote, from about 10,000 in 1880 to 150,000 four years later; the widespread belief that Prohibitionist votes in New York state had tipped the national balance of power; submission of prohibition amendments to many state constitutions, and their adoption in Iowa, the Dakota territory, and Rhode Island; introduction of a national prohibition amendment in the Congress; and gains registered in state elections during 1885-1887, all encouraged party men to believe that they would soon supplant the Republican party as the standard-bearers of reform.[1] Suiting their strategy to their vision of a national party, they sought to reach out to all types of voters.

Prominent members of the party presented the case for proselytizing various minority groups to Executive Committee meetings and to the national convention of 1888. The party responded by ordering copies of the platform printed in German and the Scandinavian languages and by providing for subsidized distribution of a Minnesota Roman Catholic paper. Aiming toward both nativists and organized labor, Prohibitionists reversed their stands of 1872, 1876, and 1884 for unrestricted immigration and advocated enforcement of the restrictive immigration law of 1882. In their Sabbath observance plank, they stood "for the preservation and defense of the Sabbath

as a civil institution, without oppressing any who religiously observe
the same on any other than the first day of the week." During the
1888 campaign its publishers raised funds to send free copies of
the New York *Voice,* the party's national organ, to 60,000 ministers
and 500,000 farmers. By its nomination for President of Clinton
B. Fisk, former Union General and influential Methodist layman,
the party expected to draw massive support from that temperance-
minded denomination. Hoping to repeat their determining role
in the election, party leaders decided to concentrate upon "pivotal"
states.[2]

Prohibitionists in 1888 were not alone in believing that the
near future might see the supplanting of the Republican party by
a less tarnished agent of reform, the Prohibition party. During the
Prohibitionists' national convention in Indianapolis, Congressman
James B. Weaver, a former Greenbacker presidential candidate,
sent greetings to a Prohibitionist leader:

> It is clear to the thoughtful observer that the National
> Prohibition Party is destined in the near future to be
> the dominant political force in American politics, and
> rightfully so. The Political Storm center now rests on
> Indianapolis, and if you make no mistake in your plat-
> form, you will discharge the thunderbolt that will unite
> all true elements of reform and bring on a rain that will
> refresh and fructify the whole continent.[3]

Likewise, Bishop Henry M. Turner, the most prominent black nationalist of the late nineteenth century, sought after 1884 to lead black
voters into the Prohibition party, which he saw as the rightful heir
to the Republican antislavery tradition.[4]

Turner could have been right. Two-thirds of the men and women
who led the Prohibition party during 1890-1913 were former Republicans, and over half left the party of Lincoln during the years
1880-1887, although for Prohibitionists the Republican "farewell
to the bloody shirt" was probably only one indication among many
that Republicanism no longer meant reform. Nineteen of the
125 party leaders born before 1841 called themselves former abolitionists, and thirteen others recalled early lives in abolitionist
families.[5]

Having recently left the Republican party, Prohibitionists framed their approach to reform within the model provided by the Republican party of the 1880s. Thus, they carried with them into the Prohibition party the racial dilemma of Republicanism. It sprang from the inability to reconcile their antislavery heritage with their desire to become a "truly national" party, which they felt necessitated an appeal to the white South.[6] As the Republican party sought to bring together businessmen and former Whigs in both North and South, Prohibitionists tried to unite "decent citizens" of both sections.

At their 1888 national convention, Prohibitionists made obeisance to the antislavery tradition by listening to an address by Bishop Turner and adopted the "supplementary" resolution offered by a black delegate from North Carolina: "RESOLVED: That we hold that all men are born free and equal, and should be made secure in all their civil, legal and political rights."[7] General Fisk, their presidential nominee, a former Freedmen's Bureau official and founder of Fisk University, also symbolized the antislavery connection.[8] The real difficulty came, however, with the woman suffrage plank, which was apparently considered by southerners in the party to be the litmus test of its desire to appeal to their section. The South's quarrel with woman suffrage stemmed not only from the fear of enfranchising black women but also from opposition, especially by churchmen, to the widening of woman's sphere.[9] The history of the Prohibition party's tampering with its suffrage plank affords, therefore, a guide to its oscillations between the poles of postwar abolitionism and the southern white vote.

The party had appeared upon the national scene in 1872 with a suffrage plank advocating the franchise for all, restricted only by "mental and moral" qualifications. This could have meant either the normal disqualification of idiots and criminals, in which case the party would have been promoting universal suffrage in effect, or it could have implied an educational qualification which could be used against uneducated blacks and other lower-class citizens, leading to a class-based franchise. In 1876 the Prohibitionists advocated an unrestricted franchise. Another ambiguous qualification appeared in 1880 when the party promised to support the ballot for women for their "protection."[10] Frances Willard shortly before this had subverted the WCTU's resistance to woman suffrage by sneaking through a declaration for the "home protection" ballot, which allowed women to vote when questions of liquor control ("protection of their homes") were to be decided. Seen in this context, the party's 1880 plank may have represented a position somewhat short of universal, unrestricted suffrage.[11] In 1884 Willard, the leader of the woman suffrage forces in the party, was so impressed by the need for placating the South, to which she had just devoted several long organizing tours, that she personally inserted into the suffrage plank the most drastic qualification yet. She had the party "enunciate the principle" of the "home protection" ballot only, but "relegate the practical outworking of this reform to the discretion of the Prohibition party in the several states, according to the condition of public sentiment in those states."[12] In 1885 the Prohibition party made a concerted effort to woo the temperance sentiment of the white South, sending nationally prominent lecturers through the section.[13]

In the 1884 presidential election the Prohibition party made substantial gains in the South, but the Northeast remained the base of its mass support. Three-fifths of the party's vote came from the six states of Massachusetts, New York, Pennsylvania, Michigan, Ohio, and Illinois.[14] Consequently, some revision of the woman suffrage plank was felt to be necessary in 1888. J. B. Cranfill expressed the need for a plank "that would read for woman suffrage in the North and against it in the South."[15] A vigorous debate over the nature of that revision occupied the central place at the Indianapolis convention. A majority of the Committee on Resolutions reported a plank designed to break both horns of the race dilemma. It proposed

> that the right of suffrage rests on no mere circumstance
> of race, color, sex or nationality, and that where, from
> any cause, it has been withheld from citizens who are
> of suitable age, and mentally and morally qualified
> for the exercise of an intelligent ballot, it should be
> restored by the people through the Legislatures of the
> several States, on such educational basis as they may
> deem wise.[16]

This was obviously a two-headed plank: one head looked to northern reformers and spoke to them in idealistic tones of an inalienable right which, having been "withheld," should be "restored";

the other looked to southerners and northern conservatives, allowing them, through the provisions for "mental and moral" qualifications, an "intelligent ballot" and an "educational basis" established by the states, to continue to withhold from women and blacks the inalienable right promised in the first section. It would have the effect of localizing the party's appeal within the educated classes to which most of its leaders belonged. Delegates from Kentucky, Georgia, and Missouri supported the majority report because they felt that it would be acceptable to the South.[17]

The minority report, offered by a Wisconsin delegate, generally repeated the provision of 1884 that the woman suffrage question be referred to the states for decision.[18] Thomas C. Richmond and other supporters charged that the majority report would prevent the party from ever becoming a "truly national" party by alienating southerners as well as antisuffragists.[19] All speakers for the minority report claimed to be supporters of woman suffrage.[20] The old warrior Neal Dow, also a woman suffragist, made clear to the convention just where he thought antisuffragist sentiment was strongest: "The Presbyterian Church, the Reformed Church, the Episcopal Church, the Congregational Church, the Methodist Church, the Baptist Church," he pointed out, "are almost unanimously opposed to Woman Suffrage." Their pleas were in vain, however, for the educational qualifications brought to the suffragist forces enough southern strength to carry the majority report by a large margin.[21]

The convention majority of 1888, in its attempt to speak to many different segments of society, pushed through a broad platform consisting of eight planks not directly concerned with prohibition in addition to the first four prohibition-related demands. But the delegates also listened to a minority which insisted that the party could gain success only by limiting its platform to the single issue of prohibition. In conceding to this minority the last plank of the platform, the so-called dominant-issue plank, the broadgauge forces handed their opponents a weapon which would be used to defeat them eight years later. The plank sounded innocuous enough at the time. It read:

Recognizing and declaring that prohibition of the liquor traffic has become the dominant issue in national politics we invite to full party fellowship all those who, on this

one dominant issue, are with us agreed, in the full belief
that this party can and will remove sectional differences,
promote national unity and insure the best welfare of
our entire land.[22]

In the election of 1888 the Prohibition party found its outstretched
hand refused. The national vote climbed to 250,122 from 150, 957 in
1884. In the South as a whole the vote increased, and in some states
it increased spectacularly (fivefold in Tennessee, sixfold in North Carolina,
and tenfold in Georgia and Virginia), but the final totals and, worse,
percentages of the popular vote were still unimpressive (1.96 percent,
0.98 percent, 1.26 percent, and 0.55 percent, respectively, in the
four states mentioned).[23] Worse still, the party lost the national
balance of power it had claimed to hold in 1884, and the election
seemed to turn not on prohibition, as the party leaders had hoped
and expected, but rather on the tariff issue precipitated by President
Grover Cleveland's message. In states such as North Carolina,
where the party had frightened the dominant political powers
since its founding in 1885, its strength was tested in 1888 and found
to be negligible, leading to a loss of influence.[24]

James R. Turner has claimed that the election of 1888 made the
Prohibitionists a more genuinely national party than they had been
in 1884. The trend was away from almost complete dependence
upon the Northeast.[25] The columns for 1884 and 1888 in Table 5
present the evidence upon which he bases this claim. As we can see,
the distribution of the party vote did shift from the Northeast toward
the South and West.

Focusing upon these two elections, however, obscures a more
important countertrend. Table 6 presents the Pearsonian correlations
derived from comparisons of the state-by-state distribution of the
party vote in paired elections from 1872 through 1912. The closer
Pearson's r approaches +1.0, the closer the association between the
distributions of party strength. More important than the dispersion
between 1884 and 1888 was the long-term trend toward stabiliza-
tion. In fact, the distributions of the 1884 and 1888 votes were more
closely related than those of any previous pair of elections. The
significant fact in 1888 was not that the party's appeal was spreading,
but that it was spreading less than ever before.

TABLE 5: REGIONAL DISTRIBUTION OF THE PROHIBITION PARTY VOTE, 1872-1912
IN PERCENTAGES

Region	1872	1876	1880	1884	1888	1892	1896	1896N*	1900	1904	1908	1912
New England	6.9	5.4	13.3	12.5	8.0	7.0	7.0	0.4	6.5	3.7	4.3	3.8
Middle Atlantic	32.8	38.6	35.1	30.8	23.6	26.4	31.2	6.2	27.2	23.7	25.4	20.0
East North Central	60.3	27.8	39.3	34.6	36.5	36.5	23.2	58.1	30.2	38.9	34.6	30.5
Total *Northeast*	100.0	71.8	87.7	77.9	68.1	69.9	61.4	64.7	63.9	66.3	64.3	54.3
South Atlantic	0.0**	0.1	0.0**	3.0	5.2	5.7	13.0	2.8	6.5	4.1	4.7	5.3
East South Central	0.0**	8.4	2.9	3.2	4.8	4.6	8.0	0.0**	5.0	3.5	2.7	1.9
West South Central	—	—	—	2.6	2.2	0.8	1.4	6.4	1.5	2.0	1.1	2.3
Total *South*	0.0**	8.5	2.9	8.8	12.2	11.1	22.4	9.2	13.0	9.6	8.5	9.5
West North Central	—	19.5	8.7	10.4	15.8	13.0	10.4	14.8	16.0	16.5	16.2	14.7
Mountain West	—	—	—	0.5	0.9	1.2	1.7	2.8	2.5	1.9	3.3	3.5
Pacific West	—	0.0**	0.5	2.3	3.0	4.8	3.4	8.5	4.8	5.6	7.6	17.9
Total *West*	—	19.5	9.2	13.2	19.7	19.0	15.5	26.1	23.3	24.0	27.1	36.1
Total States Casting Prohibition Votes	6	18	18	34	37	41	41	18	40	40	39	40
Total Vote (In Thousands)	6	10	10	151	250	271	131	14	210	260	253	210

*1896N: National Party (see Chapter 4).

** 0.0 signifies that the party received some votes, but less than .05 percent.

Source: Petersen, *Statistical History,* pp. 43-79.

TABLE 6: THE CHANGING DISTRIBUTION OF THE
PROHIBITION PARTY VOTE, 1872-1912

Election Pairs	Pearson's r (see footnote*)
1872/1876	+.5208 (+)
1876/1880	+.7084 (+)
1880/1884	+.7402 (+)
1884/1888	+.8458 (+)
1888/1892	+.9782 (+)
1892/1896	+.8446 (–)
1892/1900	+.9068 (–)
1896/1900	+.9130 (+)
1900/1904	+.9258 (+)
1904/1908	+.9574 (–)
1908/1912	+.8467 (–)
1892/1896N**	+.5240
1896/1896N**	+.2156
1896N**/1900	+.4438

*(+): Rising vote from first to second paired election.
(–): Falling vote from first to second paired election.
**1896N: National party (see Chapter 4).

Source: Petersen, *Statistical History*, pp. 43-79.

This performance led to disappointment among Prohibitionists
and among many gave rise to a gnawing doubt.[26] An anonymous
correspondent of the Wisconsin party paper summed up the feeling:

> The prohibition party has reached a critical period in its
> history. . . . The hopes of immediate victory, which inspired
> its early votaries, have not been realized. The problem with
> which it has been wrestling is yet unsolved. . . . there are
> many misgivings concerning the future. "What next?" is the
> anxious inquiry of many who in years past have sacrificed
> and toiled for the success of this cause.

He hastened to add, "This question is asked, not because those who

have given their support to this principle have any thought of abandoning the cause they have so unselfishly espoused, but because they would be sure that they are in the true line of advancement."[27]
In search of another "line of advancement," party leaders in Pennsylvania and Washington flirted briefly with nonpartisan methods.[28]
Other leaders merely carried on in the same ways. At postmortems in 1888 and 1889, the National Committee and National Executive Committee resolved to continue the party's appeals to the South as well as to Germans and other "citizens of foreign birth." At a National Committee meeting in 1889, James B. Cranfill of Texas asked the Mississippi State Chairman "whether objection was raised in Mississippi, that woman suffrage included Negro woman suffrage and thus doubly complicated [the] race question."
The Mississippian "replied 'Yes,' but thought the educational qualification proposed in our platform fully answered such objection."
A meeting of leaders in 1891 decided to write a platform in the following year that would "not differ materially from the one of -88."[29]

Those who had fought against that platform in 1888 not surprisingly found the cause of the party's disappointing performance in the broadness of its demands and therefore urged limiting the platform either by retention of the dominant-issue plank or by trimming to the single plank of prohibition. Thomas C. Richmond became the center of this effort until, in January 1892, Frances Willard convinced him that the party's best hope lay in coalition with the Populists through the adoption of a broad platform. Until that time, Richmond argued that the party's potential constituency lay among "thinking, practical, business men" and pointed out that "men may be too radical at times, as well as too conservative" and "compromise is not a crime." Richmond saw his proposed single-issue platform as the means of uniting "the intellectual power and moral worth of the best manhood in America" and urged the kind of political sellout of southern blacks which Booker T. Washington advocated.[30]

Responding in 1891 to pressure from Richmond's group, *The Voice* queried party leaders on their preferences for a dominant-issue or single-issue platform. From without, a Catholic writer denounced the party for having allowed itself to be "barnacled" with "the standing army of crack-brained, visionary cranks, who here in America take up with every fad—free love, anarchism, etc., etc. (you cannot mention an absurdity which they will not insert

in their creed)." Within the party National Chairman Samuel Dickie
urged Ohio Prohibitionists to concentrate on their main issue, "a
question of vastly greater moment than the silver question, the
tariff or the tin-plate humbug."[31]

The direction of Dickie's warning was significant, for while
national party leaders continued to operate within the Republican
model, state Prohibition parties were beginning to move in a new
direction, shaping their vague reformism into specific critiques of
the economic system designed to ally them with discontented
farmers and laborers. This change of direction was evident in Washington where the party's new alignment with the "wrong" side in
class conflict drove out older leaders. In Tennessee, the Methodist
minister who won the party's gubernatorial nomination simultaneously attracted the party's largest vote ever, persecution from his
bishop, and charges of sympathy with blacks by seeking support
from "farmer and mechanic" through an economic reform program.
Perhaps in response to these developments, the Prohibition party's
National Committee in 1889 listened courteously to a fusion
proposal from the leaders of the Union Labor party, but such a
possibility, never very great, shriveled with the decline of the
weak Union Laborites.[32]

The rise of the Farmers' Alliances as they turned to political
activity after 1889 required from Prohibitionists a more positive
response. A writer in the reformist *Arena* of Boston urged in
1891 the union of Prohibitionists and labor reformers in a new party,
socialist in all but name. A veteran Ohio Prohibition party leader
suggested shortly afterward that "our party has very special
relations to, and ought to be in very close sympathy with the farmers
in their political movements."[33]

Other, powerful voices within the party urged caution. In November
1890 Chairman Dickie felt it necessary to issue a party circular on
the question of fusion. Finding "cause of rejoicing and hope of
strength" in "the numerous labor organizations, and in the agricultural
organizations of the West and South," and believing that such organizations' "complaints are well founded," he stated, "While we do
not believe that the mere suppression of the dramshops will accomplish
the reforms so much desired by the laboring and agricultural classes,
we do believe that such suppression must be the first step and will
be a very long step in that direction." Therefore, he set two conditions
as prerequisites to fusion:

1st. If it [the organization to be allied with] hold any
other tenet of political faith as of more importance than
prohibition, that tenet must be one which we esteem of
minor concern, and upon which we can agree to disagree
while we shall together accomplish that which the present
membership of the prohibition party hold to be of chief
moment. 2d. That party must be so clearly and so honestly
committed to prohibition . . . that it will deliberately prefer
defeat with prohibition to victory without it.

He concluded, "For my own part I know of no political party to which
we can make or from which we can consider a proposition to unite
without stultifying ourselves, becoming the laughing stock of the
nation and doing the principle we represent irreparable injury."
Other Prohibitionist leaders, including the editor of *The Voice,* con-
trasted the class-based character of the farmers' movement to the
Prohibitionists' selflessness in warning against fusion.[34]

FIRST STEPS TOWARD POPULISM: CINCINNATI, 1891,
AND CHICAGO, 1892

Prohibitionists entered the 1890s in a state of tension which
reflected the conflicting motives for their reform. They searched
for order, but that order could take either of two forms: consensus
or pluralism. The idealism of the Prohibitionists led them to believe
that a consensus with those less fortunate than they was both possible
and necessary. The class interests of the Prohibitionists at the same time
impelled them toward a political stance which would set them apart
from and in conflict with those who refused to share their values
and life-style. Both courses required sacrifice. Consensus could be
achieved only if the middle class which the Prohibitionists represented
relinquished a portion of the property which constituted its members'
stake in society in order to give others a similar stake. A pluralistic
society would require the sacrifice of Prohibitionist idealism envisioning
a united society. The rise of Populism provided the Prohibitionists
with their decisive opportunity to take the path which led to consensus.
Prohibitionists found in the rise of Populism both promise and threat.
One source of gratification was the fact that many, if not most,
of the Populist rank and file seemed to share Prohibitionists' hostility

toward the liquor traffic. Affinity led to political cooperation in four
states during 1890, with the Populists adopting a prohibition plank
and the Prohibitionists agreeing to Populist economic and political
demands. One of the only two Prohibition party Congressmen ever
elected won as a coalition candidate in Minnesota. The most prominent
Populist leaders from every section supported prohibition and, with
less unanimity, woman suffrage.[35] Thus, Prohibitionists could greet
the farmers' success as the triumph of a parallel movement composed
of like-minded though not wholly enlightened reformers.[36]

Prohibitionists found distressing, however, the possibility that
Populism would divert Prohibitionist support into other channels,
leaving their party high and dry. In Texas, the Prohibitionists'
first gubernatorial candidate abandoned their leaky boat to swim with
the rising tide of Populism.[37] The fear that others were reaching
similar conclusions lurked beneath the surface of a *Voice* editorial
early in 1891 which pointed out that the People's party arose from
the same rural districts where Prohibitionists found their sources
of greatest strength. The same fear bubbled to the top of numerous
attempts to discredit the sincerity of Populist prohibitionism.[38]

Actually, neither party as it was constituted in 1892 had much
chance of wooing away the other's supporters. If the town-country
hostility found by Stanley Parsons in Nebraska was general among
Populist voters, they were not likely to see much value in a party which
was led by urban dwellers and based in the most highly urbanized
and industrialized sector of the nation, and which had historically
shown no interest in farmers' problems.[39] As a Prohibitionist farmer
pointed out, party leaders were too much subject to "city dweller's
attitudes."[40] For their part, the Populists could offer Prohibitionists
little more than dry good will and a mutual though uniquely originated dissatisfaction with the workings of American society. As it
turned out, Prohibitionist fears of Populist incursions were largely
groundless. The correlation between the distributions of the Prohibition vote in 1888 and the larger vote of 1892 was nearly perfect:
+.9782 (Table 6). The Populist vote in 1892 correlated with the
Prohibition distributions of 1888 and 1892 at -.0478 and -.0513
respectively. The Populists did take away some Prohibitionist voters,
even in the Ohio Valley bastion, but they failed to make a significant
dent in party strength.[41] Together, the two reform parties spanned
the nation, attracting voters in its most urban and most rural, most

industrial and most agricultural areas. But to unite those voters
would require cooperation at every level.

Party Chairman Samuel Dickie articulated the negative response
to this situation: sit tight, he and others warned, and wait until
the shock of political conflict makes clear to the farmers the preeminence of prohibition. Meanwhile, the chaos of multi-party
politics would break the ties of loyalty which alone kept nascent
Prohibitionists from joining the true reform party. Populism itself
might serve as a bridge for Republicans and Democrats to cross to
the cold-water forces. John P. St. John claimed that "the Alliance
party, as such, can never permanently attain power in this country,
for the reason that it is a class organization. But it is loosening
political shackles and stirring up the pool of politics, so to speak, and
when it is settled politics will be clearer and purer than . . . before."[42]
Implicit in this position was the hope that Prohibitionist ties would
not be loosed at the same time, a hope founded upon the belief
that Prohibitionists did not sympathize with the Populist economic
critique, and therefore were not susceptible to the appeal of a "class
party." Antifusionist thinking thus displayed the class bias characteristic among most other opponents of Populism.

For Frances Willard, reform was not divisible according to the
class antecedents of reformers. Reform included a socialist economic
program as well as prohibition and woman suffrage. Union of the
most powerful groups of reformers thus became for her the prerequisite to successful reform.[43] Since a Prohibitionist decision for
coalition was impossible until the national convention in June 1892,
she and her allies in the Prohibition party sought first to influence
Populist gatherings in Cincinnati in May 1891 and St. Louis in
February 1892.

Willard believed that Populist adoption of a prohibition and
also, as she hoped, a woman-suffrage plank would create the lever
to swing Prohibitionists into the arms of the Populist party. She
found, however, that despite earlier assurances by their leaders,
Populist conventions tended to place the effect of such planks upon
their own developing consensus above her dream of a grand coalition.
A premature attempt at Cincinnati to push prohibition into the
platform ran head-on into the Populists' need for internal unity.[44]
Introducing the Cincinnati platform, Ignatius Donnelly had
explained the situation: "We believed that we had better concen-

trate upon a few planks of an invulnerable platform, rather than
to spread ourselves on that which might be doubtful . . . . We feel
that we are not here so much to proclaim a creed as to erect a
banner around which the swarming hosts of reform could rally."
Kansas Senator William A. Peffer put it more bluntly: "There were
many in the convention who would have voted for it [a prohibition
plank], but they didn't think it expedient."[45] Much of the opposition
to the prohibition plank had come from leaders of the Knights of Labor,
whose support was anxiously sought by Populists pursuing the ever-
lasting dream of American radicals, a farmer-labor coalition.[46]

To antifusionist Prohibition party leaders, the type of reform
represented by the Cincinnati convention was inadmissible. John P.
St. John, who had been present, declared that "as a reform convention
it is the biggest failure I ever saw." Mixing perceptive criticism with
denunciation, he pointed out that not only did it reject prohibition,
but "the only thing that distinguished it from the old party conventions
was its visionary sub-treasury scheme," which "would be the worst
species of class legislation. It would afford no relief whatever to
the very poor, the class that needs relief most." Further, "no other
party convention was ever more subservient to the liquor interests
. . . . It is simply the birth of a third whiskey party."[47] The editors
of *The Voice* warned against fusion, repeating their charge that the
farmers' movement supported "class legislation," but proposed to
send free copies of the paper to 100,000 selected Farmers' Alliance
members for six months as a means of capitalizing upon the latter's
discontent with the status quo.[48]

In June 1891 the utopian novelist and Populist supporter Edward
Bellamy published a proposal which fusionists might have made into
a basis for coalition. This was the "nationalization of liquor," a plan
whereby the federal government became the sole dispenser of liquor
through government stores.[49] It seemed to fit in with Populist
sentiment for extension of government responsibility; indeed, the
Populist Senator from South Dakota, James H. Kyle, wrote to
The Voice that "this plan is in perfect harmony with the principles
of the party upon money and transportation." The Ohio, Massachusetts,
and Minnesota Populist parties adopted it as a platform plank.[50]

The nationalization scheme, however, was no panacea for the political
problems of either Prohibitionists or Populists. Although Bellamy
and his Nationalists promised that state conduct of the liquor traffic

would eliminate the corrupting influence of saloons, the profit motive, and impure liquor, most Prohibitionists saw it as simply a method for granting the public blessing to an immoral and socially disastrous habit.[51] And to Populists seeking a national coalition, any proposal which could be construed as opposition to drinking was anathema. Nevertheless, friends of compromise and fusion outside the Prohibitionist ranks—particularly Bellamy's Nationalists—continued to advance the proposal in the hope that its merits could be shown to outweigh these disadvantages.[52]

About two months after the Cincinnati Conference, a notice appeared in Prohibition party papers which indicated that antifusionist leaders of that party were amenable to cooperation with discontented farmers if such cooperation could take place on the antifusionists' terms. Entitled "An Official Call For a National Conference of the Friends of the Farmers Alliance who Believe in Prohibition," the notice began with the statement, "It is universally conceded that the basis of a nation's material prosperity consists chiefly in its agricultural interests." It continued by attacking "the power of money in politics" and advocating the return of government to the people, but asserted that "we believe that one of the first steps to be taken to insure this end is to destroy the legalized liquor traffic." Therefore, a nonpartisan conference was to be held in August 1891 at Prohibition Park on Staten Island for "simply an exchange of views." The signers, who claimed to be "identified with the farmers' organizations of the land, or otherwise deeply interested in them," included leaders of the antifusionist wing of the party.[53] No more was heard of the conference after this announcement; it illustrated the oft-expressed belief of this faction that the "class movement" of the farmers could serve only as a means of breaking their allegiance to the major parties and setting them free for eventual alignment with the Prohibition party. The antifusionists, that is, recognized the growing strength of the farmers' movement without realizing the weak position of their own party.

Less impressed by Prohibitionist strength, Frances Willard in the fall of 1891 began to gather her forces for the great effort at St. Louis. She proposed to anticipate and if possible to control the actions of the St. Louis conference by securing agreement beforehand from Prohibition and People's party leaders upon a mutually acceptable platform. The platform agreed upon by the

leaders would then, she hoped, be accepted by the conventions
of the two parties and fusion achieved. In October she began to
explore the possibilities of a conference of reform leaders; in
December she issued invitations for a "private" meeting at the
Sherman House in Chicago on January 27, 1892.[54]

In her search for agreement, Willard excluded from her conference as many sources of controversy as she could while retaining
an appearance of representativeness. No labor leaders or southern
Populists were present. General James B. Weaver and Ignatius Donnelly
were Willard's prize catches from the People's party. Chairman
Herman Taubeneck had to be invited because he was the titular
party leader and lived in Illinois, and George F. Washburn, the Boston
Nationalist who served as Populist national secretary, also came,
bringing with him a liquor nationalization plank which was promptly
rejected. The conference was packed with prohibitionists, most of
them members of the WCTU, and National Chairman Dickie came
as a more or less official representative of the Prohibition party.

After some rhetorical maneuvering, the general discussion began.[55]
Three Populist veiwpoints became evident. General Weaver wanted
a platform including planks on land, money, transportation, prohibition, and woman suffrage. Another Populist leader said that he
had formerly been a prohibitionist, was now wavering on the question—
along with public sentiment—and thought that nationalization of
liquor was the only true solution. Herman Taubeneck said flatly
that the People's party would not accept prohibition or woman
suffrage planks because of their unpopularity in the South.[56]

The liquor plank in the final address was the result of a compromise
but still did not suit the chairman of either party. The committee on
resolutions, dominated by Prohibitionists, presented a plank calling
for "annihilation" of the saloon. Donnelly, who favored the nationalization scheme, suggested that "abatement of the liquor traffic"
(a wording that he felt would permit acceptance of nationalization)
be adopted, and Taubeneck turned his suggestion into a motion.
Donnelly said that he felt it unwise to declare open war on the saloon
because of the German voters in the party. E. J. Wheeler suggested
a compromise on "suppression" of the saloon, and with that the
plank was adopted. The final liquor plank read: "[Resolved,]
That the saloon is the great enemy of reform and the chief fountain
of corruption in our politics. We denounce its pernicious influence
upon our country and demand its suppression."[57]

The other planks called for government issue of legal-tender money, government control of public transportation and communication, and "municipal suffrage for women, with an educational qualification," and denounced speculation and alien ownership in land. The "municipal" and "educational" qualifications of the woman suffrage plank were probably aimed at assuring harmony with southern Populism, for, as we have seen, a similar "educational qualification" for the ballot, to be determined by the states, had been inserted into the 1888 Prohibition party platform for the purpose of easing the political burden of southern Prohibitionists. In its retreat from state to municipal suffrage, the Chicago plank compromised even the weak position of the 1888 Prohibitionist platform.

The final address carried the signatures of Ignatius Donnelly and James B. Weaver for the Populist, and Frances Willard and E. J. Wheeler for the Prohibitionist side. Taubeneck and Washburn, the officers of the People's party, refused to vote on the final liquor plank, and Taubeneck told the group that the Populists at St. Louis would not accept the saloon plank and consequently its adoption at Chicago "was not a wise step toward a union of forces."[58] Nor did Chairman Dickie sign the final address. Although Frances Willard had her platform of reform leaders, the adoption of a liquor plank acceptable to most Prohibitionists had cost the support of the Populist National Chairman. Yet she had the approval of Donnelly and Weaver, names to conjure with in reform ranks for the past twenty years. That this was not enough became evident at St. Louis.

A DECISION AT ST. LOUIS

Shortly after the Sherman House conference, Willard's *Union Signal* tried to prepare Prohibitionists for fusion by outflanking the antifusionist stand on "principle": it was right, the WCTU organ said, to stand for principle, "but there are many ways of expressing our principles, there are many subsidiary movements that we might advocate which all really conduct to prohibition and not away from it." If fusion should be achieved, it "would mean more to the people of this country than any single event since the declaration of peace at Appomattox."[59] Prohibition party papers in Illinois and Wisconsin saw the moderate tone of the industrial

and monetary planks adopted at Chicago as indicators of the
probability of fusion but conceded that the pronouncements
of single-issue and dominant-issue Prohibitionists would tend
to alienate the Populists.[60] Edward J. Wheeler in *The Voice* encouraged Prohibitionist support for the Sherman House agreement: "Speaking for Prohibitionists we believe we can say that they are ready to
live up to that suggested basis of union in spirit and letter. If the
People's party can do the same, there is no formidable obstacle to a
union that will be a chemical not a mere mechanical union."
Further compromise by the Prohibition party, however, might be
difficult: "The entire question concerning a union of forces depends
then on whether the People's party has moral courage enough
to espouse it."[61]

    Wheeler's remarks did not apply to antifusionists Mrs. Helen
M. Gougar and John P. St. John, for, believing that Frances Willard
had stolen a march on them with her Sherman House meeting, they
came to St. Louis determined to block her attempts at fusion. Their
weapon was an informal meeting of the National Executive Committee
and other Prohibition party members, held on Monday morning,
February 22, just before the opening of the Industrial Conference
on Monday afternoon. At a reunion held on Saturday, February 20,
participants in the Sherman House meeting had reaffirmed support of
their month-old agreement.[62] Mrs. Gougar directed her attack at
that agreement. She told the assembled Prohibitionists that the
Sherman House conference was an attempt to sell out the Prohibition
party to the Populists, attacked the Sherman House prohibition
plank as an endorsement in effect of the liquor nationalization
proposal (because it opposed the "saloon" rather than the "liquor
traffic"), and denounced the woman suffrage plank as a compromise
of the principle of equal suffrage, as in truth it was. Miss Willard and
E. J. Wheeler denied the charges. After voting down, 28-13, a
resolution repudiating the prohibition and woman suffrage planks
of the Sherman House agreement, the assembled group appointed
a committee which included the prominent protagonists on each
side to determine whether those two planks correctly represented the
sentiment of their party. The Prohibitionists instructed the committee
to fight it out and report at eight the following morning, then adjourned
to attend the opening of the Industrial Conference.[63]

    At the meeting's resumption on Tuesday morning, the five-member
committee returned with two conflicting reports. The impasse

was broken by adoption of a resolution, proposed by National Chairman
Dickie, that the Prohibition party would not deal with any party
not committed to "the principle and policy of Prohibition" and
therefore would not participate "as a body" in the Industrial Conference. "It will be time enough," the resolution continued, "to
consider the question of organic union when such orgainzation or
party [referring to the farmers' movement] shall have placed
itself in open hostility to the liquor traffic." The meeting then adjourned,
and Willard made haste to explain to reporters that this resolution
"did not in the least interfere" with efforts to obtain from the
Industrial Conference a platform on which fusion could be effected.[64]
Nevertheless, it was clear that her position had been eroded by the
action of the Prohibition party antifusionists. The party's Executive
Committee had not, however, closed the door to fusion; the decision
for or against union with the People's party was now in the hands of
the Industrial Conference. A prohibition plank was to be the price
of fusion.[65]

On Tuesday afternoon, delegates to the Conference cheered
the admission of Willard and other WCTU leaders to their gathering,
seated her upon the platform, and elected her a vice-president of
the meeting. In addition, Willard became the chairwoman of the
subcommittee on miscellaneous planks, which was implicitly charged
with the formulation of prohibition and woman suffrage planks.
Shortly after 4:15 on Wednesday morning, the resolutions committee
completed its work on the three main planks and turned to the Willard
group's recommendations. Despite the opposition of southern
delegates, the full committee adopted the woman suffrage plank by
a 55-25 vote. Willard's prohibition plank, to which the committee
turned next, was a curious mixture. The first sentence duplicated
the wording of the Sherman House plank, with the substitution of
"liquor traffic" for "saloon." The remainder of the plank demanded,
as a southern Populist leader had suggested before the Conference,
that the federal government refrain from interference with state
regulation of the sale of intoxicants.[66] This time the arguments
of the opposition, that the campaign could not carry both woman suffrage
and prohibition, prevailed upon the committee to table the prohibition
plank. Frances Willard left the committee room at 7:30 A.M., and
the remaining committee members reconsidered and voted down the
woman suffrage plank before adjourning at 8:00 A.M.[67]

Undaunted by the committee's action, Willard presented her

two planks to the convention the following afternoon as a minority
report of the platform committee. Jerry Simpson of Kansas immediately
moved to table her report. On this crucial test the convention split
evenly in a voice vote.[68] Before a roll-call vote could be taken, a Mrs.
Curtis of Colorado offered a substitute for Willard's report which read:
"We demand that the question of universal suffrage be submitted to
the Legislatures of the different States and Territories for favorable
action."[69] The substitution was made "amid cheers." The cause
of fusion was now lost with the prohibition plank, and Frances Willard
and her companions left the platform and slipped out of the hall.[70]

Behind her she left the Industrial Conference in the throes of
indecision. The threat of a split between prohibitionist western farmers
anxious to woo their southern comrades and antiprohibitionist Knights
of Labor favoring woman suffrage was overcome by a Donnelly compromise
relegating the Curtis plank to the limbo of "supplementary resolutions."[71]
Once again, Populist delegates had acted upon their need to cement a
farmer-labor alliance before proceeding to consider a coalition with
the Prohibitionists.[72]

A DECISION AT CINCINNATI

The result of this rebuff by the Populists was not the retreat
from radicalism which might have been expected. Instead, the
Prohibitionists in 1892 accomplished a different kind of fusion: a
fusing of the concern for blacks engendered by their abolitionist
heritage with a new openness to economic radicalism. They could
do this in 1892 for two reasons: the appeal to the white South,
which had compromised their convictions during the 1880s, had shown
singularly unfruitful results in 1888; and most Prohibitionists, while
recognizing the strength of the demand for economic reform, could
not yet apprehend the enormous success of the Populist party in
channelling that demand. Prohibitionists did see that they were competing with the Populists for the allegiance of a growing mass of
voters disaffected by the economics as well as the politics of the major
parties. Furthermore, Prohibitionists themselves were beginning to
suspect that the sins of the ruling parties extended beyond their loose
attitudes toward liquor into a disquieting range of favors for special
interests[73] Consequently, the Prohibition party sought at its national
convention in Cincinnati to rally northern reformers behind a semi-
Populist economic program.

Frances Willard arrived in Cincinnati on June 28 with the mad
dream that the Prohibitionists might consent to withdraw their
presidential candidate if the Populists' Omaha convention nominated
a "satisfactory" candidate. After assessing the mood of the convention,
however, she quickly withdrew the idea.[74] The antifusionists were
in control of the convention from the start. St. John laid down their
position in his keynote speech: "From this hour let no fusions,
no deals, no compromises be our motto." Willard, on the defensive,
stated that she had never favored fusion that would destroy the
Prohibition party's identity. She rested with a declaration that:
"I simply believe that we are the same sort of people in rank and file
as the people in St. Louis, and the people in Omaha [at the Populists'
nominating convention], only they are better educated on economical
questions than we, and we better educated on Prohibition."[75]

Although the hopes of the fusionists had gone a-glimmering
at the Industrial Conference, the Prohibitionists still found plenty
to fight about. Conflict centered upon four planks proposed by the
majority and minority reports of the resolutions committee: two
on currency, one on tariff and taxation, and the dominant-issue
plank of 1888. St. John, leader of the committee's majority,
successfully fought before the convention for a plank advocating gold,
silver, and paper currency issued by the government, against a plank
declaring for a paper currency alone. He also won approval for a fiscal
plank that leaned in the direction of free trade and demanded a tax "on
what the people possess instead of what they consume." This implied
a system of progressive taxation intended to act as a levelling device.[76]
The convention united to adopt a plank favoring "the limitation
of individual and corporate ownership of land," a demand noticeably
more radical than even the Populists' land plank in 1892.[77]

St. John lost his battle for a free-coinage-of-silver plank by a
vote of 596-335, but the arguments against free silver came at least
partially from the profarmer point of view presented by Thomas R.
Carskadon, a West Virginia farmer and former Radical Republican.
The Chicago *Lever* summarized Carskadon's speech:

> He admitted and indorsed all that had been said on the
> subject of grinding monopolies and grasping money-sharks,
> but was not in favor of unbusiness methods. There are great
> business principles which must be recognized, and even on
> Wall street there are men who, in their own interests, desire

business to follow its legitimate channels. He himself had
been a loyal member of the National [Farmers'] Alliance,
and is yet a loyal member of the order, but he had un-
swervingly stood up to defend the farmers against wild
crazes that are more dangerous than the present evils.
It was folly to believe that the hocus pocus of free coinage
could destroy the infernal combinations which threaten labor.[78]

St. John also lost his fight against the 1888 dominant-issue plank presented
by the committee minority, largely because National Chairman Dickie
threw behind it his considerable prestige.[79] The St. John group gained
a final victory when the convention nominated its presidential
candidate, John Bidwell of California, who was considered to stand
closer to Populism than his principal opponent, William Jennings
Demorest, the retired fashion-magazine editor from New York.[80]

Perhaps the most significant action of the Prohibition party convention occurred when the delegates confronted their old bugaboo, the
race question. In contrast to their behavior in 1888, the convention
showed no mercy to the South, voting down the southern delegates'
attempt to secure the full state vote for their half-filled delegations.
An antilynching plank appeared in the platform for the first time.
Most important, the convention adopted an unqualified declaration
for woman suffrage, the strongest in the party's history, and coupled
with it a demand that "equal labor should receive equal wages without
regard to sex."[81] As if to underscore the racial implications of this
action, the entire convention threatened to leave its hotel in support
of black delegates to whom the management had refused use of the
dining facilities.[82] The convention appropriately closed with "shouts
of approval" when a black female Michigan delegate stood on a
chair as the delegates began to leave the hall and denounced the discrimination practiced by Cincinnati hotel-keepers and hypocritical
white northern Republicans.[83]

State Prohibition platforms supported and in some cases extended
the position taken by the national convention. In Nebraska, for
example, although the national party had ventured only as far as
a demand for "control" of "railroad, telegraph, and other public
corporations" by the government, Prohibitionists asked in their state
platform for government ownership.[84] In Tennessee the Prohibition
party platform declared that "economic law requires each citizen to be

a producer, to receive as such his equitable share of the profits of his production and to bear his proportionate share of the burden of the state."[85]

The events of early 1892 showed that the Prohibitionists had abandoned the Republican model and were now seeking—and beginning to find—a new model for reform which fused their anti-slavery heritage with the new perspective of Populism. One month after the Prohibition party national convention, Frances Willard asked her party comrades the essential question for an assessment of Prohibitionist radicalism: "The question is, are we willing to help on the labor movement when it costs us something— perhaps in our social status, perchance in our worldly goods?"[86] As of July 1892, the answer seemed to be No, not yet; the dominant sentiment in the party looked for the discontented farmers to come to the Prohibition party, not for the party to go to the farmers as Willard had tried to do at St. Louis.

Nevertheless, Willard and other Prohibitionists had stimulated significant changes within their party. As it entered the campaign of 1892, the party stood further to the left in its demands for government control of business, progressive taxation, inflationary monetary policies, and racial and sexual equality than it had ever stood before. In the election its candidates won more votes than the party received in any presidential election before or since. Yet, because of the rapidly changing political climate, Willard had failed to keep the Prohibition party in the vanguard of reform, and her failure set the stage for the transformation of the party four years later.

NOTES

1. For a semi-official statement of this Prohibitionist self-image, see E. J. Wheeler, *Prohibition: The Principle, the Policy, the Party* (New York, 1889), pp. 157-160. Wheeler was editor of the party organ, *The Voice.* Throughout this study, "prohibitionist" designates a supporter of the prohibition policy; "Prohibitionist" identifies a member of the Prohibition party. This method follows contemporary usage.

2. Minutes of National Executive Committee (NXC) meetings, June 1, 1888, Indianapolis; June 23, 1888, New York City; 1888 Convention Proceedings, "Minutes of the National Committees,

Conferences and Conventions of the Prohibition Party," vol. 1,
pp. 6, 7-8, 9, 11, 14, 15, 22, 23, 24-25, Michigan Historical
Collections, Ann Arbor; David Leigh Colvin, *Prohibition in the United
States: A History of the Prohibition Party and of the Prohibition
Movement* (New York, 1926), pp. 93, 111, 159, 191, 193-194;
James R. Turner, "The American Prohibition Movement, 1865-1897"
(Ph. D. dissertation, University of Wisconsin, 1972), p. 408;
John Sobieski, *The Life-Story and Personal Reminiscences of Col.
John Sobieski* (Shelbyville, Ill., 1900), p. 242.

    3. J. B. Weaver, House of Representatives, Washington, D.C.,
to John P. St. John, May 27, 1888, St. John Scrapbooks 7, St. John
Papers, Kansas State Historical Society (KHS).

    4. Edwin S. Redkey, "Bishop Turner's African Dream,"
Journal of American History 54 (September 1967): 283.

    5. For evidence of the "striking kinship" between antislavery
radicals and Prohibitionist radicals in Washington state,
see Norman H. Clark, *The Dry Years: Prohibition and Social Change
in Washington* (Seattle, 1965), pp. 64-65.

    6. Sobieski, *Life-Story*, pp. 192-195. The Independent Order
of Good Templars, to which many Prohibition party leaders belonged,
had suffered an international split lasting from 1873 to 1887 over
the admission of blacks on an integrated basis. Turner, "American
Prohibition Movement," pp. 201-203.

    7. 1888 Convention Proceedings, "Minutes," vol. 1, pp. 13, 18.

    8. Turner, "American Prohibition Movement," p. 336.

    9. James B. Sellers, *The Prohibition Movement in Alabama,
1702 to 1943* (Chapel Hill, 1943), pp. 59, 80. A historian of the
WCTU attributes southern resistance to "states' rights" feelings,
general conservatism on social questions, and a fear of enfranchising
black women. Samuel Unger, "A History of the WCTU" (Ph.D.
dissertation, Ohio State University, 1933), p. 113.

    10. Colvin, *Prohibition in the U.S.*, pp. 93, 110, 127.

    11. Mary Earhart, *Frances Willard: From Prayers to Politics*
(Chicago, 1944), ch. 10.

    12. Frances E. Willard, *Glimpses of Fifty Years: The Autobiography
of an American Woman* (Chicago, 1889), pp. 400-401. See also
pp. 328-329, and Turner, "American Prohibition Movement," p. 260.

    13. Colvin, *Prohibition in the U.S.*, p. 168.

    14. Svend Petersen, *A Statistical History of the American
Presidential Elections* (New York, 1963), p. 194.

    15. James B. Cranfill, *Dr. J. B. Cranfill's Chronicle: A Story
of Life in Texas* (New York, 1916), p. 369.

16. Minutes of NXC meeting, June 23, 1888, New York City, "Minutes, vol. 1, p. 22; Colvin, *Prohibition in the U.S.,* p. 191.

17. 1888 Convention Proceedings, "Minutes," vol. 1, pp. 16-17; Willard, *Glimpses,* pp. 444-445.

18. 1888 Convention Proceedings, "Minutes," vol. 1, p. 16; George L. Case, "The Prohibition Party: Its Origin, Purpose and Growth, "*Magazine of Western History* 9 (April 1889): 710.

19. 1888 Convention Proceedings, "Minutes," vol. 1, pp. 16-18. Thomas C. Richmond, who will figure prominently in the following chapter, was born of Protestant parentage in Ulster in 1848. Emigrating to the United States in 1860, he enlisted in the Union Army four years later and served until the end of the Civil War. He studied law at the University of Wisconsin and Boston Law School and, after some years as a teacher and superintendent of small-town schools in Wisconsin, opened a law practice in Madison. A former Republican, he joined the Prohibition party in 1882 and immediately became prominent in its affairs, first in Wisconsin and by 1888 on the national level. Louis E. Van Norman, ed., *An Album of Representative Prohibitionists* (New York, 1895), pp. 198-199.

20. Willard, *Glimpses,* p. 444.

21. 1888 Convention Proceedings, "Minutes," vol. 1, pp. 17, 18; Willard, *Glimpses,* p. 445; Case, "Prohibition Party," p. 710; Sobieski, *Life-Story,* pp. 196-197. Dow had been doing this sort of thing for a long time: see Frank L. Byrne, *Prophet of Prohibition: Neal Dow and His Crusade* (Madison, 1961), pp. 55-56.

22. Minutes of NXC meeting, June 23, 1888, New York City, "Minutes," vol. 1, p. 23.

23. Petersen, *Statistical History,* p. 194.

24. Daniel J. Whitener, *Prohibition in North Carolina, 1715-1945* (Chapel Hill, 1945), p. 86.

25. Turner, "American Prohibition Movement," p. 344.

26. William R. Dobbyn to T. C. Richmond, July 26, 1890, Richmond Papers, State Historical Society of Wisconsin (WHS); *Northwestern Mail* (Madison, Wis.), July 10, 1903; Turner, "American Prohibition Movement," pp. 344-349, 365-366.

27. *Northwestern Mail,* December 17, 1891.

28. Earl C. Kaylor, Jr., "The Prohibition Movement in Pennsylvania, 1865-1920" (Ph.D. dissertation, Pennsylvania State University, 1963), vol. 1, p. 265; Clark, *Dry Years,* p. 43.

29. Minutes of NXC meetings, December 11, 1888, Pittsburgh, and November 8, 1889, Louisville; National Committee (NC) meeting, February 15, 1889, Louisville, "Minutes," vol. 1, pp. 26-30,

31-32, 35, 37, 43; J. B. Cranfill to T. C. Richmond, July 21, 1891, Richmond Papers.

30. *Northwestern Mail,* May 29, October 2, 1890. See also *Northwestern Mail,* September 17, 1891; M. P. Hanson to Richmond, March 17, 1891, Richmond Papers.

31. Editor of *The Voice* to Richmond, August 19, 1891, Richmond Papers; J. V. Tracy, "Prohibition and Catholics," *Catholic World* 51 (August 1890): 670-671; *Northwestern Mail,* October 29, 1891.

32. Clark, *Dry Years,* pp. 45-46; Paul E. Isaac, *Prohibition and Politics: Turbulent Decades in Tennessee, 1885-1920* (Knoxville, 1965), pp. 65-68; James Cannon, Jr., *Bishop Cannon's Own Story: Life as I Have Seen It,* ed. Richard L. Watson, Jr. (Durham, 1955), p. 79; Minutes of NC meeting, February 15, 1889, Louisville, and NXC meeting, November 9, 1889, Chicago, "Minutes," vol. 1, pp. 35-37, 43.

33. Edwin C. Pierce, "The True Politics for Prohibition and Labor," *Arena* 4 (November 1891): 723-729; *The Voice,* December 3, 1891.

34. *Northwestern Mail,* November 27, 1890; *The Voice,* May 1, August 7, 1890, January 8, February 12, 1891.

35. Jack S. Blocker, Jr., "The Politics of Reform: Populists, Prohibition, and Woman Suffrage, 1891-1892," *The Historian* 34 (August 1972): 615-617; Michael P. Rogin, *The Intellectuals and McCarthy: The Radical Spectre* (Cambridge, Mass., 1967), pp. 140, 181-182.

36. See, for example, *The Voice,* February 6, 27, 1890; *Northwestern Mail,* August 14, 1890; *Union Signal,* January 14, 1892; *Spirit of Kansas,* October 3, 1891.

37. Roscoe C. Martin, *The People's Party in Texas: A Study in Third Party Politics,* University of Texas Bureau of Research in the Social Sciences Study No. 4 (Austin, 1933), p. 81; Ernest H. Cherrington et al., eds., *Standard Encyclopedia of the Alcohol Problem,* 6 vols. (Westerville, Ohio, 1925-30), vol. 2, pp. 826-827.

38. *The Voice,* November 20, 1890, February 12, May 14, 1891.

39. Stanley B. Parsons, *The Populist Context: Rural Versus Urban Power on a Great Plains Frontier* (Westport, Conn., 1973); Turner, "American Prohibition Movement," pp. 409-410.

40. Turner, "American Prohibition Movement," p. 410.

41. Paul Kleppner, *The Cross of Culture: A Social Analysis of Midwestern Politics, 1850-1900* (New York, 1970), pp. 137-140, 142.

42. *The Voice,* February 12, 1891. See also the report of a party strategy conference in *Northwestern Mail,* February 26, 1891.

43. "President's Address," *Minutes of the N.W.C.T.U.* (Chicago, 1891), pp. 118-119; Earhart, *Frances Willard*, pp. 287-289.

44. Blocker, "Politics of Reform," pp. 618-619. See also Larry G. Osnes, "The Birth of a Party: The Cincinnati Populist Convention of 1891," *Great Plains Journal* 10 (Fall 1970): 11-24.

45. *Cincinnati Commercial Gazette*, May 21, 1891; *The Voice*, June 4, 1891.

46. *Journal of the Knights of Labor*, May 7, 21, 1891; *The Voice*, June 4, 1891.

47. *Kansas City Star*, May 23, 1891. St. John was quite correct in his comment on the subtreasury; the plan reflected clearly the farmers' economic position, which was marginal rather than totally submerged.

48. *The Voice*, May 21, 28, 1891.

49. *New Nation* (Boston) 1 (June 20, 1891) : 325-326.

50. *The Voice*, February 11, 1892; *New Nation* 1 (September 26, 1891): 556, and 1 (December 29, 1891): 707; *Journal of the Knights of Labor*, August 20, 1891; *Minutes of the N.W.C.T.U.* (Chicago, 1891), p. 168. See also *Topeka Advocate*, January 6, 1892.

51. *The Voice*, January 21, 1892.

52. See esp. *The Voice*, September 3, 1891.

53. *Northwestern Mail*, July 16, 1891.

54. Frances E. Willard to Henry Demarest Lloyd, October 22, 1891, Lloyd Papers, WHS; Earhart, *Frances Willard*, p. 228.

55. Dickie had just issued another party circular in which he declared that "as prohibitionists, we cannot enter into any deals, combinations or alliances, nor contemplate for a moment any reorganization and union of our own and other party forces that does not make Prohibition the issue of first importance," thus softening his position of November 1890. *The Voice*, January 28, 1892; *Northwestern Mail*, January 28, 1892.

56. *Chicago Times*, January 28, 1892.

57. *St. Louis Republic*, January 29, 1892; *The Voice*, February 4, 1892.

58. *Chicago Times*, January 28, 1892.

59. *Union Signal*, February 18, 1892.

60. *Northwestern Mail*, February 4, 11, 1892; *The Lever* (Chicago), February 4, 1892.

61. *The Voice*, February 4, 1892.

62. *Union Signal*, March 3, 1892. I doubt that Taubeneck and Washburn were present.

63. Ibid.; *The Voice*, March 3, 1892; *Kansas City Star*, February

23, 1892; *The Lever*, February 25, 1892. The official minutes
of the meeting do not mention the conflict which occurred.
Minutes of NXC meeting (informal), February 23, 1892, Southern
Hotel, St. Louis, "Minutes," vol. 1, p. 49.

64. *The Voice*, March 3, 1892; *Kansas City Star*, February 23,
1892. Compare *Union Signal*, March 3, 1892, where Willard claimed
that the resolution included woman suffrage as well as prohibition.

65. Willard's biographer, Mary Earhart *(Frances Willard,*
pp. 233-236), contends that the action of the Prohibitionists in
refusing to join the Industrial Conference was decisive in bringing
about the defeat of fusion. Her argument ignores the fact that
the Prohibitionists did not reject the possibility of fusion at all;
they only set a single condition, the acceptance of a prohibition
plank by the Conference, for consideration of such a course
of action.

66. *Chicago Tribune*, February 25, 1892; *Kansas City Star*,
February 24, 1892. The substitution of "liquor traffic" for
"saloon" seems to have been an attempt to eliminate the
nationalization loophole. It is significant that by this step, and
by the expansion of the woman suffrage plank from the "municipal suffrage, with an educational qualification" of the Sherman
House address to an unequivocal demand for universal suffrage,
Willard had tried to meet the demands of Mrs. Gougar.

67. *Union Signal*, March 3, 1892; *The Voice*, March 3, 1892;
Kansas City Star, February 24, 1892; *Journal of the Knights
of Labor*, March 3, 1892; Milton W. Small, "The Biography of
Robert Schilling" (M.A. Thesis, University of Wisconsin, 1953),
p. 271.

68. *Chicago Tribune*, February 25, 1892. I have found no
source which contradicts this estimate.

69. Ibid. *The Voice*, March 3, 1892, claimed that Mrs. Curtis,
as a member of the resolutions committee at Cincinnati, had cast
a decisive vote against the prohibition plank there. Mrs. Curtis'
St. Louis suffrage plank was essentially the same as the suffrage
resolution adopted at Cincinnati.

70. *Chicago Tribune*, February 25, 1892; *The Lever*, March 3,
1892.

71. *Journal of the Knights of Labor*, May 7, 28, 1891, March 3,
17, 1892; *Chicago Tribune*, February 25, 1892; *The Voice*,
March 3, 1892; *Kansas City Star*, February 25, 1892. The Populists'
Omaha convention on July 4, 1892, dropped the woman suffrage
plank from the final version of the platform, refusing even to

include it in the "resolutions" appended to the main body
of the platform.

72. See esp. *Union Signal,* April 7, 1892.

73. For a complementary discussion of the Prohibitionists'
stance in the 1890s, see Joseph J. Rumbarger, "The Social Origins
and Function of the Political Temperance Movement in the
Reconstruction of American Society, 1825-1917" (Ph.D. dissertation, University of Pennsylvania, 1968), pp. 200-202.

74. *Kansas City Star,* June 28, 1892; *Union Signal,* June 16,
1892; *The Voice,* June 30, 1892.

75. *Kansas City Star,* June 29, 30, 1892; *The Voice,* July 7,
1892; *The Lever,* July 7, 1892.

76. John P. St. John, "The Great Issue," *The American
Journal of Politics* 1 (August 1892): 417-418.

77. Compare the two planks in Colvin, *Prohibition in the
U.S.,* p. 248, and John D. Hicks, *The Populist Revolt*
(Minneapolis, 1931), p. 443.

78. *The Lever,* July 7, 1892.

79. *The Voice,* July 7, 1892. Dickie had been unanimously
reelected to his position by the new National Committee.
Minutes of NC meeting, June 29, 1892, Cincinnati, "Minutes,"
vol. 1, p. 52.

80. *The Voice,* July 7, 1892.

81. Ibid.; *The Lever,* July 7, 1892.

82. Frederick W. Adrian, "The Political Significance of the
Prohibition Party" (Ph.D. dissertation, Ohio State University,
1942), p. 81.

83. *The Voice,* July 7, 1892.

84. *Union Signal,* March 10, 1892.

85. Quoted in Isaac, *Prohibition and Politics,* p. 68.

86. *The Voice,* July 28, 1892.

3

Troubled times, 1893-1895

*T*he election of 1892 demonstrated the failure of the Prohibition party's attempts to appeal to the forces of discontent. It also made clear that the People's party had replaced the Prohibitionists in the forefront of American reform. As a result, Prohibitionists intensified and broadened their debate over the nature of the party and the character of its constituency. Three interrelated issues formed the bones of contention: the breadth and content of the platform; the desirability and feasibility of an alliance with the People's party; and the appropriate attitude of Prohibitionists toward the Christian, and especially Protestant, churches. All three had their origins in intraparty debate before 1892, but after the party's disappointing showing in the election they appeared at the head of new alignments and sparked a more bitter conflict than the organization had ever before seen. The conflict produced two irreconcilable positions which caused a party split in 1896, and the positions crystallized with the formation of two Prohibition parties.

The battle waged by the two factions during 1893-1896 concerned nothing less than the nature of the prohibition movement in America. Would it be radical or conservative in its attitude toward established wealth and power? Would it align itself with the producers or possessors of wealth? This was the debate that never took place within the prohibition movement in later years when prohibitionists actually did have power to affect social policy. Instead, it occurred at a time when prohibitionists were confused and frightened, not only by the depressed state of their movement, but also because of the all-too-apparent failures of their society. Because they were confused, prohibitionists could entertain radical proposals that they would not have considered a few years before. But because they were frightened, they finally closed the debate by turning back reluctantly to the shaky but at least familiar confines of the dominant middle-class institutions.[1]

THE PLATFORM: BROAD- OR NARROW-GAUGE?

Like the election results of 1888, those of 1892 stirred Prohibitionists into questioning whether they stood in "the true line of advancement." The optimistic sophistries of the party press could not conceal Prohibitionists' realization that their share of the total vote (2.25 percent, up from 2.20 percent in 1888) represented a peremptory halt to their progress.[2] The depression which struck in the following year seemed to turn attention from moral to economic problems, and in August 1893 one of the party's prominent lecturers wrote to his National Committeeman: "The times are so 'out of joint' just now that our work suffers with everything else."[3]

The facts of the situation as Prohibitionists saw them pointed to serious questions regarding the party method. They believed that widespread support for the cause of prohibition existed in America. *The Voice* claimed early in 1895 that "no single issue in America can begin to poll as many votes as Prohibition. In 19 State votes alone Prohibition has received 1,676,603 votes."[4] In depressing contrast stood the total of 271,111 votes cast for the party in 1892. The obvious conclusion seemed to be that drawn by a Wisconsin party leader: "The people as a whole do not consider the Pro. party & its methods *practicable.*"[5]

Acting on this assessment of the situation, some party Prohibitionists in 1893 began to turn toward nonpartisan political action. In that same year major-party prohibitionists in Ohio and Washington, D.C., formed the local antisaloon leagues which were to create a national organization to ride this method to the triumph of a constitutional amendment twenty-six years later. Since the Civil War the nonpartisan method had occupied a place subordinate to the activities of the third party, and its attraction had always sprung from an unwillingness

to cast off loyalties to the major parties. In 1885, at the height of the
Prohibition party's success, two staunch Republican prohibitionists
had founded the National League for the Suppression of the Liquor
Traffic, a nonpartisan organization for moral and legal action against
saloons.[6] After its collapse, one of the two, Mrs. J. Ellen Foster,
led a seceding group out of the WCTU in protest against its support
of the Prohibition party. The Non-Partisan WCTU, which Mrs. Foster
founded in 1890, lasted into the Anti-Saloon League years, small
in numbers but vociferous in its opposition to the third-party affiliation of its parent.

Southern Prohibitionists after 1892 seemed particularly susceptible
to nonpartisanship. In 1893 Tennessee Prohibitionists rejected a
proposal to merge with the Populists and adopted instead the nonpartisan approach.[7] The Prohibition party in Virginia took up another
line of what was to become the Anti-Saloon League strategy by
dropping advocacy of immediate prohibition in favor of efforts to
inaugurate local option elections in the larger cities of that state.[8]
In 1895 a Maryland correspondent of T. C. Richmond urged abandonment of the Prohibition party—"We have long since given up hope
of any results favourable to the cause of prohibition through the
blind striking of that party"—and suggested formation of a single-issue,
nonpartisan organization which would adopt the supposed tactics
of the liquor interests by wielding a decisive balance of power
between the two major parties, which he thought would be Republicans
and Populists.[9]

Most party leaders in the mid-1890s, however, avoided the nonpartisan approach, for two reasons: outside of a very few states, no
organization advocating such an approach existed; and where one did,
they suspected it of being no more than a vehicle operated by major-
party politicians for the purpose of shuttling them back to their old
loyalties. They agreed with E. J. Wheeler that the Prohibition party
should be strengthened rather than abandoned for nonpartisan
activity.[10] The means of strengthening it was the question over
which conflict arose.

The most obvious phase of the conflict in the years 1893-1896
was the debate over the breadth of the party platform. Both sides
had won victories in the writing of the 1892 platform. The "broad-
gauge" faction, led by John P. St. John, had secured the adoption
of its entire economic program with the exception of the free-coinage-

of-silver plank, while the "narrow-gauge" forces behind Chairman
Dickie had countered with the dominant-issue plank, which required
for party membership allegiance only to prohibition.[11] After 1892
both factions moved to more extreme positions. The broad-gaugers
attacked the "dominant" prohibition plank and proposed a more
radical program than in 1892, but headed it once again with the
demand for free coinage of silver. The purpose of their broad-gauge
platform was to forge an alliance with the forces of protest against
economic injustice. The narrow-gaugers held to their dominant-issue
plank until September 1895. They then moved toward support of
a single-issue platform aimed directly at church members who could
not stomach economic radicalism. Thus, both of the contending
factions used the debate over the breadth of the platform to forward
their notions of its proper content and the constituency to which
it should appeal.

The first stage of the debate began when the broad-gaugers renewed
an earlier attack upon the party's basic demand for immediate
prohibition, proposing instead Edward Bellamy's plan for nationalization of the liquor traffic. A similar plan had won national attention
when Governor Ben Tillman, who, although a Democrat, was
commonly regarded as a Populist, instituted in 1893 state conduct
of the liquor traffic in South Carolina. Prohibitionists in general
had denounced Bellamy's plan when it first appeared in 1891,
but the failure of the Prohibition party and the success of the Populists
in 1892 realigned some perspectives.

In 1893, thinking that the disappointment of 1892 might make
Prohibitionists amenable to compromise, E. J. Wheeler reopened
the debate by speaking editorially in *The Voice* in cautiously favorable
terms of the state conduct, or dispensary, system. T. C. Richmond
immediately spoke out, advocating the nationalization of the liquor
traffic "as a plan on which we may hope to unite at the ballot-box
all men who believe in temperance, and who hope in some way, at
some time in the future, to suppress the beverage traffic in intoxicants."[12]
With Wheeler's editorial and Richmond's approval, the debate
was on. Many Prohibitionists immediately sided with Richmond
and Wheeler,[13] basing their action upon two arguments: (1) the
nationalization plan was a step toward ultimate prohibition by the
removal of the saloon's power in politics and could also be made to
fit prohibitionist morality, for its backers claimed that state conduct

eliminated from the sale of liquor the element of profit, or greed; (2) adoption of the nationalization plan could serve as a basis for union between the two reform parties of the country.[14] This development held crucial implications: it showed that the need for success as reformers could even wean some Prohibitionists away from prohibition itself.

As Wheeler should have known, he was addressing an audience experienced in deploying arguments against halfway measures. Prohibitionists unamenable to fusion quickly pointed out that state conduct meant complicity with the evil traffic.[15] Some even rephrased an argument used by Wheeler himself in a different context only a few years before:

> The liquor traffic can never be legalized without sin.
> To nationalize the liquor traffic is to legalize it. There-
> fore the liquor traffic can never be nationalized without
> sin. Any man or paper that consents to sin is a sinner.
> The nationalization of the liquor traffic is a sin. There-
> fore the man or paper that consents to the nationalization
> of the liquor traffic is a sinner.

Chairman Dickie and the National Executive Committee weighed in with an address repudiating both nationalization and fusion.[16] The vehemence of the counterattack caused Wheeler and his supporters to draw in their horns temporarily.

Meanwhile, the debate over the breadth of the party platform and the primacy of the prohibition plank, dormant since the 1892 convention, revived once again. In a characteristic flood of evangelical rhetoric, the Methodist farmer Thomas R. Carskadon denounced the broad-gaugers for seeking to attract to the Prohibition party "money loving, unsanctified brother farmers" and "a host of uncircumsized Philistines," by offering a shortcut to righteousness. He claimed that votes attracted to the party by its economic reforms would not remain with it and proposed instead that "to succeed, we must bring to us that steady, Christian, patriotic element now constituting the best elements of the old parties, and the Populist party, too." An appeal to these men required the subordination of the economic planks upon which they disagreed to the morally dominant issue of prohibition. In answer, the leader of Nebraska

Prohibitionists, while affirming the moral dominance of the prohibition issue, denied its political importance. "The real dominant issue in the politics of the country is always that upon which the people at that time feel most deeply and which influences most votes." Correctly noting that the dominant-issue plank had been adopted "as a means to evade suffrage and other issues," he advocated its rejection. Finally, the Nebraskan rejected Carskadon's conception of the party as a congregation of the like-minded. "Ours is a political party, and not a church. . . . If we do not desire votes and take measures to secure them, we had better go out of politics and organize a hard-shell temperance society at once."[17]

E. J. Wheeler, while in 1893 favoring the designation of prohibition as the dominant issue, tried to develop a basis for his position apart from the moral absolutism of the Dickie wing. For Wheeler and his supporters, the prohibition issue was dominant not because it was a moral question or because it was the only moral question to be decided: "Every question which affects the home, the church, and State, are [sic] great moral questions." The prohibition issue was the dominant one because of the supposed political power of the liquor interests which was used to block "the channels of legislation" through which all reforms must pass. Therefore, for those who desired reforms other than prohibition, the first task and dominant issue was the removal, through prohibition, of the power of the liquor interests in politics and government: "To put an end to gin-mill government is the *first*, but by no means the last, thing required in order to reach a satisfactory solution of other industrial problems."[18] This argument took the sting out of the dominant-issue debate for the moment, and a *Voice* poll of the party's National Committee in mid-1893 found an overwhelming majority in favor of prohibition as the dominant issue, including some who were to belong to the broad-gauge, seceding faction at Pittsburgh three years later.[19]

Nevertheless, the continuing success of the People's party in 1894, in contrast to the failure of the Prohibition party to regain its lost position, soon brought the question of Prohibitionist platform tactics again to the fore. E. J. Wheeler, reacting to the Populist advances in 1894 and the reversal of the Democratic victory of 1892, predicted "an earthquake in national politics," a disintegration of major-party loyalties, and a consequent increase of opportunity for Prohibitionists to augment their forces.[20] Chairman Dickie responded to the unsettled political conditions by reaffirming the allegiance of the party to its dominant issue, giving as his reason the divisions of opinion among Prohibitionists upon other questions.[21]

The conflict between the broad-gauge and narrow-gauge factions was renewed in March 1895 when T. C. Richmond proposed a union of the reform forces of the country upon a prohibition plank calling for the destruction of the saloon system through state conduct of liquor sales.[22] E. J. Wheeler then organized and to some extent directed a conference at Prohibition Park on Staten Island which recommended a union of reformers upon an eight-plank platform, including: direct legislation; government ownership of monopolies; popular election of the president, vice-president, senators, and civil service officers; woman suffrage; prohibition of speculative land ownership; "prohibition of the liquor traffic for beverage purposes, and government control of the sale for medicinal, scientific and mechanical uses"; issue of money only by the government; and free coinage of gold and silver at 16 to 1.[23]

The Prohibition Park conference stimulated a series of attempts by members of the Richmond wing to broaden the Prohibition party platform so as to bring about a union with the Populists or, if fusion was impossible, to attract to the party those who had been estranged from old allegiances by the unsettled economic and political conditions. These efforts in turn set off a violent response by the Dickie wing and produced a new offensive which did not stop with the demand merely for a dominant-issue platform but pushed on to more exposed ground by calling for a platform limited to the single issue of prohibition uncompromised.

In a letter to *The Voice* in September 1895, Alphonso Alva Hopkins, vice-chancellor and professor of political economy at the American Temperance University, Harriman, Tennessee, opened the counter-attack. In his proposal Hopkins provided an argument for the single-issue platform that went beyond the mere assertion of the absolute moral righteousness of prohibition. He assumed, to begin with, that the proper constituency of the Prohibition party should be the "church element." Hopkins then asserted that the nonprohibition planks in the party platform, on which the opinions of the "church element" were divided, gave church members an excuse not to vote for the prohibition demands supported by their church assemblies and the Prohibition party. The conclusion was obvious: the Prohibi-

tion party should appeal directly to its true constituency by dropping
from its platform planks extraneous to the moral question of prohibition.[24]

Other members of the Dickie wing quickly adopted Hopkins's
argument. One leader wrote, "I would like to see the Christian
conscience of the country have one chance to test itself on the
liquor issue alone." Another asserted that "a political platform, if
it is anything, is the creed of the party that promulgates it; a
declaration of its faith."[25]

Another element crept into the debate when some single-issue
leaders began to make clear what they meant when they spoke of
the "moral element in the community." Chairman Dickie thought
that the vast majority of party members opposed the broad-gauge
policy, "and conspicuously is this true among those safe and
conservative business men whose influence is, after all, of the greatest
value to our movement."[26] A. A. Stevens of Pennsylvania, a lawyer
and vice-president and general manager of the American Lime &
Stone Company, saw the situation in the same terms:

> I am not one of those who believe that wealth dis-
> qualifies the possessor from being a prohibitionist, or
> to whom a successful business man is more objectionable
> as a political associate than an unwashed anarchist. Industry,
> sobriety, honesty, and economy produce wealth, and
> these qualities are generally found predominating in a
> large majority of Prohibitionists, who have no sympathy
> with those who are continually crying out against capital,
> monopolies, trusts, etc., but who, in their own business
> affairs, have not developed business capacity enough to
> manage or accumulate anything for themselves, or any person
> else; and whose income, be it what it may, comes largely
> from the liberality of the very class they denounce. . . .
>
> What is to be gained by the Prohibition Party becoming
> the champion of all so-called reforms? What public good
> will be served by mixing such political leaders and reformers
> as Waite, the bloody rider, of Colorado; Altgeld, of
> Illinois, the friend of Anarchists; Coxey, of Ohio, the
> leader of the late Tatterdemalion; Most, of New York, the
> champion of the red flag; and others, leaders in reforms

that the advocate of a 'broad' platform would have the
Prohibition Party incorporate in its platform that these
reform(?) leaders might unite their influence with ours
to bring about what?[27]

Defense of the business community was not by itself, however,
a completely reliable guide to the make-up of the single-issue wing,
for some of its leaders, such as James B. Cranfill of Texas and Thomas
R. Carskadon of West Virginia, denounced the policies of "safe and
conservative business men" as strongly as Dickie and Stevens defended
them.[28] Neither were attitudes toward the maintenance of the gold
standard a sufficient guide to Prohibitionists' positions on the single-
issue question, for staunch supporters of free silver, such as Cranfill
and the Reverend J. S. Hughes, could be found backing Chairman
Dickie, an opponent of free silver.[29] Defense of the churches and
rejection of both fusion with the Populists and the economic
radicalism they represented were the three characteristics of the
single-issue wing, and Prohibitionists could find a place within it
by endorsing any of the three.

Wheeler mounted a counterattack against the arguments of the
single-issue spokesmen through the editorial columns of *The Voice,*
claiming that Hopkins's proposal would mean abandonment of the
party's necessary task, the attainment of political power, and reversion
"to a sort of non-partizan or balance-of-power party."[30] The Dickie
wing then gained a valuable advantage when the Funk & Wagnalls
Company Executive Committee, presumably directed by Dr. Isaac K.
Funk, dumped Wheeler as editor of *The Voice* in late February 1896,
Funk himself becoming editor-in-chief.[31] Beginning with the issue of
February 27, *The Voice* reversed the editorial policy established by
Wheeler and thenceforth stood squarely in the single-issue camp,
arguing the point largely on the basis of Hopkins's rationale:

Never was the public so ripe for Prohibition. All the
churches, all the Christian Endeavor Societies, the Epworth
Leagues and other similar church organizations, the
Salvation Army, the Catholic and Protestant temperance
societies, the great club movement among women, are all,
with scarcely an exception, making rapid progress our
way.[32]

The Richmond wing continued its attempts to maintain a broad platform so as to appeal to the disaffected voters of other parties until they were, as they saw it, driven out of the party at Pittsburgh on May 28, 1896. In February 1896, however, T. C. Richmond, disgusted at the attitude of unbending rectitude assumed by his opponents and perhaps foreseeing their victory at Pittsburgh, delivered a bitter comment that can serve for the moment as his closing statement in the long debate over the party platform. Responding to a Prohibitionist's letter to *The Voice* which asserted, "We are opposed to the whole vote-catching business," Richmond wrote:

> Now, if it is not out of order, I rise at this point in the discussion merely to suggest that we put something in the platform that will, if possible, prevent any one from voting the party ticket. I frankly admit that our efforts in the past along this line have come very near securing the desired result, and I am fully persuaded that one more trial, if made in good faith, will place the party where whatever other troubles it may have to contend against it will not be embarrassed or overburdened with votes.[33]

TO FUSE OR NOT TO FUSE?

The immediate objective of the fusionist Richmond wing was of course the People's party. Two qualities of the People's party attracted the Prohibition party fusionists: success and presumed availability. The election of 1892 demonstrated clearly that the Populist leaders had succeeded in mobilizing the discontent of over one million voters and directing their protest along reformist lines. The election results stimulated a renewed effort by T. C. Richmond, E. J. Wheeler, Frances Willard, and other Prohibitionists who had worked for fusion early in 1892 and also presented the possibility of success through fusion so tantalizingly to such antifusionist leaders as John P. St. John and Helen M. Gougar that they changed their positions in the party conflict and worked for fusion.[34] The fusion debate, initiated in 1891 with the first signs of Populist power, continued in full force from the closing of the ballot-boxes in 1892 until December 1895, when the Prohibition party National Committee decided against further attempts

at fusion. At that point the debate became a more generalized intraparty
conflict over the best means of attracting disaffected voters to the
Prohibition party.[35]

Serious efforts for fusion on the state level were made in Illinois
(1894), Virginia (1894), Wisconsin (1894), and Mississippi (1895).[36]
Most of these efforts foundered upon the refusal of the Populists
to adopt the uncompromised prohibition plank insisted upon by the
Prohibitionists. In Georgia (1894), North Dakota (1894), Mississippi
(1894), Wisconsin (1894), and Kansas (1895), Populists nominated or
endorsed party Prohibitionists, and in Boston the Socialists joined
a Populist-Prohibitionist coalition in 1895.[37]

Personal contact with public support for the issues raised by
the People's party brought John P. St. John to the fusionist position
by early 1895. After his defeat for a third term as governor of Kansas
in 1882, St. John had left his law practice and turned to public
lecturing on prohibition as the means for earning a substantial living.[38]
He sustained a successful career as a prohibition lecturer until the
early 1890s when the usefulness of his career as governor of Kansas
and as the 1884 Prohibition party presidential candidate and general
interest in prohibition began to fade away simultaneously. Engagements
for prohibition lectures grew fewer and fewer. St. John, however,
rescued his lecturing career by switching to advocacy of Populist
issues, for some of which he had entertained sympathy in the 1880s.[39]
With his change in emphasis to the Populist side of the land, transportation, and, especially, money questions, St. John's popularity
as a lecturer revived in both the East and the West and his income
again reached a satisfactory level during 1895 and 1896.[40]

By January 1895, St. John had deduced from the course of his
lecturing career and the failures of the Prohibition party that a
change in party tactics was necessary, and he began to move, at
first secretly, from support of Dickie and into the Richmond wing.
On May 17 he addressed a confidential letter to T. C. Richmond:

> I am disgusted with our party management—or rather
> with the utter lack of management. Personally Dickie is
> a pleasant man. He would make an efficient college pres-
> ident, but as a political general he is a *failure*. His dominant
> issue policy has stood in the way of all progress and party
> growth, and the only way I see out of the trouble is to go

to the next prohibition convention in such force as to
accomplish a thorough reorganization and go into the next
campaign with a broad liberal platform, upon which all
real reformers can unite. Something of that kind has got
to occur, or the prohibition party will die of dry rot. . . .
Dickie spoke to less than 50 persons last week at
Providence, R. I. on 'dominant issue' lines. No
admission fee. I made a *free coinage* speech there last
Tuesday (rainy) night, to 500, when they chged *[sic]*
25 cts. admission. Enthusiasm was great.[41]

The most obvious quality of the arguments for fusion was their
almost complete lack of ideological content. A few vague references
to forestalling revolution and restoring "good government" appeared
occasionally, but on the whole arguments for fusion with the
Populists ignored the question of the substantive goals of such a
coalition and instead addressed themselves to the problem of
effecting it.[42] Many Prohibitionists even indicated during the
debate over nationalization of liquor in 1893 and the intense debate
over fusion in 1895 that they would be willing to compromise the
demand for immediate prohibition of the liquor traffic which the
antifusionist wing held so dear.[43] One letter-writer from Ohio went
so far as to declare, "Let the reform forces get together, platform or
no platform."[44]

Nor did the questions of free silver, woman suffrage, or the
conflict between capital and labor provide unifying themes for the
fusionist arguments. If a "Populist wing" existed within the
Prohibition party, it can be identified with the fusionist wing only
by the fusionists' determination to unite with the Populists and
not necessarily by their commitments to the Populist positions
on land, transportation, and money.[45] At the Prohibition Park
conference in mid-1895, the climax of the efforts for fusion,
St. John and E. J. Wheeler, two of the leading fusionists, clashed
over the question of free silver, St. John supporting free coinage
and Wheeler arguing for the broader principle of government control
of the money supply.[46] The editors of the *Union Signal,* in plumping
for fusion, declared that, while they could not accept the theories
of the free-silver advocates, they did not believe that a trial of
free silver or indeed of the single tax would leave the country in

worse financial troubles than it was then experiencing.[47] Nor did
T. C. Richmond consider an essential part of a fusion platform the
woman suffrage plank which Frances Willard, Helen Gougar, and the
WCTU prized.[48] Richmond hoped at times to "appeal to the
practical business, conservative men of the country," while St. John
and others denounced Wall Street in general and, within the Prohibition
party, William T. Wardwell, party secretary and treasurer of the
Standard Oil Company, in particular.[49] E. J. Wheeler approved of
the Populists' attempt at "destroying private wealth" and suggested
only that their position would not be logically complete until
they included among their enemies the liquor power as well as the
money power.[50] The motive for the fusion attempts seemed to
spring from the simple fact of Prohibition party failure, and the
fusionists directed their efforts toward a goal defined only as
"success."[51]

But if the fusionists gave no indication, beyond "success," of the
goal of their efforts, they did offer some hints as to the character
of the constituency for and to which they assumed to speak.
Like the Dickie wing, the fusionists saw in the community both
"good" and "bad" elements, but they did not distinguish them on
the basis of the "moral character" valued so highly by their
opponents. When speaking of themselves and of those reformers with
whom they wished to unite, members of the Richmond wing used,
instead of "moral" or "righteous," words such as "sensible,"
"rational," "brainiest," or "level headed."[52] The object of the
reformer's concern should be the "average man," or "the average
voter," who should first be enlisted in a reform movement, then
"educated up" to the standards of the reformers.[53]

The fact that the fusionists did not share a consistent ideology
can easily be misleading. Behind such remarks as "Let the reform
forces get together, platform or no platform" lay a perception of
polarization, with the "reform forces" opposed by the forces of the
status quo. With hindsight we know that such a perception, while
overstated, was substantially accurate. Recent studies of voting
behavior in the 1890s have shown that no one was very happy with
the major parties' conduct of affairs: during 1890-1892 the voters
made a massive shift to the Democrats; during 1894-1896 they
executed an equally massive shift to the Republicans.[54] Yet,
as the election of 1896 showed, a crucial distinction existed between

those who had more to lose than to gain from an untested mode
of change and those who had more to gain than to lose from any
change, no matter how novel. Thus, in an atmosphere of polarization, it seemed more important whose side one was on than what
policies one approved.

The paternalism expressed by the fusionists seems to have served
two purposes. First, it imputed to Prohibitionists a social position
superior to those with whom they proposed alliance, thus assuaging the
feelings of lost status which Willard had recognized would be the
price of coalitionist endeavors. Second, paternalism promised an
eventual assimilation of the lower class into the moral, and
perhaps social, world of the Prohibitionist.[55] It thus revealed an
openness toward their social inferiors which, though qualified by
a tendency toward manipulation, still constituted a rare quality
among the middle class during the troubled 1890s.

The arguments of the antifusionists contained two themes:
(1) the compromise of the principle of prohibition necessary
for coalition was morally wrong; (2) as a practical matter, a coalition with the People's party would not advance the cause of prohibition because many Populists could not accept prohibition and
many Prohibitionists could not accept the radical programs of the
Populists.[56] The conception of the Prohibition party as the uniquely
moral element of the nation appeared in both arguments.[57] As one
Prohibitionist put it, a coalition of the Prohibition and People's parties
"would be an indiscriminate mixing of the good and bad elements of
society, and a consequent extinction of the influence of the moral
element of the nation."[58] A member of the National Committee
used both arguments in expressing his impatience with political
unions:

I believe in the union of nothing except God and humanity
as against the devil. Union with other political forces, and
upon questions on which we are divided, is no union, only
in name. Such a union would weaken our forces and
result in possible destruction. I believe in a straight temperance and Prohibition platform, on which we ought to
stand, and stand until it wins, even if we have to wait until
the millenium comes.[59]

Thomas R. Carskadon made explicit the contrast between prohibition
and politics with his characteristic religious imagery:

> I do most emphatically favor taking most "active steps
> toward union of reform forces" in heaven's own appointed
> way by lifting up that Christ who has assured us that if
> thus lifted up, He will draw all men unto him, but not
> by calling together scheming and disgruntled politicians.[60]

Another Prohibitionist argued against fusion by citing the
qualifications necessary to join his movement: "The temperance
masses will come to it [the Prohibition party platform] so soon
as they are soundly converted. We do not want them before."[61] That
was the nub of the difference between fusionists and antifusionists.

WHOSE GOD VOTES FOR PROHIBITION?

Just as the Richmond wing held out its proposed broad-gauge
platform as bait to tempt the Populists into alliance, so the narrow-
gaugers sought the single-issue platform as a lure for the church
voters of America. In urging this course, the Dickie wing contradicted
party history as fully as did the Richmond wing in its attempts at
fusion. The history of the evangelical Protestant churches' attitudes
toward the liquor traffic in the nineteenth century was a record of
increasing hostility, but the history of Prohibitionist relations with
those churches was a story of frustration engendered by the gap
between Prohibitionists' expectations and the churches' performance.
From the earliest days of the movement's revival after the Civil War
this gap was evident.[62]

Frustration sprang partly from proximity. Nearly all of the party
leaders were members of the evangelical Protestant denominations. E. J. Wheeler, the son of a Methodist minister, described
in 1900 the tone this imparted to party gatherings:

> A Prohibition convention has a very religious cast throughout.
> It is a custom to hold a prayer and praise meeting for several
> hours preceding the convention proper; and it is not unusual,
> in New York State, at least, for the delegates, on the various
> railroad trains that take them back to their homes, to hold

enthusiastic prayer-meeting in the coaches, much to the surprise of other passengers. Every mass-meeting and nearly every committee-meeting must open with prayer, and the usual methods of manifesting approval of a speaker or the points of his speech are the Chautauqua salute of waving handkerchiefs and shouts of "Amen!"[63]

Feeling obligated to support prohibition as a "moral reform," yet at the same time anxious to avoid association with a political party, evangelical Protestantism in the early 1890s refused support for the Prohibition party while offering vociferous rhetorical opposition to the saloon.[64] This situation drove party Prohibitionists to distraction and stirred in many of them an increasingly bitter hostility toward the churches, which in turn alienated church members from the party still further. The escalation of mutual hostility continued at least until 1896, when the single-issue wing gained control of the party and offered friendly overtures toward the churches. The hostility between the churches and the prohibition movement as a whole did not disappear until the Anti-Saloon League constructed its base in the churches during the years after 1900.

To understand the uncertain course of the evangelical Protestant churches' relations with the prohibition movement in the late nineteenth and early twentieth centuries requires a broader view of the secularization process than has normally been taken. Prohibitionists unquestionably contributed to the decline in ecclesiastical authority which historians agree was taking place in the late nineteenth century.[65] They did so by employing arguments for temperance which, although they often began in an attempt to demonstrate the relevance of sacred texts to the modern condition, ended by citing drink's moral and physical effects upon society and the individual rather than the authority of scripture.[66] With such friends, the churches needed no enemies. Organized evangelical Protestantism had two choices, neither of which looked very promising. It could retain the scriptural basis for social action and at the same time keep a healthy distance between itself and the prohibition movement. This was the course taken during the late nineteenth century. Unfortunately, espousal of temperance coupled with refusal to aid the political advocates of temperance created an appearance of hypocrisy—a weakness which Prohibitionists quickly perceived.

Yet prohibitionists, like churchmen, insisted that both personal identity and social progress had meaning only in ultimately transcendent terms. Faced with noncooperation from the churches, they were forced reluctantly toward an "invisible religion": a religion without a church.[67] Attempting to avoid such a radical innovation, they first created institutional alternatives in the form of prohibition "churches."

By the turn of the century, however, the churches were to become receptive to new prohibitionist overtures. Although Anti-Saloon League arguments for prohibition were couched in the same worldly terms as those of their predecessors, such arguments were subordinated to the promise of institutional regeneration through political action. Apparently feeling more isolated than before, many churches took League promises at face value. Like the symbol of social purity, the prohibition cause "permitted cooperation across denominational lines and acted as a moral cement for religionists as they applied themselves to social reconstruction."[68] Thus, organized evangelical Protestantism implicitly gave up the scriptural basis for social action in exchange for the promise of social influence through political cooperation with the Anti-Saloon League, only to find itself by 1933 bearing the double burden of failed politics and, in urban alienation and rural Fundamentalism, diminished intellectual hegemony.

Within the Prohibition party, differences in personal religious beliefs underlay the disagreements between the Richmond and Dickie wings over the proper attitude of the party toward the churches. Leaders of both groups diverged from the party standard, though in different directions. Samuel Dickie was a layman active in national Methodist affairs, and Joshua Levering, the single-issue wing's candidate for President in 1896, played a similar role in the Baptist church.[69] Dr. Isaac K. Funk was trained as a Lutheran minister and held pastorates in Ohio and Brooklyn for seven years, and Thomas R. Carskadon was reported to have held all positions open to laymen in the Methodist church.[70] In contrast, Thomas C. Richmond was an agnostic who invited the famous skeptic and lecturer Robert Ingersoll to Madison; John P. St. John was a former Congregationalist who turned to Christian Science about 1887 and later experimented with spiritualism; and Jesse Yarnell, a fusionist National Committeeman from Los Angeles, described himself as a "heathen."[71]

Frances Willard's grievance with the churches issued directly from her personal experience. In 1888 she had been one of five women elected by their conferences as delegates to the General Conference of the Methodist Episcopal church. The General Conference, after a heated debate, denied the women the seats to which they had been elected, and subsequent quadrennial conferences continued the practice of exclusion until 1904.[72] Willard got her revenge by proposing formation of a "Church Union" composed of those protesting against government of the churches by their male minorities. The requirements for membership consisted solely of endorsement of the Apostle's Creed, a pledge of "social purity," and total abstinence from liquor and tobacco. The Union would ordain and license women as ministers and encourage them to participate in its special work "among the masses of the people and in foreign lands, especially among women." By 1890 the WCTU had been forced to dissociate itself from its leader's proposal, but by her endorsement of secession from lethargic and undemocratic churches, Willard had set the pattern for other temperance reformers dissatisfied by the churches' lukewarm attitude—as they saw it—toward their special cause.[73]

The most drastic expression of Prohibitionist frustration with the churches appeared in a remarkable series of *Voice* editorials during the period September-November 1891. Probably written by E. J. Wheeler, they may have been in conscious imitation of William Lloyd Garrison's blasts at the churches of his day for their reluctance to condemn slavery. The shock of these editorials reverberated through the Prohibition party for the next twenty years. In view of this fact and because it put the issue in such stark terms, the first of the editorials, "The Ungodly League of Church and Saloon," deserves quotation at length.

> Prohibitionists of America, the time has come for a new warfare. The ungodly league between churches and saloons must be broken, if the churches have to be split from turret to foundation stone in order to do it. A church that will any longer palter or stammer in the presence of these 140,000 gaping hells in America is one that is an enemy to God and a menace to the moral health of the nation. The minister that any longer supports by his ballot or his silence the policy of license or a license party is as guilty before God on this subject as a bar-keeper, and no longer worthy to be a religious instructor or moral guide. The time has come when the truth must be shown in all its nakedness. The saloon exists because it is legalized and protected. Its legalization rests upon

the voters of America. There is the responisbility for all this immeasurable woe and sin. Men who deliberately shut their eyes to this fact are men unfit to take communion at God's table, and a church that will let them do it is unfit any longer to be called a church. We say this in all deliberation, conscious of all that it implies. If we cannot condone this sin in a party or a political leader, much less can we do it in a church or minister. . . .

What is to be done about it? There is but one thing to do. The guilt which we refuse to share politically is one we should refuse to share religiously. The Church must be purged of this guilt. . . . If any church or any minister or church paper refuses hereafter to free itself or himself from complicity with this 'traffic in human blood,' every true Prohibitionist, in our opinion, ought to repudiate such a church or minister or paper and withdraw his or her support. [74]

Shortly afterward, *The Voice* advised party Prohibitionists to find or organize "prohibition churches" which allowed into fellowship only voters for the party or, "if you can't find one or organize one, take the Prohibition Party in lieu of a church until you find one free from guilt, and our word for it you will find God just as near you as before." [75] On September 24 and October 8, 1891, *The Voice* distingished between Christianity and the Christian churches, asserting that Prohibitionists could be true to the former by indicting the latter.

Many party leaders wrote to *The Voice* approving its position, and most of them were later to become leaders of the broad-gauge faction. John P. St. John's name was notable among them, as was that of Helen Gougar, who wrote, "We need less prayer-meeting politics and more practical politics." [76] Neither Mrs. Gougar nor T. C. Richmond, however, had yet adopted all of the arguments they would advance five years later, for Gougar was still arguing that the Populists were "without principles," and Richmond's was practically the only voice raised in defense of the churches. [77] Meanwhile, a manufacturer and member of the party wrote to congratulate *The Voice*, enclosing his withdrawal from the Presbyterian church. [78]

Prohibitionist frustration with the churches simmered during 1892, while Willard was making her attempt to turn the party toward the Populists, then erupted with new force after the presidential election. In January 1893 a Chicago Prohibitionist wrote in *The*

Voice, "We may not speak against legalized immorality, and refrain from speaking against baptized immorality."[79] Helen Gougar refused to argue whether Christ had approved of wine: "If I believed that Christ, knowing the nature of intoxicating wine and foreseeing what a terrible curse its use would bring upon the human race, justified this use by His example, I would repudiate Him as a Saviour. I would be an infidel rather than believe in such a Christ."[80] She claimed that "Prohibitionists make no pretence to extra piety, and are not necessarily Christians, though all Christians must in the very nature of the case, be Prohibitionists." She closed by chiding the Methodist church for not backing up its conference declarations at the ballot box.[81]

Other voices took up the indictment and repeated it through 1895.[82] At intervals, they revived *The Voice*'s 1891 demands that major-party voters be expelled from the churches and that, failing this, Prohibitionists withold their support or withdraw from the churches. In some cases action followed words. Christian Prohibitionists held conferences in 1893, 1894, and 1895 to announce their dissatisfaction with the churches and to discuss the problem of bringing the Christian voter to the Prohibition party, forming the Men's National Christian Prohibition Union in September 1893 to accomplish the latter task.[83] More important, congregations favoring prohibition through the party founded churches in Newburg, New York; Cleveland, Ohio; San Francisco, California; and Chicago, Illinois, by 1895.[84] In 1896 another prohibition church sprang up in Buffalo, New York.[85]

Perhaps the strangest characteristic of the debate over the party and the churches was that it virtually had only one side. Until A. A. Hopkins offered the single-issue plank as the means of appealing to church voters in September 1895, few voices were raised in defense of the churches. Before then, the distinction on this question between those who were to secede in 1896 and those who were to remain with the party, directing their appeal to the churches, was one of degree. While Samuel Dickie warned the Methodist church that it had better expel the license voter or accept the saloon-keeper, Frances Willard, John P. St. John, Helen Gougar, and John Bidwell publicly endorsed the movement for a Christian Prohibition alliance which threatened to sever the bonds between Prohibitionists and their churches.[86] The two sides in this debate would not become clearly distinguishable until the national convention of 1896.

It may be noteworthy that the appearance of Prohibitionist

hostility toward the churches paralleled the growth of a similar
disaffection among Populists. From Populist strongholds in the
Plains States and in the South, as well as from Prohibitionist redoubts
in the East and Midwest, came the charge that organized Protestantism
had failed to carry out its obligations to all who needed its support or
succor.[87] Rebellion against the major parties had sensitized both
Populists and Prohibitionists to the deficiencies of other institutions.

WHICH SIDE WERE THEY ON?

The turbulence and conflict which disturbed American society in
the 1890s divided the Prohibitionists in their opinions upon public
issues as well as in their debates over the nature and direction of their
movement. In their pronouncements upon these public issues they
exhibited a flexibility and diversity which were largely absent from
their conflicts over the issues of platform, fusion, and relations with
the churches which directly involved their interests as reformers. Prohibitionists' concern with nearly every movement for social change
was evident in the notices and symposia carried by *The Voice* in 1890,
which included Nationalism, the single tax, charity work, woman suffrage,
cooperative colonies, ballot reform, immigration restriction, tariff
reform, Christian Socialism, Socialism, Spencerian laisser-faire, Indian
welfare, the Consumers' League, civil service reform, anarchism,
altruistic and anarchistic Communism, and labor reform.[88] The "do-
everything" policy of the WCTU was notorious.

The depression which struck in 1893 not only confirmed many
Prohibitionists' doubts about the ethics of their economic system but
also forced them to look beyond liquor as the cause and prohibition
as the sole remedy for injustice. Even before the depression, *The Voice*
had responded to Alexander Berkman's attempt to assassinate Henry
Clay Frick by observing calmly that it was becoming "increasingly
difficult to reconcile the teachings of Christ, who said, 'bear ye one
another's burdens,' with the competitive system of to-day that
says, 'get what you can, keep what you get, and devil take the hind-
most.'"[89] By 1896 the Congregational minister who edited Wisconsin's
Prohibition party paper found among the causes of economic breakdown
"the present competitive wage system" and "our present currency system"
as well as "the drinking habits of the poorer class stimulated by the

saloon." He concluded by calling upon Prohibitionists "to proclaim the tidings of industrial liberty to the enslaved."[90]

Discussion of class conflict which filled the air in the first half of the 1890s led Prohibitionists to examine the company they kept. For those who identified themselves with the interests of the downtrodden, this resulted in attacks upon successful capitalists within the prohibition movement, men such as the reputed millionaire William Jennings Demorest and William T. Wardwell of Standard Oil.[91]

When the Pullman strike broke out in 1894, *The Voice* initially opposed the strike and supported both the Wood-Grosscup injunction and the use of federal troops against the strikers. A speech by Illinois Governor John Peter Altgeld in Cooper Union two years later, however, led the editors to believe that perhaps President Cleveland had not really been justified in his use of the troops.[92] The *Union Signal,* published in Chicago, also took the side of the employers at first, but with the caution that "we can but feel that it is a great mistake to regard the wage-earning classes as a menace to the country, when in fact they are themselves the country, nor do we believe that as a class they have been guilty of endangering or destroying life and property."[93] After the strike ended, disclosure of the Pullman Company's oppression of its workers swung the *Union Signal* to the latter's support.[94] The WCTU editors also urged a paternalistic sympathy for Jacob Coxey's Commonweal Army in 1894.[95] They disapproved, however, of Altgeld's pardon of the surviving Haymarket anarchists. *The Voice,* while crediting Altgeld with sincerity and conceding the bias of the trial, insisted that the anarchists "had murder in their hearts, and got no more than their moral deserts when they were hung and imprisoned."[96]

Socialism was a different matter. One prominent New York City Prohibitionist served as a speaker for the Socialist Labor party, and a fusionist Michigan cranberry-grower wrote treatises promoting Christian Socialism.[97] *The Voice* advocated government ownership of railroads and telegraph systems, and chided those who were frightened by a socialistic label: "It is time that the American people quit this silly habit of being frightened by mere bogies into acquiescence while they are being trampled over and jumped on miscellaneously by overgrown monopolies and unscrupulous corporate combinations." A year before Coxey's march, the *Union Signal* endorsed the proposal to employ a million unemployed workers upon public works projects which were to be financed by an expansion of the currency to $50 per capita.[98]

Debate over currency within the Prohibition party after 1892 reflected the polarization of political opinion that was affecting the rest of America. A faction led by John P. St. John and Helen Gougar spoke out for the free coinage of silver, while other Prohibitionists supported the gold standard or took the eventual Republican position of 1896 by demanding international agreement before America abandoned its current system.[99] Some of the Prohibitionist opposition to free silver came from men like George W. Gere of Illinois, "general counsel for the Illinois Traction system and district attorney for the Big Four railroad."[100] Some Prohibitionists continued to hold to their old arguments that prohibition was the best solution to the nation's economic troubles.[101] St. John solved the problem of the primacy of prohibition by asserting that, while prohibition was actually the "greater" question in the election of 1896, silver was the "dominant" question.[102] E. J. Wheeler tried to avoid entrapment on the question of free silver by consistently taking a position similar to that of Edward Bellamy, Henry D. Lloyd, and other radical Populist leaders. Like them, Wheeler acknowledged "the necessity of some radical changes in our industrial system and the importance of making this land an industrial republic as well as a political republic"; asserted that the basic question was, *"Shall the Government issue the nation's currency, or shall private banking corporations do it for private profit?"*; denied that free coinage of silver actually embraced this question; and deplored "the way in which those industrial reformers who have no interests involved in mines are being diverted into this utterly barren fight for free silver."[103] Wheeler's analysis may have been economically sound, but it became less and less useful politically as the forces of reform came increasingly to be identified only by their allegiance to free silver. Other Prohibitionists, unable to swallow the free-silver panacea but unwilling also to align themselves against the cause of reform which it represented, followed a vacillating course.[104] The *Union Signal* contented itself with placing the whole currency debate within the march of progress from a competitive to a cooperative system and recommending the standard free-silver tracts as reading for the WCTU.[105]

The rise of the nativist American Protective Association (APA) in the early 1890s also created divisions among Prohibitionists. The party gave its support to the movement for English-language teaching in the public schools and against state appropriations to "sectarian" schools.[106] E. J. Wheeler, however, attacked the APA, chiefly on the grounds of the society's secret nature which, he contended, would "become a shield and a cloak for intriguers, and for assassins of character." Because of its secrecy the APA could hinder the movement for separation of church and state.[107] He received in reply letters from Prohibitionists defending the APA. One writer contended that "in its ranks are thousands of your subscribers—preachers, Prohibitionists and temperance men of the strongest kind."[108] In 1895 a Prohibitionist was reported to have been elected Mayor of Nashville, Tennessee; he had run on a "Good Government" ticket and had won support from the APA.[109] In 1896 A. A. Hopkins advocated his single-issue platform as a means of attracting the southern Democrat, who "is intensely American, and . . . realizes that the loudest outcry against Prohibition is shouted with a foreign brogue."[110]

The continuing tension between their need for the southern white vote and their antislavery heritage appeared in other acts of Prohibitionists beside the quadrennial debates over their woman suffrage plank. Advocating "progressive measures" in 1890 to solve the "Southern problem," *The Voice* suggested "a restriction of the suffrage for whites and black alike, upon a rigid educational basis," but added in conclusion, "Methods for the improvement of social conditions are, however, vastly more important."[111] When an unprecedented wave of lynchings broke out in 1892 and 1893, *The Voice* condemned the practice, noting that lynchings in the North were as unjustifiable as those in the South. It warned the South that the wave of lynchings "is bound to have an unfavorable effect upon the flow of capital, the development of industries and the increase of immigration."[112]

In May 1894 a municipal election in Norfolk, Virginia, gave party Prohibitionists the only chance they ever had to wield power in America. In their campaign, Prohibitionists had produced a unique blend of nineteenth- and twentieth-century idealism, promising the white suburbs an end to corruption, bringing their prime black orator from Canada to appeal to the ghetto, and wrapping it all together in a series of cataclysmic revival meetings. Once in power, they created stronger, though not prohibitory, liquor regulation, reformed the police department to secure enforcement, and replaced whites with black street-cleaners. Having given Norfolk all the reform it wanted (and, in the appointment of blacks, more than it wanted), they were turned out in 1896 by voters anxious to protect Democratic hegemony.[113]

The attitudes of Prohibitionists upon the social questions of the
time reflected the party's confused and divided state in the years
before its split in 1896. For a party in power, or even a party hopeful
of approaching success, these divisions might not have been fatal.
But for the Prohibition party, operating in a context of electoral
failure and declining interest in its main issue, some resolution of
the conflict and definition of its nature was necessary. This resolution came in 1896, but its achievement destroyed the party as a
force for social change.

The party split of 1896 was to smooth the path of the Anti-Saloon
League by demonstrating the failure of the party's method. The
intraparty debate of the years 1893-1896 also prepared the way for
the coming of the League. Every major point of what was to be the
League's program was involved in the debate. The faction that "won"
by retaining control of the party machinery and the greater share
of its vote prescribed for the prohibition movement a single-issue
appeal to that portion of the middle class identified with the churches.
When the League made this approach central to its strategy, Prohibitionists could offer in opposition nothing but dogmatic insistence
upon uncompromised prohibition backed by a party whose failure
had been clearly demonstrated. The debate opened the eyes of
Prohibitionists to alternative strategies; the defeat of the faction
advocating an appeal to the lower class on the basis of economic
as well as moral criticism foreclosed the only available alternative
to the tacit support of the economic system represented by the
Anti-Saloon League.

This is not to say that the leaders of this defeated faction
were ready to become part of a proletarian revolution, a prospect
which even the Populists contemplated only in their most apocalyptic
moments. The Prohibitionists who added their voices to the Populist
critique of the economic system did so primarily as part of an attempt
to ally with or to attract discontented farmers. Their economic ideology
was based upon a vague and paternalistic reformism. They are
significant because, in contrast to their opponents within the Prohibition
party, they were willing to express the discontent with middle-class
society which they all shared in terms severely critical of the economic
system. They were ready, moreover, to manifest that criticism in
a political alliance with the system's victims. And in quest of that
they were even prepared to abandon prohibition. The key to their

radicalism did not lie, however, only in the distrust of established economic institutions which they held in common with the Populists, nor in the alienation from the established political parties which they shared with other Prohibitionists; it lay primarily in their profound disaffection from the churches of America, the moral center of middle-class society. Their willingness to revolt against all of these institutions of middle-class America in the interests of change made their position the most dangerous possible alternative to the accommodationist approach of the Anti-Saloon League.

NOTES

1. For some remarkably accurate guesses in the same direction, see John Joseph Rumbarger, "The Social Origins and Function of the Political Temperance Movement in the Reconstruction of American Society, 1825-1917" (Ph.D. dissertation, University of Pennsylvania, 1968), pp. 192-193.

2. Svend Petersen, *A Statistical History of the American Presidential Elections* (New York, 1963), p. 61; *The Voice,* November 17, 1892, January 12, April 20, June 22, September 14, November 16, 1893; *Union Signal,* June 22, 1893.

3. Volney B. Cushing to N. F. Woodbury, August 26, 1893, Woodbury Papers, Michigan Historical Collections (MHC), Ann Arbor.

4. *The Voice,* January 31, 1895.

5. J. F. Cleghorn to T. C. Richmond, November 14, 1894, Richmond Papers, State Historical Society of Wisconsin (WHS), Madison. Another indication of failure was the reduction by one-half of the subcription list of the Wisconsin Prohibition party paper, published in Madison, between 1892 and 1896. See Account Book of the *Northwestern Mail,* H. A. Miner Papers, WHS.

6. James R. Turner, "The American Prohibition Movement, 1865-1897" (Ph.D. dissertation, University of Wisconsin, 1972), pp. 305 ff.

7. Paul E. Isaac, *Prohibition and Politics: Turbulent Decades in Tennessee, 1885-1920* (Knoxville, 1965), pp. 69-70.

8. C. C. Pearson and J. Edwin Hendricks, *Liquor and Anti-Liquor in Virginia, 1619-1919* (Durham, 1967), pp. 218-219.

9. E. E. Ewing to T. C. Richmond, January 17, 1895, Richmond Papers.

10. *The Voice,* April 23, 1896; *Northwestern Mail* (Madison, Wis.), April 30, 1896.

11. Frances Willard's voice became fainter and fainter in party

circles as she made longer and more frequent rest-seeking trips
to England after her exertions in behalf of coalition in 1892.

12. *The Voice* January 12, 26, 1893.

13. *The Voice,* a weekly, printed 61 letters favoring the plan during
the period May 11-September 7, 1893.

14. *The Voice* found encouragement for the belief that the Populists
could be brought into an alliance in the adoption in 1893 of planks
demanding state conduct by Populist state conventions in South
Dakota, New York, and Iowa. *The Voice,* July 13, August 24,
September 14, 1893.

15. *The Voice* printed 70 letters opposing nationalization during
the period May 11-September 7, 1893.

16. *The Voice,* June 1, 1893.

17. Ibid., August 17, September 14, 1893.

18. Ibid., May 4, June 8, September 14, November 30, 1893.

19. Ibid., June 29-August 24, 1893.

20. Ibid., January 3, 1895.

21. Ibid., December 20, 1894.

22. Ibid., March 28, 1895.

23. Ibid., July 11, 1895. See Ch. 4 below for a full discussion of
the Prohibition Park conference.

24. *The Voice,* September 26, 1895.

25. Ibid., January 23, March 5, 1896.

26. Ibid., January 2, 1896.

27. Ibid., January 23, 1896.

28. Ibid., March 5, 1896; *Union Signal,* August 22, 1895.

29. *The Voice,* August 1, 1895, March 5, April 2, 1896.

30. Ibid., September 26, 1895, January 2, 1896.

31. Ibid., March 26, 1896.

32. Ibid., February 27, May 21, 28, 1896.

33. Ibid., February 13, 1896.

34. For Helen Gougar's conversion to fusionism, see *The Voice,*
December 17, 1892.

35. For the fusion debate, see *The Voice, Union Signal,* and the
Richmond Papers, 1892-1895, and *Minutes of the N.W.C.T.U.* (Chicago,
1894, 1895).

36. G. M. Miller to T. C. Richmond, June 15, 1894, John C.
Martin to T. C. Richmond, August 19, 1894, E. B. Knowlton to
T. C. Richmond, November 13, 1894, Richmond Papers; *The Voice,*
June 7, July 5, 1894, January 10, 17, 1895; William DuBose Sheldon,
Populism in the Old Dominion: Virginia Farm Politics, 1885-1900
(Princeton, 1935), pp. 107-109.

37. *The Voice,* June 28, September 13, 1894; William Monroe to

T. C. Richmond, November 11, 1894, W. A. Curl to T. C. Richmond, April 3, 1895, Richmond Papers; *Union Signal,* December 5, 1895.

38. In the first years of his lecturing career, St. John earned $10,000-$12,000 yearly. Edna T. Frederickson, "John P. St. John, the Father of Constitutional Prohibition" (Ph.D. dissertation, University of Kansas, 1930), pp. 224-225.

39. Ibid., pp. 296-306. St John's position in favor of the free coinage of silver in 1895 was, however, the opposite of his views of 1878; also, his hostility to the railroads in the 1890s contradicted an earlier attitude of neutrality, if not cooperation, toward Kansas railroads during his terms as Governor. Ibid., pp. 185, 310. It was said that his stand on free silver was connected with his ownership of silver mine properties; by 1899 such a connection certainly existed, but it cannot be determined whether he held such properties four or five years earlier. Ibid., p. 307; St. John to W. C. Dickinson, July 19, 1899, St. John Letterpress Books, vol. 4, pp. 422-425, St. John Papers, Kansas State Historical Society (KHS), Topeka.

40. Frederickson, "John P. St. John," p. 308.

41. John P. St. John to T. C. Richmond, May 17, 1895, Richmond Papers. Similar views are expressed in St. John to Richmond, January 16, 1895, Richmond Papers.

42. Jesse Yarnell to T. C. Richmond, May 30, 1895, Richmond Papers; *Union Signal,* December 15, 1892; "A Call for a National Conference," 1895, Pamphlet Collection, WHS.

43. See above, pp. 71-72; letters to *The Voice,* January-May 1895.

44. *The Voice,* February 28, 1895.

45. Compare Joseph R. Gusfield, *Symbolic Crusade: Status Politics and the American Temperance Movement* (Urbana, Ill., 1963), p. 7.

46. *Union Signal,* July 11, 1895.

47. Ibid., July 18, 25, August 1, 1895.

48. *The Voice,* December 15, 1892, August 1, 1895.

49. Ibid., November 22, 1894, January 3, 1895, June 4, 1896; W. A. Curl to T. C. Richmond, January 23, 1895, Richmond Papers.

50. *The Voice,* October 20, 1892.

51. Ibid., March 28, 1895; John P. St. John to T. C. Richmond, January 16, 1895, E. W. Chafin to Richmond, January 19, 1895, H. S. Wells to Richmond, March 31, 1895, Richmond Papers.

52. *The Voice,* November 22, 1894; Jesse Yarnell to Richmond, May 30, 1895, T. C. Richmond to E. J. Wheeler, April 27, 1895, Richmond Papers; *Union Signal,* December 15, 1892.

53. *The Voice,* January 17, 1895; Edward Evans to T. C. Richmond, January 18, 1895, Richmond Papers.

54. Paul Kleppner, *The Cross of Culture: A Social Analysis of Midwestern*

Politics, 1850-1900 (New York, 1970); Richard Jensen, *The Winning of the Midwest: Social and Political Conflict, 1888-1896* (Chicago, 1971); Samuel T. McSeveney, *The Politics of Depression: Political Behavior in the Northeast, 1893-1896* (New York, 1972).

55. For a definition and discussion of assimilative reform, see Gusfield, *Symbolic Crusade,* pp. 61-86.

56. Chairman Dickie incorporated both themes in his pronouncements. *The Voice,* April 18, 1895.

57. See *The Voice,* January-May 1895.

58. Ibid., March 9, 1893.

59. Ibid., December 12, 1895.

60. Ibid., December 12, 1895.

61. Ibid., February 21, 1895.

62. Earl C. Kaylor, Jr., "The Prohibition Movement in Pennsylvania, 1865-1920," 2 vols. (Ph.D. dissertation, Pennsylvania State University, 1963), vol. 1, pp. 67-68; Turner, "American Prohibition Movement," ch. 1, and pp. 134-135.

63. E. J. Wheeler, "The Prohibition Party and Its Candidates," *Review of Reviews* 22 (September 1900): 330.

64. Charles H. Hopkins, *The Rise of the Social Gospel in American Protestantism, 1865-1919* (New Haven, 1940), p. 17. The antiliquor resolutions of church councils, most notably of the United Presbyterian General Assembly (1889), Presbyterian General Assembly (1892), General Conference of the Methodist Episcopal Church (1892), General Conference of the Methodist Episcopal Church, South (1894), National Congregational Council (1892), and American Baptist Home Missionary Society (1890), may be found in *The Voice,* October 18, 1894, and *Northwestern Mail,* September 24, 1896.

65. David J. Pivar, *Purity Crusade: Sexual Morality and Social Control, 1868-1900* Westport, Conn., 1973, pp. 81, 120, 158-159, 245, 260.

66. Turner, "American Prohibition Movement," pp. 63-65.

67. Thomas Luckmann, *The Invisible Religion: The Problem of Religion in Modern Society* (New York, 1967).

68. Pivar, *Purity Crusade,* p. 157.

69. *Union Signal,* June 11, 1896.

70. W. D. P. Bliss, ed., *New Encyclopedia of Social Reform,* p. 529; *Union Signal,* May 7, 1896; *Northwestern Mail,* April 16, 1896.

71. J. L. Ingersoll to T. C. Richmond, July 27, 1891, J. N. Baker to Richmond, August 1, 1891, Richmond Papers; John P. St. John to James St. John, June 16, 1899, St. John Letterpress Books, vol. 4, p. 356 (St. John's biographer mistakenly dates his conversion

to Christian Science in 1912. Frederickson, "John P. St. John," pp. 361-362); Jesse Yarnell to Richmond, May 30, 1895, Richmond Papers.

72. *Journal of the General Conference of the Methodist Episcopal Church, New York, May 1-31, 1888* (New York, 1888), pp. 92-103; Frances E. Willard, *Glimpses of Fifty Years: The Autobiography of an American Woman* (Chicago, 1889), pp. 617-621; Norton Mezvinsky, "The White-Ribbon Reform, 1874-1920" (Ph.D. dissertation, University of Wisconsin, 1959), p. 224.

73. Samuel Unger, "A History of the National Woman's Christian Temperance Union" (Ph.D. dissertation, Ohio State University, 1933), pp. 154-155.

74. *The Voice,* September 3, 1891. See also *The Voice,* September 10-November 12, 1891

75. Ibid., September 17, 1891.

76. Ibid., September 17, October 1, 8, 1891. See also letters of H. S. Taylor (*The Voice,* September 17) and John Bascom (October 8).

77. *Northwestern Mail,* November 5, 1891. The only substantial rebuttal I have found is instructive for two reasons: (1) it was published anonymously, and (2) the author built his case upon historical revisionism which discredited the sincerity and effectiveness of antebellum abolitionists. Thus he was able to assert that the anti-ecclesiasticism of the Prohibition party would hinder the achievement of prohibition, just as the fanaticism of the abolitionists had obstructed the abolition of slavery, which the influence of the churches would have otherwise accomplished without the necessity for civil war. "Abolitionists and Prohibitionists; or Moral Reform Embarrassed by Ultraism," *New Englander and Yale Review* 262 (January 1892): 1-25.

78. *The Voice,* October 1, 1891. See also E. G. Durant to T. C. Richmond, November 6, 1891, Richmond Papers. For qualified support of *The Voice'* s position by the Wisconsin Prohibition party paper, see *Northwestern Mail,* September 24, October 15, 1891.

79. *The Voice,* January 5, 1893.

80. Helen Gougar, "Christ and the Liquor Seller," *Arena* 7 (March 1893): 462.

81. Helen Gougar, "Is Liquor Selling a Sin?" *Arena* 8 (November 1893): 711, 716.

82. See letters and editorials, too numerous to list, in *The Voice,* 1893-1895.

83. *The Voice,* January 12, February 2, April 27, September 28, 1893, September 27, 1894, May 16, 1895.

84. Ibid., October 3, 1895.

85. Ibid., January 16, 1896.

86. Ibid., May 16, October 31. 1895. After the split, however, one single-issue leader claimed that broad-gaugers "have been the loudest in censuring the church." John Russell, "Some Reasons Why I Cannot Go with the Seceders," *Prohibition Party Campaign Text-Book, 1896* (Albion, Mich., 1896), p. 24.

87. Leland L. Lengel, "Radical Crusaders and a Conservative Church: Attitudes of Populists toward Contemporary Protestantism in Kansas," *American Studies* 13 (Fall 1972): 49-59; Peter H. Argersinger, " 'The Prayers of the Oppressed': Religion and Populism," Paper presented at the annual meeting of the Organization of American Historians, Washington, D.C., April 8, 1972; Argersinger, "The Divines and the Destitute," *Nebraska History* 51 (Fall 1970): 302-318; Frederick A. Bode, "Religion and Class Hegemony: A Populist Critique in North Carolina," *Journal of Southern History* 37 (August 1971): 417-438.

88. *The Voice*, February-November 1890.

89. July 28, 1892.

90. *Northwestern Mail*, April 30, 1896. See also *Union Signal*, August 22, 1895, and *The Voice*, January 30, 1896.

91. L. B. Howery to T. C. Richmond, September 7, 1894, Richmond Papers. E. J. Wheeler later exaggerated when he described Wardwell as "the financial mainstay of the party." E. J. Wheeler, "Prohibition Party and Its Candidates," *Review of Reviews*, p. 330. For evidence that Wheeler's statement was an exaggeration, see the financial statements of the party in its papers at MHC.

92. *The Voice*, July 12, 1894, October 22, 1896.

93. *Union Signal*, May 17, July 12, 19, 26, 1894. See also "President's Address," *Minutes of the N.W.C.T.U.* (Chicago, 1894), p. 115. Compare Mezvinsky, "White-Ribbon Reform," p. 229.

94. *Union Signal*, January 3, 1895.

95. Ibid., April 5, May 10, 31, 1894.

96. Ibid., October 19, 1893; *The Voice*, July 6, 1893.

97. T. W. Organ to T. C. Richmond, March 31, 1895; S. H. Comings to T. C. Richmond, February 6, 1895, March 30, 1895, Richmond Papers; Comings, "Competition vs. Co-operation," Proceedings of the Kansas Co-operative Congress, *The Nequa* (Topeka, Kansas) 1 (June and July, 1896): 20-27.

98. *The Voice*, March 21, 28, May 30, October 10, 1895, August 27, 1896; *Union Signal*, January 5, 1893.

99. St. John was the Prohibitionist in attendance at the Chicago meeting of the American Bimetallic League in August 1893. *Chicago Tribune*, August 1, 2, 1893. *Union Signal*, August 27, 1896. For the arguments of the gold standard and international agreement

advocates, see *The Voice*, August 1, 1895; *Union Signal*, September 10, October 8, 1896.

100. *American Advance*, June 24, 1911.

101. Rev. W. R. Brown to T. C. Richmond, July 25, 1893, Richmond Papers, reporting the resolution of Wisconsin Good Templars; *The Voice*, June 18, 1896.

102. Clipping, St. John Scrapbooks, vol. 15, St. John Papers.

103. *The Voice*, August 3, 1893, February 7, 1895, May 21, 1896. For a similar lack of devotion to free silver by the Populist Governor of Kansas, see Speech of Governor Lorenzo D. Lewelling, July 26, 1894, Kansas City, in Populist Documents, KHS.

104. *Northwestern Mail*, August 6, 13, October 1, 1896.

105. *Union Signal*, March 14, 1895, July 9, 1896.

106. Platform demands along these lines were adopted in 1895 by Prohibitionists in Ohio, Iowa, Nebraska, Maryland, New York, and Massachusetts, and in 1896 in Illinois. *The Voice*, June 20, 27, July 11, August 8, September 5, 26, 1895; *Northwestern Mail*, April 16, 1896.

107. *The Voice*, November 16, 30, 1893, May 31, June 21, 1894.

108. Ibid., November 30, 1893, January 4, February 15, March 22, June 28, 1894.

109. Ibid., October 24, 1895.

110. Ibid., January 16, 1896.

111. Ibid., January 23, 1890.

112. Ibid., September 28, 1893.

113. G. Clifford Boocks, "Experiment in Municipal Reform: The Prohibition Party in Norfolk Politics, 1892-1896" (M.A. thesis, Old Dominion College, 1967).

4

Farewell to reform: the party split of 1896

Much more than the silver issue caused the Prohibition party split in 1896. As we have seen, Prohibitionists since 1888, and vigorously since 1892, had been debating with each other—and with themselves—over the place their movement should occupy within American politics. The issues of the platform, fusion, and the proper attitude toward the churches provided the terms of this debate. If free silver, or any other one of these issues, had been the sole basis for disagreement, the wounds of the party might have been patched up. But by 1896 polarization between those holding different conceptions of the party had become so complete that the members of the winning faction at the party convention could not bring themselves to compromise with the losers, and the losers could see no alternative but a reluctant secession. And because the party disaster of 1896 had such deep roots in the general crisis of the 1890s, prohibitionists within and outside the party could only turn after 1896 to new means and a new organization to help them define themselves in American society.

THE FUSIONIST OFFENSIVE, 1895

The fusion debate early in 1895 produced numerous calls for a general reform conference to unite the scattered forces.[1] The pressure for union seemed to be so strong within the Prohibition party that even leaders like National Chairman Samuel Dickie,

who would never have consented to fusion without strong guarantees
of the primacy of the prohibition issue, were compelled to acquiesce
grudgingly to the call for such a conference. On April 9, E. J. Wheeler,
managing editor of *The Voice,* forwarded to Thomas C. Richmond
a copy of a letter he was sending out over the signature of his publisher,
Isaac K. Funk, listing the names of a broad cross-section of reform
leaders whose approval Wheeler hoped to gain for the conference.
Wheeler noted in his postscript, however, that he was disappointed
by the lack of attention devoted to the movement for fusion by
Populist papers.[2]

On April 25 *The Voice* published "A Call to Confer," which
announced a national conference of reformers to be held in the
University Temple, Prohibition Park, Staten Island, June 28 to
July 4, for "an interchange of views" on the questions of the day.
In its final leaflet form, the call distinguished eleven issues to be
discussed: (1) prohibition; (2) tariff; (3) antimonopoly; (4) government ownership of railroads, telephones, and telegraphs; (5) civil
service reform; (6) woman suffrage; (7) tax reform; (8) bimetallism;
(9) government issue of currency; (10) direct election of U.S. senators;
and (11) proportional representation. "If possible, without a violation
of principle," it concluded, "the friends of political reform should
enter the next Presidential campaign united."[3]

The call carried 144 names of reformers who supported it, but
the scope of the views they represented was more restricted than
that of Wheeler's original list of prospective signers sent to Richmond
two weeks before. From the left, Wheeler had failed to secure the
signatures of the Socialist Labor party chieftain Daniel DeLeon,
Nationalist Edward Bellamy, Socialist W. J. Ghent, single-taxer
Henry George, and labor spokesmen John Swinton and T. V. Powderly.
From the right, he had been unable to win approval from William
Jennings Demorest and William T. Wardwell, representatives of the
Prohibitionist business community. He did, however, manage to
use the names of five labor leaders, including James R. Sovereign,
Powderly's successor as Grand Master Workman of the Knights
of Labor. Socialism was represented among the signers of the call
by the Christian Socialists W. D. P. Bliss and George D. Herron.
As for the Populists, Senator James Kyle of South Dakota was the
most influential of a small group of signers which also included the
vocal but powerless Henry D. Lloyd, Mary Lease, Annie Diggs,
and two obscure party officials.

Wheeler's greatest success was among the Prohibition party leadership, from which he managed to secure the signatures of chieftains of both warring factions. From the antifusionist wing, Samuel Dickie, Isaac K. Funk, T. R. Carskadon, John G. Woolley, A. A. Stevens, and A. A. Hopkins signed the call. The insincerity of their support for fusion was evident five days later when Dickie issued a statement—claiming for it the support of Carskadon, Woolley, and Stevens—that "under present conditions it is useless to attempt a union of reform forces."[4] An easy victory was apparent in the appearance of the names of sixteen WCTU state presidents on the call, as well as that of National President Frances Willard.

Wheeler's call did not elicit complete support from other fusionists in the Prohibition party. While agreeing on the timing of the effort for union, western fusionists preferred to meet at a location more central than Staten Island, observed critically that Wheeler's call was signed primarily by Prohibitionists, and suggested that instead of holding a conference, the Prohibition party Executive Committee be pressured into appointing ambassadors to the People's and other parties.[5] A California National Committeeman pointed to one of the obstacles in the path to fusion: "I fear the trouble with too many Eastern Prohibitionists is, that they *do not want* a union of forces fearing the financial and other planks may not be satisfactory to them."[6]

Perhaps because of the limited segment of the political spectrum which its participants represented, the Prohibition Park conference came off amicably. The only noticeable conflict occurred when the two fusionist leaders, John P. St. John and E. J. Wheeler, clashed over the question of free silver.[7] The conference harmoniously adopted the eight recommendations of its fusionist Resolutions Committee and proceeded as well to set up the mechanics of union.[8] The conference made the unsurprising choice of E. J. Wheeler as its Secretary and ordered him

> to communicate with the authoritative heads of the
> Populists, Prohibitionists, Socialists, Silver Party, Single
> Taxers and any other reform elements, requesting them
> to call an instructed convention of these reform forces,
> to be held in Chicago or some other central city, some

time between Oct. 1 and March 1, next, to consider the
resolutions passed and the union of reform forces.

It also requested "the heads of these reform parties to hold their
conventions for nominating the President of the United States in
1896 at the same city, and on the same day."[9]
The promoters of the Prohibition Park meeting hoped that subsequent
local, state, and regional conferences would add support to the national
conference's demand for fusion upon the Staten Island basis of union.
The Voice reported several such mass meetings: 3,000 Populists and
Prohibitionists in Cambridge, Maryland; 5,000 farmers in Battle Creek,
Michigan; 5,000 Prohibitionists at Lycoming, Pennsylvania; and 1,500
farmers and 3,000 Prohibitionists in Indiana. Aside from these, *The
Voice* could discover no signs of a widespread popular movement for
fusion, although approval of the conference's action came from the
Populist Senator Kyle, the Populist *Topeka Advocate,* John P. St. John,
and the *Union Signal.*[10]
The movement for fusion also brought out the Prohibition party
reactionaries. A Colorado professor threw rocks at the Populists
and fusionists from behind the wall of the middle-class success myth:

There is a wide difference between us [Prohibitionists and
Populists] . . . . What these masses need is a strong moral
party to rise and abolish these sources of crime and poverty,
take away these irresistible temptations, and turn the price
of labor into legitimate channels of trade that will bring
comfort and contentment into the home. Labor organizations
ought to aid us in this, and, instead of constantly demanding
higher wages, should systematically teach their members
how to save what they do earn and how to get the most real
good out of it. "By industry and economy one becomes
rich" is old but always and eternally true. All ages have
been oppressive to those who "have wasted their substance
with riotous living."[11]

Other Prohibitionists shuddered at the thought of associating with
"revolutionaries." "We had better die a natural death, and leave an
honorable record behind us, than be choked to death in the attempt
to swallow socialism, communism, and anarchism in one gulp."[12]

Look at history, and point to an epoch in which the
ragamuffin elements of society have won a battle. You
will find ambuscades and bloody streets. You will not
find a case in which civilization has been advanced. When
you have brought into the Prohibition Party Debs and
Altgeld and Coxey, and Blood-to-the-bridle Waite,
and all their tattered and dirty followers, and have washed
from them the stains of the gutters, and shall have
neutralized their saloon breaths, you shall have a sight to
behold. But while you are drawing these men in, you are
proclaiming to the world that Prohibition is an associa-
teism [*sic*] with all those which speak of disorganization
and revolution. . . . There is a way to build up a party in
America, and this is to build on American principles.[13]

These hysterical reactions by antifusionists foreshadowed the
bitter conflict on December 11, 1895, which put an end to the hopes
aroused by the Prohibition Park conference. The battlefield, ironically,
was the Sherman House in Chicago, which had been the birthplace
of the fusion movement in January 1892. The occasion was the
regular meeting of the Prohibition party National Committee to
plan the convention of the following year.

For the fusionists, it turned out to be the wrong battlefield at
the wrong time. They had apparently begun their effort early in 1895
in the hope of avoiding the late start and vulnerability to the whims
of a convention which they felt had killed their chances in 1892.
But by entrusting the fate of their movement to the leaders of the
Prohibition party at a meeting to which they neglected to bring
their full strength, the fusionists guaranteed defeat for their cause.

Wheeler's only strength at the National Committee meeting
consisted in signatures and resolutions; his side was fatally short on
votes. In November he had issued the proclamation required by the
Prohibition Park conference, requesting the National Committees of
the People's, Prohibition, and Socialist Labor parties each to appoint
a committee charged with calling an official union conference of
the three parties. The proclamation was signed by four members each
of the Populist and Prohibition National Committees as well as
by several other reformers.[14] Wheeler also had assurances of support

from the 1895 national convention of the WCTU, which, however, controlled few votes in the three parties or their National Committees.[15]

The Prohibition party National Committee included two members from each state and territory. Only about half of the membership appeared at the Sherman House meeting, but, probably because Chicago lay in the heartland of Prohibitionist strength, the thirty-seven who attended represented areas which had provided 80 percent of the party's vote in 1892.[16]

The crucial vote came when Chairman Dickie presented Wheeler's proclamation of November 14 under the latter's cover letter urging its endorsement. Committeeman Robert J. S. White of New Jersey moved "that the secretary be instructed to return the communications and to inform Mr. Wheeler that it is the judgment of this committee that it is not in the province of this committee to consider his communication nor has it the power to act in the matter"—in effect, a flat refusal even to explore the possibility of fusion. A North Dakota fusionist moved to table the communications, apparently in an attempt to save the chance, but the committee defeated the tabling motion by 29-8. White's motion to refuse the fusion attempt prevailed by five votes, 21-16.[17]

Analysis of this key vote reveals that an East-West antagonism, seen by many within the party, did indeed exist on the question of fusion. Of the twenty-six Committeemen from states east of the Mississippi River, eighteen voted for White's motion and thereby against the fusion cause, while eight of the eleven western Committeemen voted against the motion. The losers could not claim that they were defeated by the representatives of states in which the party was weak, for the antifusionists came from areas which had provided 43.9 percent of the 1892 party vote, while the fusionists represented only 36.6 percent.[18]

Simultaneous with the National Committee meeting, *The Voice* polled its membership by mail on the question put to the Sherman House meeting by Wheeler's proclamation.[19] Comparison of the results of this poll with the vote at Chicago shows that the antifusionist majority of five did not reflect the alignment within the National Committee. Wheeler's side lost the support of twenty National Committeemen favorable to a fusion conference either through absences (eighteen) or a proxy's voting contrary to the expressed position of his Committeeman (two); the antifusionists lost ten votes through

absences (eight) and proxy switches (two). A decisive factor in the
defeat of fusion was thus the failure of the fusionist wing to bring its
troops to the field of battle. Nor could the fusionists plead in their
behalf an unfair location, for the geographical distribution of the
missing committed delegates was nearly the same for both sides.
Following the rejection of Wheeler's call, John P. St. John
resigned from the Executive Committee and was replaced by James
B. Cranfill. The National Committee then scheduled the convention
for May 27 and 28 in Pittsburgh.[20]

The negative vote of the Prohibition party National Committee
killed the cause of fusion in 1896. The Populists were thus able to
continue to avoid the embarrassing question of prohibition, which
together with the woman suffrage issue had nearly split their party in
February 1892.[21] Shortly after the Sherman House meeting, National
Chairman Herman Taubeneck of the People's party refused the request
of the Prohibition Park conference which was forwarded to him in
Wheeler's proclamation.[22]

THE SINGLE-ISSUE COUNTERATTACK

Emboldened by the defeat of the fusionists in December 1895,
eastern and southern leaders of the Prohibition party began shortly
thereafter to press for the adoption of a single-issue platform at the
1896 national convention. Some, like Dickie and Stevens, proposed
such a platform as a means of avoiding entanglement with the lower-
class support for free silver, but all agreed with the need to turn the
party toward the "moral element" found primarily among church
voters. In their drive to replace the dominant-issue plank of 1888 and
1892 with the more extreme single-issue platform, they created a
small but aggressive and influential faction which came to Pittsburgh
in May 1896 convinced that the best defense against the economic
radicalism of the broad-gaugers would be a concerted attack under
the single banner of prohibition.

Those who rallied behind the position presented by A. A. Hopkins
in his *Voice* letter of September 1895 found themselves joined by
one who had been moving toward the single issue and church voters
for several years. John G. Woolley was a worthy successor to the
beloved John B. Gough as the greatest of prohibition orators. Like

Gough, Woolley was a reformed drunkard. Two years after Gough's death in 1886, Woolley finally cured his alcoholism "by grace" and, as he later put it, joined the church and the Prohibition party "at the same instant."[23] Since 1888 Woolley had been on the lecture trail, and his overriding theme was the need for church voters to "vote as you pray."[24] In 1895 he had come to the Prohibition Park conference to present his new plan for prohibitionist success. "It is," he told the conference, "that we [Christian Democrats, Republicans, Populists, and Prohibitionists] combine politically in the name of Jesus Christ, the Conqueror, and form an Inter-Partisan Order of Independent Voters whose entire scope shall be *the head of the ticket,* in federal, state, judicial and municipal elections." All other issues than prohibition were to be ignored "for the present."[25] Woolley's plan drew little support from the fusionists at Prohibition Park, but clearly he was ready to lead an appeal to church voters on the single issue of prohibition. Consequently, he attacked the Staten Island basis of union, the adoption of which, he claimed, "would be to throw away a diamond drill and attack the rock of error with a rake."[26]

One advantage of the single-issue platform lay in its novelty, for many Prohibitionists blamed the broad-gauge policy for the party's failure to take advantage of the aroused prohibition sentiment of the 1880s. The party in Oregon, which had aligned itself in the 1880s with agrarian radicalism, showed the new direction of some Prohibitionists' thinking. Reorganizing in 1894, Oregon Prohibitionists abandoned their radical tendencies and elevated to leadership a dedicated single-issue man.[27]

Some evidence of the strength and nature of the single-issue faction appeared in the December 1895 *Voice* poll which asked the National Committee where it stood on fusion. Inquiring, "Do you believe the Prohibition Party should confine its platform to a single issue?" *The Voice* found among the forty-six who replied only twelve who answered in the affirmative. Twenty-eight National Committeemen opposed the single-issue platform, three called for a dominant-issue platform, and the other three were undecided.[28] Of the twelve single-issue advocates, nine came from states of the New England, Middle Atlantic, South Atlantic, and West South Central regions. Opposition to the single-issue platform was not confined to the West, however, for only twelve of the twenty-eight answering in the negative represented states lying west of the Mississippi.

In the early months of 1896 the single-issue men kept their cause before Prohibitionists through the party press.[29] A Kentucky Prohibition orator outlined the shape of a single-issue platform: "I would like to have our national platform this year condense into a preamble the declarations of the church conferences, synods, presbyteries, associations, etc., on the liquor question; follow that with one plank emphatically declaring for the abolition of the traffic—and then quit."[30] From Chicago a Prohibitionist minister cried, "In God's name give us an issue that appeals, without incumbrance of any kind, to the conscience of Christians."[31] As the convention approached, *The Voice* urged upon its readers the merits of the single-issue platform.[32]

Thomas C. Richmond helped to maintain the broad-gauge side of the argument. Writing in April, he addressed the claim that advocacy of issues other than prohibition would divide the party: "If it be suggested that to take up the money question or the tariff question is to divide the party, I answer [that] they *are* up for discussion, they *are* here for settlement." When an old friend countered that "nothing we can say on either side of them, will have a particle of influence in their settlement," Richmond pointed to the existing lines of political division within the country and denied the possibility, much less the realism, of Prohibitionists' taking a stand aloof from the battle.

> Those who would debauch our people with liquor, double
> their debts with a dishonest dollar, enslave the toiler and
> lay the heaviest burdens of taxation on the poor, are united
> in support of these indescribable wrongs, while reformers are
> fighting in factions. . . . He who thinks we can get the
> voters of the country this year to drop all other issues and
> settle the liquor question, is too visionary to deserve,
> and certainly will not get, the respectful attention of the
> people.[33]

When the WCTU editors spoke out, they noted that "THE UNION SIGNAL votes broad-gauge."[34]

Single-issue advocates, of course, thought themselves the realistic ones. They based their argument upon two propositions: (1) church voters were in fact a significant political force, and (2) church voters could be mobilized in support of their churches' anti-liquor resolutions by an appeal to them upon that issue alone. The first proposition rested upon findings such as those published in *The Independent* of

February 1895 by the Stated Clerk of the Presbyterian General
Assembly: the estimated percentages of church voters in the electoral
population ranged from 7.3 percent in the Western Division of the
census to 50.1 percent in the South Atlantic Division.[35] A test of the
second proposition depended upon whether single-issue men could
persuade the Prohibition party to make the appeal. In early 1896
the single-issue wing began to mount its appeal to church voters
through the party press, and *The Voice* offered special subscriptions
to all clergymen.[36]

State conventions of the Prohibition party previewed the conflict
that was to erupt at the national convention. At the Wisconsin
gathering two weeks before the national meeting, single-issue forces
made an effort spearheaded by the address of National Party Treasurer
Samuel D. Hastings, a founder and one of the most revered figures
in the Prohibition party. The *Northwestern Mail* noted that Hastings's
support came from "older and more experienced leaders," while
"many of the younger men were in favor of broadening out." The single-
issue men mustered a majority in the Resolutions Committee and
presented a platform limited to prohibition alone. The minority
report stood for "free silver, free trade, a single tax on land system,
government ownership, equal suffrage, Sabbath observance, free schools
taught in the English language and against any government appropriations
for sectarian schools." The convention hammered out a four-plank
compromise platform including prohibition as well as the first,
fifth, and seventh planks of the minority report. The vote on the
free-silver plank ended in a tie which was broken in favor of free
silver by the vote of the convention chairman. As the *Northwestern
Mail* pointed out, "The real issue in the debate was not on the
merits of the different planks presented in the minority report, but
on the policy of presenting any other issue than prohibition to the
people of this state for their suffrage." The convention closed by
nominating Joshua H. Berkey, a single-issue leader, as the gubernatorial candidate of Wisconsin Prohibitionists.[37]

RESOLUTION

By the time delegates began to arrive in Pittsburgh on Tuesday,
May 26, the small but influential single-issue faction had established
its position as the leading alternative to the plans of the broad-gaugers.

The issue of free coinage of silver, which many then and since have seen as the decisive dividing question, was in fact no more than a symbolic reference point for both sides.[38] While delegates to the convention knew that the decisive test of strength would come in the vote on a free-silver plank, they also realized that the two sides in the voting would be determined not by their respective feelings on the currency question but rather by their deep-seated beliefs about the character of the Prohibition party and the course it should pursue.

The uselessness of attitudes toward free silver as indices of the broad-gauge alignment at Pittsburgh has been noted above.[39] It was even more clear when the broad-gauge faction proposed the Nebraska Baptist minister and farmer Charles E. Bentley as its candidate for President. Asked in March 1896 about the potency of free silver in solving the country's money problem, Bentley replied, "I do not regard it as a solution at all."[40]

Meanwhile, the single-issue men found themselves in the company of conservative opponents of the Prohibition party who for years had been blasting the party for loading itself with "isms."[41] A single-issue man later reported that the resentment of broad-gaugers toward the party's prominent entrepreneurs had been enhanced by the belief that *The Voice*'s simultaneous dumping of Wheeler and switching to the single-issue side had been dictated, "not by a change of belief in its editorial force, but by the capitalistic interests of the company that published it."[42]

The first group to meet on May 26 was the single-issue caucus, consisting at that time of about one hundred delegates.[43] The sentiment emerging from their meeting held that no planks should be adopted to which a large portion of the convention was opposed, and that prohibition by itself would solve many of the financial problems confronting the nation. As one reporter noted, "This action, if indorsed by the convention, will eliminate any reference from the platform to the financial question, woman suffrage, government control of railroads and telegraphs, anti-monopolies, and all other issues that would tend to create discussion or division in the party." The caucus appointed a narrow-gauge steering committee led by Samuel Dickie, A. A. Stevens, Isaac K. Funk, J. B. Cranfill, and John G. Woolley. The broad-gauge caucus also met, decided on Bentley as its presidential nominee, and form its own steering committee led by John P. St. John and Helen Gougar.

The following day, May 27, the narrow-gaugers held another caucus, which attracted between 400 and 500 delegates. Chairman Dickie was reported to have asked the women delegates not to press for a woman suffrage plank in the convention, apparently to leave the way clear for the single-issue platform. The narrow-gaugers voted that they would support a motion that the platform not include any issue which failed to command the support of three-quarters of the convention.

Forty-eight members of the new National Committee, selected by their respective states, met on the evening of the twenty-sixth. Their only important business was selection of a temporary chairman for the convention. In this opening skirmish between the two factions, the single-issue men won decisively, electing A. A. Stevens over E. J. Wheeler by 32-16. St. John asked Chairman Dickie if he would rule out of order a minority report to the convention proposing Wheeler. Dickie declined to answer the question, referring it instead to the National Committee—a safe move in the light of the voting just concluded. The broad-gaugers tried anyway with a motion by Oliver W. Stewart of Illinois that the Chairman be directed to present to the convention all names given him by members of the Committee. As Dickie knew it would, the National Committee voted the motion down, 31-12, thereby setting the stage for the convention's first battle.

Dickie presented Stevens for temporary chairman at the opening of the convention's first session on May 27. Immediately, a California National Committeeman leaped to his feet and submitted a minority report signed by himself and ten colleagues on the Committee, proposing E. J. Wheeler for temporary chairman. Dickie ruled him out of order. The Californian asked for an appeal from the decision, but Dickie handed the gavel to Stevens. Stevens ruled that no appeal could be taken to the unorganized body which the convention then constituted. Tumult reigned but was eventually calmed, first by the playing of the band and then by Wheeler's withdrawing his name in hope of harmony.[44] This brief but bitter conflict brought to the surface the broad-gaugers' resentment of the party's managers.

Single-issue resentments were aroused in turn when Gougar, chairwoman of the Credentials Committee, presented the name of the broad-gauger Oliver W. Stewart for permanent chairman as the "unanimous" report of her committee; only the broad-gauge majority had voted that the report be "unanimous."[45] William P. F. Ferguson of New York submitted a minority report nominating A. A. Stevens.

After a heated debate, the broad-gaugers won their first victory when
Stevens withdrew his name and Stewart was thereupon seated.

The two sides clashed again on the evening of the twenty-seventh
at a mass meeting. John G. Woolley spoke first, reiterating the value
of the single issue as a means of winning the church vote. St. John
followed with an address urging adoption of a broad platform so
as to align the party with the forces of reform. He opened by proclaiming, "We are not here as a methodist campmeeting, a Salvation
Army or a church. We are holding a political convention." He went on
to decry the single-issue faction's solicitude for church voters.

> For 25 years the Prohibition party has been run by narrow-
> gauge managers. Tons of Prohibition literature has been sent
> out, but not a leaf on any other issue. There are 20,000,000
> church-members in this country, 4,000,000 church-voters,
> and yet we can only poll 270,000 votes. It is time we quit
> slobbering over the church.

After this collision between the party's two greatest orators, no delegate
present could have been in doubt about the ground occupied by each
faction.

While most delegates were in their beds on Wednesday night, the
Resolutions Committee struggled over the platform. The single-issue men
appeared to have a majority on the 36-member committee, and they
supported a six-plank platform advocating only prohibition and aimed
directly at church voters. The broad-gauge minority, led by St. John,
proposed in addition to prohibition a fifteen-plank platform including:
(1) government issue of money and free coinage of silver; (2) land
grants only to actual settlers; (3) government ownership of railroads,
telegraphs, and other monopolies; (4) income tax and free trade;
(5) abolition of contract convict labor; (6) initiative and referendum;
(7) woman suffrage; (8) one day's rest in seven; (9) English-language
public schools and no public support of sectarian institutions; (10) direct election of President, Vice-President, and Senators; (11) liberal
veterans' pensions; (12) immigration restriction and delay of voting
rights until five years after arrival in the country; (13) delay of voting
rights until one year after naturalization; (14) international arbitration;
and (15) a plea for support from all citizens. The whole committee

approved a woman suffrage plank, 20-16. The narrow-gauge majority
also seemed to be willing, for the sake of party harmony, to accept
all of the broad-gauge platform except the "Populist" planks
on land, transportation, money, and direct legislation.

The final battle occurred on Thursday, May 28, when the
convention took up the majority report presented by Funk and the
minority report read by St. John. First incorporating the two reports
into each other, the convention then proceeded to take up each
plank in succession. The six prohibition planks of the majority
report and the woman suffrage plank all passed rapidly by large
majorities. Debate on the free-silver plank took up three hours.

Dr. Louis Albert Banks, a Brooklyn minister who claimed to be
pastor of the largest Methodist church in the world, delivered the
most passionate argument against the free-silver plank. "I plead with
you," he cried, "to give the preachers a fair chance to appeal to
the voters on the great question of Prohibition. . . . Let us for once
open every church in the land and unshackle the voice of every
preacher on this monstrous crime. . . . Give the church a chance."
He concluded by denying the need for class conflict: "Let us enable
the banker of New York and the silver-miner of Colorado to
stand shoulder to shoulder, and I assure you that every church that
I can touch will ring out death to the rum traffic." An Indiana
broad-gauger replied, "How does the pastor of the largest church
in the world expect to convert people when little children are starving
because the gold men of New York have all the gold of the country
invested in breweries, and they have another kind of it?" Dickie
added his voice to the chorus against free silver.

The arguments probably changed no one's mind. When the vote
was taken, the free-silver plank lost by 40 votes, 427-387. Of the
150 delegates from states west of the Mississippi River, 120 voted
for free silver. East of the Mississippi, however, no such unanimity
was evident, for the vote from those states stood 397-268 against
free silver, or about 60 percent to 40 percent. The four states of
Illinois, Indiana, Ohio, and Michigan confused such a crude division
by voting with the broad-gaugers by 171-56. The "West" in this
case included the Ohio Valley as well as the trans-Mississippi
states.

After killing the free-silver plank, the convention proceeded to
consideration of St. John's ninth plank, advocating English-language

public schools and opposing appropriations for sectarian institutions.
It had just voted for adoption when an obscure delegate from Illinois,
Robert H. Patton, gained the floor and dropped the convention's
biggest bombshell. Patton had supported the defeated silver plank, but he
was convinced that the party's only hope lay in either the broadest possible
platform, or the narrowest possible, not something in between. Therefore,
he had brought to the convention a single-issue platform which he
had prepared, and he now presented it as a substitute for everything
adopted and reported. Patton defended his substitute by attacking
divisive issues. "The plank before this convention at the present time
is an illustration of the folly of our party's declaring upon issues
that cause men who believe in Prohibition to refuse to cooperate
with us. It is a declaration upon an issue in American politics
fostered by the American Protective Association." Taking his
stand on the side of the "little red schoolhouse," Patton nevertheless
advised against antagonizing any possible allies: "But if there is in
America a Catholic or any other person who feels a prejudice to this
issue in American politics who will give me his hand and lend me his
help to make it safe for our boys to live, I will give him mine, and
together we will work for the accomplishment of this one thing upon
which we are agreed."

The single-issue men were probably surprised at the way in which
their position had appeared before the convention. But they were
certainly prepared to support such a platform, for they had argued
and worked for it steadily for at least eight months before the convention,
and their delegates on the Resolutions Committee had presented a platform different in form but identical in substance to the one Patton now
offered. The broad-gauge wing, angered and resentful at their defeat
after the exciting debate over the free-silver plank, joined their
opponents in pushing through Patton's motion, 650-150. St. John
spoke for it, saying that he had been defeated and now proposed to
test the sincerity of the single-issue wing. Gougar tried in vain to salvage
the already adopted woman suffrage plank.

The convention then adjourned until the evening nominating
session, and the broad-gauge wing called a caucus which included about
330 delegates from over twenty states. They claimed leaders from the
party committees of twelve states as well as fourteen members of the
National Committee. Even after the defeat of their free-silver plank
and the adoption of an uncompromised single-issue platform, they

hesitated to bolt the party and resolved instead to postpone a final
decision until after the nominations had been made that evening.
Frustrated by the seeming intransigence of the narrow-gauge party
leaders, they would wait passively to see whether the majority wished
to offer any concession at all in the nomination of a compromise
ticket.

The majority did not wish to compromise. At the evening session the
delegates shouted through the nominations of Joshua Levering of
Maryland for President and Hale Johnson of Illinois for Vice-President.
Both were confirmed narrow-gauge men; Levering was a Baltimore
coffee merchant, active in the Baptist church, who had refused before
the convention to run for office if a free-silver plank was adopted.
The only attempt at compromise hardly constituted a meaningful
gesture. New York WCTU President Ella Boole offered a woman suffrage
plank, but the convention refused to accept it as an integral part
of the platform, agreeing only to include it as a supplementary
resolution.[46]

As party leaders appealed for funds to conduct the campaign, several
hundred broad-gauge delegates ratified with their feet the decision
they felt the uncompromising single-issue men had made. Withdrawing
to another building, they formed the National party, adopted a platform
including prohibition and the entire minority report of the Resolutions
Committee, and nominated the Reverend Charles E. Bentley of
Nebraska for President and J. H. Southgate of North Carolina for
Vice-President. Leaders of the new party planned to attend the conventions
of the Populists, Republicans, and Democrats "to confer with the
dissatisfied elements."

Two conflicting visions of the nature and destiny of the Prohibition
party thus wrought themselves out in two separate parties as the
convention of 1896 ended. In splitting, the Prohibitionists set the
pattern for the two major parties, and the Populists avoided the same
fate only through desperate manipulation of their ticket. By leaving the
old Prohibition party in the hands of those who had little interest in
economic reform and less sympathy with the lower class, the broad-
gaugers removed from the prohibition movement the potential it had
once possessed for an attack on the institutions of middle-class
America.

Some participants thought the party split had been inevitable.
John G. Woolley best summed up what had taken place:

Over-freighted with priceless things, helpless with riches,
submerged to the bulwarks, our good ship has "cast off"
many times, and stood away—but vainly, for each time, when
her white sails were filling with a fair wind, her keel plowed
the reef and hung her there, a prisoner in port, while her
helm swung useless to and fro. She rides higher now, but
it cost something. Bales of stuffs as dear as life to those who
brought them on board, and bags of gold and silver had
to be put ashore, and finally part of the crew went over
the side. But the Prohibition Party has crossed the bar.[47]

TWO PATHS TO FRUSTRATION

In the aftermath of the convention, a bitter debate erupted
between the WCTU and the Prohibition party. In biting, sarcastic
editorials the *Union Signal* attacked the single-issue men for having
dropped woman suffrage from the platform. "Not even in bidding
for the Christian vote—in giving the church a chance to vote her
own resolutions," admonished the white-ribboners, "should the
party of moral reform sacrifice right to expediency."[48] They stopped
short, however, of endorsing the National party, preferring instead
to leave the choice to each WCTU member.[49] Members of the
Cleveland, Ohio, Central WCTU were so outraged at the deletion of
woman suffrage that they resolved to "withdraw our aid and influence"
from the Prohibition party.[50] Some southern Prohibitionists, such
as J. B. Cranfill, rejoiced at what was for them a triumph and vindication
in the unloading of woman suffrage, which they and their constituents
had always opposed.[51] The editors of *The Voice*, however, tried to
shift responsibility for dropping woman suffrage from the single-issue
to the broad-gauge wing, and frenziedly tried to make the white-ribboners
believe that all good Prohibitionists were really their friends. Other
Prohibitionists, such as Samuel D. Hastings of Wisconsin, affirmed their
personal support for woman suffrage but tried to persuade the WCTU
that both prohibition and woman suffrage would advance more rapidly
if each travelled alone.[52]

From its parent organization the National party drew both leaders
and strength in important areas. E. J. Wheeler later reported that all

three of the Prohibition party's living former presidential candidates supported the seceders.[53] At a Prohibition party National Executive Committee meeting in July, Chairman Dickie reported that the "division and loss" caused by the split were apparent in the states of Ohio, Michigan, Indiana, Iowa, Kansas, Nebraska, Colorado, and California. The Executive Committee recognized the party's need for a good showing in the first six of those states and authorized a special expenditure of $1,500 there.[54] *The Voice* reported that, of the twenty-eight party papers published west of Pittsburgh, seventeen supported the National party. Ten of these seventeen were in the states of Ohio, Indiana, and Michigan.[55]

For many seceders, the National party probably represented little more than a stepping-stone to the Democratic party after the Chicago convention nominated Bryan and adopted a free-silver platform and after the Populists failed at St. Louis to provide an alternative to the Democracy. In July, T. C. Richmond, who had not been at Pittsburgh, announced his withdrawal from the Prohibition party with the statement, "If it be necessary, I, for one, am willing to stay operations against King Alcohol until we overthrow King Gold." Replying to the implications of the narrow-gaugers that National party men were less than completely loyal to prohibition, he charged that "many of those now in control of the old organization were guided, in the course they pursued, more by opposition to monetary and other reforms, than by an enthusiastic loyalty to prohibition."[56] Richmond addressed free-silver meetings during the campaign and probably ended it voting for Bryan, as did St. John and many others.[57] In one town in Michigan which A. A. Hopkins visited eight years later, "there were thirty-six Prohibition voters when that campaign of 1896 began. Thirty-three of these went straight over to Bryan, two went to McKinley and only one of them remained true to Prohibition. This instance could be matched, I suspect, over and over again."[58]

In the early days of the campaign, Prohibition party leaders responded defensively to broad-gauge charges that the single-issue platform had been bought by Wall Street gold.[59] In denying the charges, however, Dickie noted several "liberal additions" to the campaign fund from "men who take this method of expressing their satisfaction at the results of the convention." He observed that a Buffalo, New York, Prohibitionist, "who has given the party only lukewarm support for several years on account of what he deemed its populistic tendencies, sends his congratulations and his check for one hundred dollars." Still, Dickie pointed out, "it will require a large amount of effort to swell the total to twenty thousand dollars, which ought to be a minimum figure for a wide awake campaign."[60]

It was in fact a shortage of funds which kept the Prohibition party leaders from pursuing to the utmost their plan to conduct a campaign directed primarily toward church voters. The Executive Committee was forced to turn down an exceedingly attractive offer from Dr. Funk to send *The Voice* to every clergyman in the country. Funk estimated that the cost of his project would be $13,000, but he offered to assume $8,000 of this if the party could guarantee the remainder. The Executive Committee could not come up with the funds, although it heartily wished to do so. Apparently, the accounts were so impoverished that the Executive Committee could not even bring itself to accept J. B. Cranfill's offer to send his paper, the *Baptist Standard* of Dallas, to 8,000 Baptist ministers at a cost of only $1,000.[61]

The shortage of campaign funds did not prevent party speakers and editorialists from mounting an unprecedented campaign for the votes of church members and the influence of clergymen. In their responses to the action of the Pittsburgh convention, leaders and the rank and file alike had expressed delight at being able at last to appeal directly to the churches on the basis of prohibition alone.[62] Woolley reviewed the problem which had been overcome. The Prohibition party "had inveighed against the church, because, having declared that the liquor traffic must be destroyed, she declined to help us to abolish the existing banking system and extend the elective franchise, when the belief was honestly held of about half the voting church that our currency laws were wise and righteous and the suffrage already too extended." But now, he said, "we have confessed our own fault and met every condition of eligibility to serve her ends and restore the honor of her name."[63] T. R. Carskadon pointed out that it was not only the party's platform which the church voters had been unable to accept.

> Having placed ourselves in the best possible position before
> the churches of the country and there having gone out from
> us those most objectionable to the churches. . . . I do most
> earnestly believe we shall have from them a largely increased
> vote, this being the first time for many campaigns that we
> have come to them with an unobjectionable platform.[64]

Woolley too prophesied an increased party vote from church members.

He did his best during the campaign to fulfill his prophecy, speaking to every Protestant gathering with a vacant spot on its program and an inclination toward prohibition, hammering constantly on the single theme of the Christian voter's duty to support the principle and the party of Prohibition, now for the first time one and the same. Other speakers rang changes on the same theme. In Massachusetts, Illinois, and Tennessee the party organizations made specific appeals directly to church voters. *The Voice* and other party papers kept up a drumfire of editorials urging Christians to square their votes with the declarations of their churches. A symposium was conducted in which ministers of New York, New Jersey, and Massachusetts gave opinions on the involvement of preachers in politics. Prohibition rallies and the party press featured declarations of thanksgiving by clergymen and church members for their heaven-sent opportunity to unite or reunite with the party now that it was no longer attacking the churches and advocating "Populistic" issues.[65]

None of this did any good. Writing in 1905, the single-issue leader William P. F. Ferguson accurately summed up the 1896 election results: "Only a few southern states made any appreciable gain over the vote of four years before, while in the states where the great bulk of the Prohibition vote had been found in the past, the balloting was a sickening slump."[66] The Prohibition party polled only 131,285 votes, less than half of its 1892 total; the National party could not claim the other half, for it attracted only 14,003 votes in eighteen states.[67] The two southern states which showed substantial increases were Alabama, where the Prohibition vote jumped almost ninefold from 241 to 2,147, and Georgia, where it went from 988 to 5,613.[68] Ironically, the gain in Georgia was achieved through a fusion of sorts when the Populists added a prohibition plank to their state platform and nominated a Prohibitionist for Governor.[69]

The "sickening slump" occurred primarily in the four states which comprised the core of the Prohibitionist heartland and whose delegates had voted overwhelmingly for free silver at the national convention. Illinois plunged from 25,870 Prohibition votes in 1892 to 9,818 in 1896; Indiana from 13,050 to 3,056; Michigan from 20,857 to 5,026; and Ohio from 26,012 to 5,084.[70] The National party drew away some of the missing voters—three-fifths of its vote came from the Ohio Valley (see Table 5, p. 45)—but not all. In none of the four states did the National vote exceed one-quarter of the difference between the Prohibition party's 1892 and 1896 totals. The fact that Prohibitionist broad-gaugers had been numerous in those states would seem

to indicate that it was Bryan rather than McKinley who benefited
from the Prohibition party's losses.[71]

Both prohibition parties thus found only frustration at the end
of the campaign trail in 1896. The single-issue men who controlled
the Prohibition party failed to make good their appeal to the Christian voter; the broad-gauge seceders, whether they stayed with the
National party or moved on to the Democrats, reaped obscurity and
defeat, respectively. The failures of both groups created a leadership
vacuum in the prohibition movement which would be filled only
after nearly a decade of drifting. More specifically, the crippling
of the Prohibition party in the heart of the Middle West made possible
the growth of a competing prohibitionist organization in that hotbed
of anti-liquor sentiment.

Two events which took place three weeks after the election demonstrated that the Prohibition party would probably do little if any
experimenting in the future with economic radicalism. At a Prohibition
conference in Poughkeepsie, New York, William W. Smith, founder of
the Smith Brothers Candy Company, stimulated with his $5,000
donation a nine-minute fund-raising drive which gathered a total
of $12,000 for the party coffers. William T. Wardwell of Standard
Oil, the symbol within the party of plutocratic rule, sweetened the pot
with a $1,000 contribution.[72] A week later the National Executive
Committee issued from Chicago a manifesto warning against deviation
from the single issue, compromise of prohibition, and fusion with
other parties.[73]

The party's failure to attract church voters in significant numbers
did however bring forth momentary doubts about the possibility of
effecting such an alliance and stimulated renewed calls for disaffiliation
from the churches.[74] John G. Woolley, piqued by failure, lashed out
at the ministry: "The godly, fearless, honest preacher is the world's
noblest citizen, but the Christian ministry in America is collectively
incompetent, irrelevant, and immaterial."[75]

These doubts could not obscure the fact that at its national convention of 1896 the Prohibition party had chosen to speak primarily to
the middle class. This decision required that the party abandon the
openness to economic radicalism and hostility toward the churches
which had haunted conservative party leaders throughout the early
1890s. Aileen Kraditor, in her study of *The Ideas of the Woman Suffrage Movement, 1890-1920,* has pointed to a similar development when

feminist leaders in the 1890s began to drop their arguments based upon natural rights in favor of arguments from expediency.[76] Use of such arguments tended to align feminists with those who feared political participation by blacks, recent immigrants, or the "ignorant masses."[77] Kraditor attributes this change to the movement's growing hopes for success. For the prohibition movement in the 1890s, however, success was so far away that it was out of sight. Not the hope of success but the pressure of Populism, operating on the lever of prohibitionist failure, caused the prohibition movement's shift to the right.

The Prohibition party had failed because it could neither attract the middle-class voters who had supported prohibition legislation in the 1880s and would do so again after 1900, nor link up with the insurgent farmers of the 1890s. It seems clear that an alliance with Populism, or even the radicalizing of the Prohibition party in preparation for such an alliance, was headed off by the narrow-gaugers of the party. They acted because of their fear of contamination by contact with men and women whose reformism admittedly stemmed from the damage inflicted upon them by the system. To the narrow-gaugers, such people were not reformers at all, and therefore they rejected them. Perhaps they felt that identification with the Populists would have threatened their own position in American society. And perhaps those other middle-class men and women, who rejected reform in both its Prohibitionist and Populist manifestations during the nineties, acted for much the same reasons.

NOTES

1. S. H. Comings to T. C. Richmond, February 6, 1895, H. S. Wells to Richmond, March 31, 1895, Chauncey H. Dunn to Richmond, April 10, 1895, T. C. Richmond to E. J. Wheeler, April 27, 1895, Richmond Papers, State Historical Society of Wisconsin (WHS), Madison; *Union Signal*, April 4, 1895.

2. Wheeler to Richmond, April 9, 1895, enclosing I. K. Funk to Richmond, April 5, 1895, Richmond Papers. See also Ignatius Donnelly to Richmond, April 14, 1895, Richmond Papers.

3. "Political Reform. A Call for a National Conference," Pamphlet Collection, WHS.

4.*The Voice*, May 9, 1895. Either Wheeler or Dickie, or both, were guilty of distorting their correspondents' views when both leaders claimed support from the same men for contradictory opinions.

5. T. C. Richmond to E. J. Wheeler, April 27, 1895 (probably never sent), Jesse Yarnell to Richmond, April 26, 1895, Chauncey H. Dunn to Richmond, May 2, 1895, William R. Dobbyn to Richmond, May 8, 1895, Richmond Papers.

6. Chauncey H. Dunn to Richmond, May 25, 1895, Richmond Papers.

7. *Union Signal,* July 11, 1895.

8. For the full list of resolutions, see Chapter 3 above. The most important were prohibition of the beverage liquor traffic, woman suffrage, government ownership of monopolies, and free coinage of silver at 16 to 1.

9. *The Voice,* July 11, 1895; *Union Signal,* July 11, 1895.

10. *The Voice,* August 22, 29, September 5, October 17, 1895. *The Voice,* September 5, 1895, also noted that New York Populists had agreed to meet with the Prohibitionists of that state in 1896. Topeka *Advocate,* July 17, 1895; *Union Signal,* July 18, 25, August 1, October 3, 1895.

11. *The Voice,* August 29, 1895.

12. Ibid., September 26, 1895.

13. Ibid., October 3, 1895.

14. Ibid., November 14, 1895; *Union Signal,* November 28, 1895.

15. *Minutes of the N.W.C.T.U.* (Chicago, 1895), pp. 44, 99.

16. Minutes of National Committee (NC) meeting, December 11, 1895, Chicago, "Minutes of the National Committees, Conferences and Conventions of the Prohibition Party," vol. 1, pp. 65-66, Michigan Historical Collections (MHC), Ann Arbor; Svend Petersen, *A Statistical History of the American Presidential Elections* (New York, 1963), p. 194. Each delegate was considered to represent one-half of his state's 1892 vote.

17. Minutes of NC meeting, December 11, 1895, "Minutes," vol.1, pp. 68-70.

18. Ibid.; Petersen, *Statistical History,* p. 194.

19. *The Voice,* December 12, 19, 1895.

20. Minutes of NC meeting, December 11, 1895, "Minutes," vol. 1, pp. 70-71.

21. See Chapter 2 above. For the inability of the Populists in Nebraska and Texas to satisfy either wet or dry voters, see Stanley Parsons, "Who Were the Nebraska Populists?" *Nebraska History* 44 (June 1963): 95, and Roscoe C. Martin, *The People's Party in Texas: A Study in Third Party Politics,* University of Texas Bureau of Research in the Social Sciences Study No. 4 (Austin, 1933), pp. 106-107.

22. *The Voice,* January 16, 1896.

23. *Proceedings of the Eleventh National Convention of the Anti-Saloon League of America* (Westerville, Ohio, 1906), p. 52. John G. Woolley

was born in Collinsville, Ohio, in 1850 and took bachelor's (1871) and master's (1873) degrees at Ohio Wesleyan University, and a law degree at the University of Michigan (1873). Woolley practiced law in Paris, Illinois, Minneapolis, Minnesota, and New York City until 1888 when he cured his drinking problem and was converted to Christianity and party prohibition. He joined the Church of the Stranger in New York City, gave up his law practice, and became a professional temperance lecturer, following that occupation until his retirement from public life in 1921. He died in 1922 while on a mission to Spain in order to study the alcohol problem in Europe. W.D.P. Bliss, ed., *New Encyclopedia of Social Reform* (New York, 1908), pp. 1309-1310; Ernest H. Cherrington et al., eds., *Standard Encyclopedia of the Alcohol Problem*, 6 vols. (Westerville, Ohio, 1924-30), vol. 6, pp. 2909-2910.

24. E. J. Wheeler, "The Prohibition Party and Its Candidates," *Review of Reviews* 22 (September 1900): 329; *The Lever* (Chicago), July 4, 1895.

25. *Union Signal*, July 11, 1895; *The Voice*, July 11, 1895.

26. *The Voice*, September 26, 1895.

27. John E. Caswell, "The Prohibition Movement in Oregon, Part I, 1836-1904," *Oregon Historical Quarterly* 39 (1938): 260.

28. *The Voice*, December 12, 19, 1895.

29. Ibid., January 23, February 13, 1896; *Northwestern Mail* (Madison, Wis.), February 27, April 9, 23, 1896.

30. *The Voice*, March 5, 1896.

31. Ibid., April 2, 1896.

32. Ibid., May 21, 28, 1896.

33. *Northwestern Mail*, April 30, May 7, 14, 1896.

34. *Union Signal*, April 23, 1896.

35. The other estimates were 20.6 percent in the North Atlantic, 24.1 percent in the North Central, and 36.5 percent in the South Central Divisions. W. H. Roberts, "The Church and Men," *The Independent* 47 (February 7, 1895): 177.

36. *Northwestern Mail*, January 30, 1896; *The Voice*, January 30, March 5, 19, 26, April 9, 16, 1896; *Union Signal*, February 13, 20, 1896.

37. *Northwestern Mail*, May 21, 1896.

38. Compare James R. Turner, "The American Prohibition Movement, 1865-1897" (Ph.D. dissertation, University of Wisconsin, 1972), p. 466.

39. See Chapter 3.

40. *The Voice*, March 5, 1896.

41. For an example of such denunciation at convention's time, see *Chicago Inter-Ocean*, May 27, 1896.

42. [William P. F. Ferguson], "St. John, the Leader of 1884," *The Vindicator*, February 13, 1914, clipping in St. John Scrapbooks,

vol. 5, St. John Papers, State Historical Society of Kansas (KHS), Topeka.

43. My account of the convention is based on the following sources: *Boston Herald*, May 27-29, 1896; *New York Times*, May 28, 29, 1896; *Chicago Inter-Ocean*, May 28, 29, 1896; *The Voice*, March 5, June 4, 18, July 2, 1896; *The Lever*, June 4, 1896; *Union Signal*, June 4, 11, 18, July 2, 1896; *Topeka Advocate*, June 3, 1896; Minutes of NC meeting, May 26, 1896, "Minutes," vol. 1, p. 73; *The Citizen* (Harriman, Tenn.) February 8, 1905; Edna T. Frederickson, "John P. St. John, the Father of Constitutional Prohibition" (Ph.D. dissertation, University of Kansas, 1930), pp. 324-326.

44. The dissenting minority of eleven National Committeemen represented the states of Kansas, Illinois, Indiana, Ohio, California, Nebraska, and Massachusetts.

45. *The Citizen*, February 8, 1905. O. W. Stewart, who began his rise to national party leadership at this convention, was born in Mercer County, Illinois, in 1867. After two years as a schoolteacher, he attended Eureka College, graduating in 1890. From 1890 to 1896 he divided his time between preaching as a minister of the Disciples of Christ and semi-professional temperance work for the Good Templars and Illinois Christian Endeavor Societies. He joined the Prohibition party upon reaching his majority in 1888. *New Voice*, December 21, 1899, October 2, 1902; *Northwestern Mail*, December 21, 1899.

46. Consideration of the woman suffrage plank took place after the broad-gaugers' departure.

47. *The Voice*, June 18, 1896.

48. *Union Signal*, June 4, 18, July 2, 1896.

49. Ibid., June 11, 18, 25, August 20, 1896; *The Voice*, July 9, 1896.

50. *Union Signal*, June 25, 1896.

51. *Baptist Standard* (Dallas), June 4, 1896, quoted in *Union Signal*, June 25, 1896.

52. *The Voice*, June 4, 1896; *Union Signal*, June 25, 1896.

53. Wheeler, "Prohibition Party," pp. 327-328; Rockwell D. Hunt, *John Bidwell, Prince of California Pioneers* (Caldwell, Idaho, 1942), pp. 349-350.

54. Minutes of National Executive Committee (NXC) meeting, July 8, 1896, Albion, Mich., "Minutes," vol. 1, p. 78. Dickie actually spent $1,443.35 in identifiable expenditures in the six states. "Report of Treasurer, May 16, 1896, to December 4, 1899," "Minutes," vol. 1, p. 117.

55. *The Voice*, June 25, 1896.

56. *Northwestern Mail*, July 9, 1896.

57. Ibid., August 27, 1896; A. W. Potter to Richmond, July 20, 1897, Richmond Papers; Frederickson, "John P. St. John," p. 326; Clipping from Utica, N.Y., *Observer*, September 9, 1904, St. John Scrapbooks, vol. 7, St. John Papers. Paul Kleppner notes reports that National party

leaders sought fusion with Bryan's Democracy, but apparently their efforts came to nought on both national and state levels. Kleppner, *The Cross of Culture: A Social Analysis of Midwestern Politics, 1850-1900* (New York, 1970), p. 355.

58. *Northwestern Mail*, September 16, 1904.

59. *The Voice*, June 4, 1896.

60. *Northwestern Mail*, June 18, 1896; *The Voice*, June 18, 1896.

61. Minutes of NXC meeting, July 8, 1896, Albion, Mich., "Minutes," vol. 1, p. 78.

62. See *The Lever*, June 4, 1896; *The Voice*, June-November 1896.

63. *The Voice*, June 18, 1896. See also *The Lever*, June 4, 1896.

64. *The Lever*, June 18, 1896.

65. *The Voice*, June 18-October 29, 1896; *Northwestern Mail*, July 23, September 24, 1896; *Union Signal*, August 6, 13, October 8, 15, 1896; Paul E. Isaac, *Prohibition and Politics: Turbulent Decades in Tennessee, 1885-1920* (Knoxville, 1965), p. 71. The party campaign book devoted 19 pages in 1896 to wooing the church voter, compared to 4-½ pages in 1892. In contrast, the space given to "labor and the liquor question" shrank from 8 pages in 1892 to 3 pages in 1896. Copies of both volumes are at MHC.

66. *The Citizen*, February 8, 1905.

67. Petersen, *Statistical History*, p. 64.

68. Ibid., pp. 194-195; James B. Sellers, *The Prohibition Movement in Alabama, 1702 to 1943* (Chapel Hill, 1943), p. 85.

69. *The Voice*, December 10, 1896; Alex M. Arnett, *The Populist Movement in Georgia*, Studies in History, Economics, and Public Law 104 (New York, 1922), p. 207.

70. Petersen, *Statistical History*, pp. 194-195.

71. This hypothesis has been partly confirmed by the findings of Paul Kleppner for selected counties in Michigan and Ohio, as well as in Wisconsin. Kleppner, *The Cross of Culture*, pp. 321,335, 353-354.

72. *The Voice*, December 3, 1896. Why these men waited until after the election to contribute as they did is puzzling. The most likely explanation is that they recognized the hopelessness of the party's campaign in the polarized situation in 1896, but sought after the election to keep the party alive, in its present form, for future campaigns.

73. Ibid., January 7, 1897.

74. Ibid., November 12, 1896.

75. Ibid., November 19, 1896.

76. Aileen Kraditor, *The Ideas of the Woman Suffrage Movement, 1890-1920* (New York, 1965).

77. As we have seen, even the Prohibitionist broad-gaugers diluted their radicalism with restrictionist suffrage proposals aimed at immigrants, possibly to offset the extension of the franchise to women.

5

Leadership vacuum, 1897-1902

*T*he continuing failure of the Prohibition party was evident in the six years following the party split of 1896. The need for definition, born of failure, continued to face Prohibitionists after the election, and in response they produced a conception of the party as a kind of museum case intended only to preserve and display the virtue of its membership. As the Anti-Saloon League came into prominence with the decline of the party, Prohibitionists began their fitful romance with the League which was to continue throughout the League's history. John G. Woolley's rise to power within the party both furthered the creation of its new definition and foreshadowed the days when the Prohibitionist daillance with the League would become more frequent and more fervent.

THE STATE OF THE PARTY

In the four years after the election of 1896 the leadership of the Prohibition party underwent considerable change in personnel, though not in policy. The turnover rate among State Chairmen in 1897 reached 58.8 percent compared to a yearly average of 28.6 percent for the rest of the nineties.[1] With its first issue of 1899 *The Voice* became the *New Voice*, a family literary weekly more than a political journal. Although the *New Voice* claimed to be as much a party organ as ever, Prohibitionist leaders believed that the Funk & Wagnalls Company entertained thoughts of abandoning the advocacy of the cause which its subsidized publication of *The Voice* had theretofore represented. Therefore, National Chairman

Samuel Dickie and John G. Woolley combined, first to buy the party's second paper, the Chicago *Lever,* then, in August 1899, to purchase the *New Voice* from Funk & Wagnalls and merge it with *The Lever* in Chicago. Apparently, most of the money used to finance the enterprise came from Dickie, and when he withdrew in November 1900, Woolley was left in sole ownership of the under-financed paper.[2]

Meanwhile, Dickie had resigned as National Chairman in December 1899 and was replaced by Oliver W. Stewart, the young broad-gauger who had won his spurs by his impartial chairing of the 1896 national convention.[3] Another new face appeared in the party's inner circles when Woolley hired single-issue advocate William P. F. Ferguson as managing editor of the *New Voice.*[4] Together Ferguson, Stewart, and Woolley engineered the adoption of a single-issue platform and the nomination of Woolley at the convention of 1900.

The party, however, possessed little of its old vitality. Overt confessions of decline and discouragement appeared occasionally in the party press.[5] The membership rolls of the WCTU had suffered continuous depletion from 1891 until the organization ceased its endorsement of the Prohibition party after Frances Willard's death in 1898.[6] One state chairman noted that his organizers encountered considerable difficulty "on account of the failure of county and town chairmen to co-operate in making arrangements for meetings."[7] In 1898, 1899, and 1900 state chairmanships of the party were occupied in only twenty-five, twenty-four, and twenty-two states respectively, compared to an average of twenty-nine in the seven preceding years.[8] Perhaps the whole situation was symbolized by the plight of a Wisconsin party organizer who went to call upon a Prohibitionist and found his host lying drunk in the December snow in the middle of the road. "We helped him in[to] the house," the organizer reported, "and went on our way sorrowing."[9]

What was to be done? In some areas Prohibitionists nearly surrendered, leaving blank slots on their tickets or accepting plans, such as the state dispensary, which fell far short of prohibition.[10] For the party as a whole, however, the period 1897-1902 was a time for experimentation with new methods of attack upon the liquor traffic. Three new methods were tried, and all three offered striking parallels to the tactics of the emerging Anti-Saloon League. The first consisted of participation in attacks upon the liquor interests which fell short of prohibition but which conceded no ground on the ultimate demand as did the dispensary plan. The best example was the campaign against the selling of liquor in army canteens, or military stores, which began in 1898 with the Spanish-American War and continued until the victory of the antiliquor forces in 1901.[11] When the canteen had been conquered, the *New Voice* immediately filled the vacuum by proposing new legislation for the protection of soldiers from liquor-sellers.[12]

The second new method consisted of employment of full-time paid organizers assigned to specific areas to replace the travelling lecturers whose speech-by-speech remuneration had irritated some party members. Indiana Prohibitionists initiated this approach in 1899 by appointing a "Prohibition Evangelist" for each of the state's congressional districts, as well as a State Evangelist. They maintained the men in the field by soliciting from each Prohibitionist an amount equal to his contribution for the support of his pastor.[13] After Indiana in 1900 quadrupled its 1896 vote, other states began to look favorably upon the plan. Wisconsin adopted it in early 1901.[14]

The third method to be adopted came down to the states from the top. In August 1901 National Chairman O. W. Stewart outlined his plan for a system of local prohibition clubs, to be called Prohibition Alliances.[15] He may have gotten the idea from a speech of A. A. Hopkins at a party conference in Buffalo the previous week when Hopkins advocated a system of clubs as a means of holding converts —as did the churches—by providing them with clearly defined organizational ties.[16] The Alliances, which met monthly, were kept abreast of party policy through meeting programs provided by the National Chairman. Members paid regular dues of an amount each could afford; a percentage of the dues remained with the local club and the remainder went to National Headquarters, which in turn sent back a percentage to the state organizations. In the opinion of the official party historian, "it was undoubtedly the best system of local organization which the Party ever put in operation."[17] A similar line of attack materialized with the National Committee's revitalization in 1899-1900 of the Inter-Collegiate Prohibition Association, a network of college clubs which sponsored oratorical contests on the topic of prohibition. The ICPA was later to furnish youthful leadership to the party.[18]

The party's openness to experimentation, however, did not extend to policy, even though those broad-gaugers who had remained within or had returned to the party continued the debate over platform policy. The debate and state declarations adopted during 1897-1902 revealed two significant characteristics of the Prohibition party after 1896: the weakness of the single-issue wing and an unwillingness throughout the party to commit it to the economic radicalism many had urged before 1896.

William P. F. Ferguson, editor of the *New Voice,* implicitly confessed the single-issue wing's weakness when he closed his columns to supporters of a broad platform.[19] Single-issue men urged that minorities ranging from one-fifth of the convention to a single delegate be sufficient to defeat any proposed plank.[20] Platforms broader than the national platform appeared in sixteen of twenty-seven states in 1900.[21] Of the ten states contributing the largest Prohibition party vote in 1900, at least six adopted broad platforms at some time during the years 1900-1902.

These broad state platforms during 1898-1902 revealed little more than tactical disagreements within the party. In 1900 only three state platforms went so far as a demand for public ownership of monopolies. The broadness of most consisted in declarations for woman suffrage, direct legislation, Sabbath observance, English-language public schools, and civil service reform.[22] Unlike broad platforms of the early 1890s, they failed to distinguish the party's position from that of the single-issue wing or from that of the Anti-Saloon League. Despite its commitment to the single-issue approach, the League did advocate similar noneconomic proposals on both state and national levels.[23]

Expressions of Prohibitionist opinion outside their platforms indicated that the party represented a group of middle-class reformers who opposed more than they accepted the prevailing orientations of their society. They still leaned heavily upon their acknowledged abolitionist heritage; at times it seemed that the only unanswerable argument in intraparty debate was that based upon analogy with antislavery tactics.[24] In line with that heritage, Prohibitionist spokesmen uncompromisingly denounced lynchings in both North and South and eloquently attacked some of the current racist ideas. When the Boer War broke out, the *Northwestern Mail* sided with neither of the white contesting armies but rather with the native blacks who stood to lose, whatever the outcome. Yet Prohibitionists still hoped to win the white South for their cause and

also welcomed statements by black prohibitionists that in the
abolition of the liquor traffic lay the solution to the race problem.[25]
Although they recognized that the foreign-born vote constituted
a major obstacle to their success, Prohibitionists were usually careful to depict the immigrant not as a source of evil but rather as
an unwilling victim of circumstance.[26]

Prohibitionists combined the popular antipathy toward trusts
and monopolies with an attack on moral and ethical grounds
against corporate greed and sordid commercial ideals.[27] Reforms
and reformers attacking political corruption won Prohibitionist
support.[28] Many Prohibitionist spokesmen regarded socialism
more as an ally than an enemy,[29] although John G. Woolley
spoke for others when he denounced the Populist and Socialist
parties as "more or less sublimated forms of materialism, which
would abolish the long, hard, necessary pick-and-shovel business
of evolution and build a better order, from the roof down." For
Woolley, the coming of the cooperative society was inevitable,
but moral reform necessarily preceded economic reform.[30] Prohibitionists refused to try to understand anarchism and usually
linked it to the saloon.[31] Expressions of sympathy for workers
were balanced by an inability to accept unions, whose activities
sometimes drove Prohibitionists back upon their individualistic
success mythology.[32] About the relative merits of city, village,
and countryside, the movement as a whole was ambivalent.[33]
Their spokesmen by no means shared the fundamentalist Protestant distrust of science, and they gave full support to the emerging
Social Gospel movement within the churches.[34] In general, Prohibitionists seemed to stand behind the government in its war with
Spain but not in its suppression of the Philippine insurrection.[35]

In Prohibition party dialogue, however, all of these questions
occupied a position distinctly subordinate to the concern which
had overridden all others after the victory of the single-issue men
in May 1896: the problem of attracting church voters into the
party. No problem engaged Prohibitionists more intimately or produced more frustration than this one.[36] In their attempts to lead,
drive, or coerce the voting church into their ranks, Prohibition
party men made substantial contributions to the growing identification between the prohibition cause and the evangelical Protestant
church. Their concentration upon the church voter revealed more
than anything else the party's crucial decision to seek its supporters

primarily among those who most closely approximated the social standing of its middle-class leadership. The exigencies of this search led them to formulate a definition of prohibition which made it the peculiar reform of a politically dominant but insecure middle class.

What was the function of the church? Prohibitionists agreed that the central and primary function of the church should be the saving of souls, but they joined their voices to the growing chorus insisting that the first step was the removal of worldly conditions fostering the sinfulness which kept men from God.[37] Advocating prohibition as one means of destroying the temptations that beset men, Prohibitionists argued the case for a church commitment to their cause on grounds of both principle and expediency. On principle the Christian voter must end his complicity with the liquor traffic by refusing to vote for parties which permitted liquor-selling; on expedient grounds the voter and the church must act to ensure the voter's salvation, the church's honor, and even the very survival of the church in an increasingly unrighteous world.[38] They found justification for their gloomy predictions when a 1900 article in the *Outlook* pointed to membership declines in both the Presbyterian and Methodist folds.[39] With redoubled zeal, Prohibitionists threatened the churches with extinction if they failed to convert their anti-liquor declarations into political activity.[40] In 1900 they shouted that the only political issue was "the honor of the church."[41]

Before the Civil War, revivalism and social reform had gone had in hand.[42] But since 1865 evangelists such as Dwight L. Moody and the Prohibitionist Sam P. Jones had made revivalism the ally of "conservative elements in religion, politics, and business."[43] Thus, it was not surprising that party spokesmen after 1896 found the churches' only hope in a predicted new wave of revivals. They insisted, however, that reinvigoration of the churches could flow only from a revival spirit that produced a simultaneous flood of Prohibition party votes. A revival without ensuing mass commitment to prohibition, it seemed, was no revival at all.[44]

From this position it was only a short step to the claim that a Christian lacking commitment to prohibition was no Christian at all. As John G. Woolley said in 1900:

Whether a man is in the church, or whether he calls himself a Christian, is largely a matter of temperament or accident. There are many inside the church who are not Christians and

many outside who are. They cannot be classified save by their
own conduct.[45]

Another Prohibitionist added, "It seems to me that calling every church-
member and every self-styled religionist a Christian is dragging the pre-
cious name of our Lord and Savior Jesus Christ down to the level [of]
. . . workers of iniquity."[46] A Wisconsin editor asserted, "It is not
Christian to vote for rum directly or indirectly. Christian men can't do
it and maintain their Christian standing."[47] Applying the argument,
The Voice in 1897 asked, "What would Christ do at the ballot-box?"
and answered, "*Would he vote the Prohibition ticket? Why not?*"[48]

In 1891 *The Voice* had established the same equation between true
Christianity and Prohibition party voting, and its powerful series of
editorials had stimulated a wave of Prohibitionist denunciations of and
withdrawals from the churches. After 1896 a few voices still suggested
that Prohibitionists "come out from the unclean thing." Attacks on
church papers were launched, and a great deal of generalized hostility
was aired. A few Prohibitionists in frustration proposed a cessation of
party appeals to church members.[49] But the majority opinion favored
a fight within the churches to force their members to stand in politics
behind the evangelical churches' strong declarations for prohibition.
Prohibitionists agreed with Samuel Dickie when he was reported as
saying that his Methodist comrades were "all right . . . so far as their
resolutions were concerned. So long as they maintained their attitude,
he proposed to stay with it; it was for the other fellows to get out.
They were the ones who were false to the church standard."[50] Dickie
suited his action to his words by serving as chairman of the General
Temperance Committee at the Northern Methodists' 1900 General
Conference.[51] Clinton N. Howard made it easier for Prohibitionists
to live within their churches through the Christian Union of Prohibition
Men, which now sought to bring church members to the Prohibition
party without requiring withdrawal from their churches. In 1897 *The
Voice* cited Prohibition party increases over 1896 in local and state
voting to prove that appeals to the churches had not been in vain.[52]

The emphasis upon Prohibition party voting as the mark of true
Christianity, together with the national party's long-term failure
to make noticeable political progress, led to the formation of a
conception of the party that was new and quite different from that
held when the Prohibitionists entertained hopes of imminent success.

The formation of this conception, as well as the simultaneous creation of intraparty bonds through the Alliances and Howard's Christian Union, represented a process of institutionalization which had become necessary to the party's survival. While Prohibitionists would not "take the Prohibition party in lieu of a church," as *The Voice* had urged in 1891, they would make their party over into an institution whose function would be to display in politics, as their church activity did in social life, the virtue which they felt to be inherent in the middle-class status that they had achieved. If they could not save the country, at least they would save themselves.

This did not mean that Prohibitionists were able to escape the dissatisfaction with American society which had driven them to the party in the first place. On the contrary, party editorialists and speakers again and again hurled jeremiads at the state of the republic.[53] John G. Woolley could still claim that the country stood "in danger of hardening into a political and commercial feudalism in which an oligarchy of manufacturers and a lobby of corporations dictate the financial policy, while bosses deal out spoils and franchises to henchmen and to slaves."[54] The cure for these ills did not, however, lie in political action as it was normally conceived. Politics, as the *New Voice* said in 1900, was "hypocrisy," "venality," "cruelty," "lies and vice and crime." Politics dealt only with "material things."[55] The true course for the righteous man did not pass through the mire of party conflict but took him instead to a position above the strife, from which his virtue could shine forth to inspire those who were still deluded by transient things.

Thus, the Prohibitionists put moral character at the beginning and the end of their analysis of American society and enthroned "righteousness" as the supreme goal for both the individual and the nation. They now began to cast their main issue less in the light of an attempt to eradicate one of many social evils and more as the decisive test of middle-class moral fiber. Henry B. Metcalf, in his letter accepting the party's 1900 vice-presidential nomination, asserted that the damage wrought by saloons went far beyond the drunkards they created. Saloons "not only wreck the lives and souls of their patrons, but, by their money payment [for licenses], they wreck the conscience of thousands who never cross their thresholds, many of whom suppose themselves to be Christians."[56] The primary goal now became not the salvation of the drunkard but rather the rescue of the Christian

voter from complicity with the drunkard-making business. Thus the
worst enemy was not greed or corruption or injustice, but hypocrisy.
Answering an old argument, Woolley claimed, " 'You can't make men
moral by law'; but you can make morality respectable by law."[57]

Prohibitionists believed that they were speaking to an easily de-
finable segment of society, although they characterized it variously
as "the moral interests," "good men," or "the Christian voter."[58]
That the audience was thought to resemble the speaker was evident
when Prohibitionists postulated the obvious and absolute character
of the righteousness they extolled.[59] The *Northwestern Mail* filled
in the Prohibitionists' self-image when it painted a word-picture of
the Wisconsin party convention of 1902:

> A large and enthusiastic gathering of intelligent, sober, clean
> and prosperous citizens—men who count for the best things
> in their home communities—not rich men, not mighty, not
> trimmers for political or financial success, but men of con-
> science, conviction, courage, independence, and an honor to
> a great and good cause; men who are willing to sacrifice year
> after year for the good of others and their country.[60]

As the Prohibition party turned inward in the years after 1896,
it made its obeisance to reality by placing the time for its success
in the distant future. Congratulations for loyal perseverance like those
offered by the *Northwestern Mail* became more frequent and more
necessary. In 1900 the *New Voice* offered engraved Certificates of
Honor to "the men who have year after year preserved the organization and kept alive the sacred flame."[61] Prohibitionist spokesmen
compensated for their postponement of success by redoubling their
insistence upon its inevitability.[62] They tried to squelch doubts about
the efficacy of righteousness by pointing to instances in which Prohibitionist loyalties had furthered a man's business or professional
career. At the same time, they denounced the ascendance of "material"
or "expedient" standards of public conduct.[63]

As Prohibitionists came to situate their triumph in an ever-receding
future, they were forced to magnify its dimensions until it began to
take on aspects of the millennium. They conceived of this millennium
not necessarily in terms of the election of a Prohibition party government,
but rather as the time when one, two, or three million Christian voters

would bring about the moral regeneration of the nation by choosing
the standard of righteousness held by the party.[64] In 1898, J. Burritt
Smith, law partner of T. C. Richmond, revealed the new doctrine
to Wisconsin Prohibitionists:

> If Christian men could awake and for one year, in pulpit
> and pew cry aloud against this awful evil, and then crys-
> tallize their conscience and prayers and labors on election
> days in the ballot box, a revival such as has not been known
> to this generation would sweep the nation. . . . A million
> votes for the prohibition party this fall would make the
> windows of Heaven rattle so that all hell would arouse
> herself; and a landslide of two or three million votes in
> 1900, would open not only those windows, but the very
> gates of the New Jerusalem, and the first flood of the
> waiting millenium would burst out and begin to over-
> flow the world.[65]

Thus, Prohibitionists rationalized their party's failure by minimizing
their own responsibility while magnifying the scope of their inevitable
triumph.

But while Prohibitionists inflated the significance of allegiance to
their party, they also began to downgrade the importance of the prohibition issue, apparently in an effort to rationalize the retreat from
the broad platform of the party's history. Now a commitment merely
to the demand for prohibition was not sufficient either for individual or
national salvation; now a commitment to prohibition must be the result
of a sincere dedication to righteousness amounting almost to a religious
conversion.[66] "If the liquor traffic were to be abolished as a mere police
regulation . . . or as a mere measure for retrenchment, it would be great
gain, but our campaign for civic righteousness would have to go right
on, with some other practical question—like war, for instance, or
labor—for a figurehead."[67] Obviously there was no true salvation without remission of sins.

Prohibitionists thus adopted a posture of passivity which accurately reflected their party's political stagnation. If its victory
would come only as a result of the general and inevitable triumph
of righteousness, what roles were left for them but to exhort—"Be
like me!"—and to wait? Abandoning political maneuver and strength-

ening bonds within their organization, Prohibitionists adopted the
preacher's role for their party during the six years after the party split.
As the *New Voice* put it in 1900, "The Prohibitionists have built up a
valuable party machinery and have maintained, and do today maintain,
a center point about which the moral forces of the country can rally for
the struggle with prevailing immorality."[68] The emphasis seemed to
lie more upon the maintenance than the struggle.

Only one event seriously disturbed their equilibrium. The advent
of Carry Nation and her direct-action prohibitionism in late 1900 created
a serious dilemma for some Prohibitionists. While people outside the
movement could deride Nation's actions as the result of insanity, those
who had preached for years the destruction of saloons had to confront,
in the spotlight of national publicity, the all-too-obvious product of
their own teachings. Most important, her actions raised the specter of
prohibitionists all over the country taking up the attack on the saloons
without assistance from the party which claimed to constitute the vanguard for the war on the saloon.

Carry Nation had begun her smashing career in February 1900 and
had enhanced her local reputation by the destruction of three saloons
in Kiowa, Kansas, in June. But she did not come to the attention of
the Prohibition party until her attack on the Hotel Carey bar in Wichita,
December 27, 1900, made her name an instant household word across
the country. John P. St. John, J. B. Cranfill, Clinton N. Howard,
J. Burritt Smith, and other Prohibitionists acclaimed her actions, and
some predicted and welcomed similar attacks on saloons in other, non-
prohibition states.[69] The *New Voice,* which had been foremost in developing the party's new self-conception, first commented tentatively
on Nation's smashing in its issue of January 3, 1901. After denying a
report that its publisher, John G. Woolley, would defend Nation in court
for her attack upon a Wichita saloon, the paper went on to say, "The
New Voice has nothing to say concerning the merits of the case further
than that, when public officials openly allow criminals to violate the
law, there is much to be said in justification of the citizen who
appeals to force." On January 10 the *New Voice* ran an article
supporting the attacks, its support based largely on the fact that a
staff member had found the "moral element" of Kansas—chiefly
WCTU leaders— in support.

On January 24, the *New Voice* announced a major conclusion that
was surprisingly hesitant and indecisive in contrast to the fiery, militant,

uncompromising positions it usually took on matters about which those
outside the movement cared very little. After demonstrating that Nation
had broken no laws (and that her acts were therefore not strictly comparable to the Boston Tea Party and John Brown's raids), the editor
concluded:

> As to the wisdom and propriety of such an appeal to the rights
> of the citizen as Mrs. Nation made it is impossible to lay down
> any general principle. . . . Whether the work begun by Mrs. Nation
> will be carried on, and other citizens of Kansas will take upon
> themselves the performance of the duty neglected by the sworn
> officials of the state; and, indeed, whether it is wise that such
> action should be taken, we shall not attempt to say.

On February 7, the *New Voice* advised its readers that "the employment
of the same measures in other states, certainly in non-Prohibition states,
would be extremely unwise and, at the present time, unwarranted."

All in all, this was an amazing performance for a journal which had
repeatedly denounced the liquor traffic as the greatest curse ever visited upon the American people. The editorials gave no reason why
smashing of saloons was "unwise" and failed to explain why the leading
theoreticians of the Prohibition party could not fully endorse, even
in legally dry Kansas, actions which seemed to be the logical result of
their impassioned calls for saloon destruction. Two considerations
appeared to underlie their reasoning. The party's new policy of courting
"respectable" church voters constituted the first. In the glare of national
publicity, these Prohibitionist spokesmen apparently felt that approval
of violent destruction of private property—even when the property in
question existed illegally and was used for immoral purposes—would
alienate those toward whom the party directed its appeal. A *New
Voice* sampling of religious journals discovered widespread though not
unanimous disapproval of Carry's actions.[70] Prohibitionists' reports
from Kansas took special pains to head off the alienation of this group
by pointing out that Carry herself was "a good Christian woman, intelligent and refined," that her smashing companions were "all members of
respected families and of good standing in the community," and that
"the best people" in Kansas sustained their smashing.[71]

The need to placate church voters does not completely explain the
New Voice's hesitancy, however, for the Anti-Saloon League, which

appealed to the same constituency, immediately leaped to Nation's defense and even made the excellent tactical ploy of threatening violent destruction of saloons in Ohio, a nonprohibition state.[72] The significant difference between the two organizations lay in the degree of insularity each represented. The League, like the party, claimed to possess the only workable method for ridding the land of Demon Rum; but the League had never claimed, as did the party, that its ranks held all of the elect. Carry Nation's hatchet not only struck the Kansas saloons, but also imperilled the wall of moral superiority which the party spokesmen were so industriously laboring to erect around their institution. As the wall grew, it became more and more difficult to admit the possibility that a prohibitionist could stand outside.

PARTY AND LEAGUE

The existence of the Anti-Saloon League gave Prohibitionists a chance to test their faith. Founded as a national organization in December 1895, by 1901 the League claimed organizations in thirty-six states and territories.[73] Shortly after its founding, the Anti-Saloon League had become a topic of intense concern to Prohibitionists, and by 1900 they had already delivered at state and national party conferences the first in a flood of papers directed to the question, "What Should Be the Attitude of the Prohibition Party to the Anti-Saloon League?"[74] During the years 1897-1902, the *New Voice* arrived at one answer: rejection. Many individual Prohibitionists nevertheless chose cooperation and few Prohibitionists knocked the League without having tried it.

The WCTU moved from rejection of the Anti-Saloon League toward cooperation with it. In 1895 the League founders had invited WCTU representation at their first national convention, but the white-ribbon executive committee had politely refused, explaining that "in the past" antisaloon movements had served more in the interest of the major parties than of prohibition.[75] After Frances Willard's death in 1898, however, the WCTU ceased to adopt resolutions of support for the Prohibition party and moved toward friendlier relations with its rival organization.[76] After a widely publicized debate, the WCTU national convention in 1901 merely expressed "gratitude to the men who at the ballot box represent the principles we are working to see incorporated in the government." The *New Voice* claimed that only party members fit into that category, but the resolution could just as easily have applied to League workers as well. A few weeks later the WCTU President accepted election to the Anti-Saloon League National Executive Committee.[77]

The *New Voice* itself moved from cooperation to rejection. In 1896, while maintaining that the triumph of prohibition would come through a party, *The Voice* nevertheless welcomed the Anti-Saloon League as a means of attaining that triumph. In 1897, 1898, and through July 1899, *The Voice* under Isaac K. Funk mounted its campaigns against the army canteen and for minor antiliquor measures, in all of which it acknowledged the cooperation of the Anti-Saloon League. At a grand conference at Prohibition Park in July 1898, even National Chairman Dickie agreed to cooperate with the League in working for limited and gradual steps toward prohibition.[78]

When Dickie and John G. Woolley took over the paper in August 1899, however, its tone began to change quickly. The second issue of the *New Voice* under the new management carried an editorial which denied that a "state of hostility" existed between the party and the League, but asserted that the League's "principle" was "wholly fallacious" and that "every gram of energy and every talent of treasure expended on it" was "lost—practically hopelessly lost."[79] Three weeks later Samuel Dickie himself, still party chairman, announced the paper's declaration of war upon the League. Advising Prohibitionists to maintain toward the League "an attitude of friendly and sympathetic inactivity," Dickie denounced it on three main counts. First, the League conducted political maneuvers based upon calculations of expediency; "In such a conflict as we wage there is no proper place for sharp practice and skillful maneuvers." Second, it attempted to elect "good men" from the major parties, ignoring the controlling party influence upon them. Finally, the League taught voters that they could perform their moral duty without joining the Prohibition party; "Decent men in the license parties are the strength, the defense and the safeguard of the rum business." The leaders of the antisaloon organization were sincere, he concluded, but their method could never succeed.[80]

From that point the *New Voice* stepped up its attack. In February 1900 the paper began a long series of attempts to expose as lies Anti-Saloon League claims of local successes and began to hint that the League's fund-raising drives served the needs of League workers more than those of the movement. In April the *New Voice* refused space to Anti-Saloon League leaders for presentation of their side.[81] A week later a staff reporter went for the jugular, attempting to discredit the League's work in its home state of Ohio by demonstrating that since its founding in 1893, the number of saloons in the state had not decreased as the League claimed. In May an editorial stated what was to become the final theme for direct attacks upon the League by postulating an inevitable and irreconcilable conflict between the two organizations: "If the Anti-Saloon League is right, the Prohibition party is wrong and has no ground for existence. . . . But if the Prohibition party is right, the League is wrong."[82]

Local option, which constituted the League's major weapon in these early years, was a slightly different matter, and the forging of a Prohibitionist position toward it required some deliberation. In March 1901, the *New Voice* presented several arguments against local option laws: they submitted a moral question to popular vote and thereby made possible the perpetuation of an evil; prohibition was not a local question; prohibition by local option was "always to a large extent futile"; and, by salving the consciences of temperance men, local prohibition "acted as an effective buffer between the saloon system and Prohibition." Once a local option law had been passed, however, the paper concluded that Prohibitionists could and should vote under its provisions against the liquor traffic.[83] Some modification of its stand appeared in December 1901 when the *New Voice* granted that the context might indeed affect one's moral decision whether or not to support enactment of local option laws. Where prohibition was already in effect, Prohibitionists should of course fight the adoption of local option, which would clearly represent a retreat. Where the state already allowed license, however, the *New Voice* conceded that local option might indeed serve as a step forward for the temperance forces and should therefore be supported, even if it might thereafter constitute an obstacle to the attainment of state or national prohibition.[84] Although the editors could not admit it, this was precisely the position of the Anti-Saloon League. Such an admission would have revealed that the antagonism between the two organizations sprang neither from differences in their hostility to the liquor traffic nor from their respective willingness to compromise as the situation required, but rather from the simple fact that they were two organizations contending for the leadership of the same movement.

Many other Prohibitionists seconded the *New Voice*'s attacks on the League. For the most part they merely repeated the main themes set forth by the national organ: the League collected too much money and accomplished too little; the major parties, not the League, con-

trolled the actions of their office-holders who had been supported by
the Anti-Saloon League; and, Prohibitionists complained most often
and most stridently, the League kept prohibitionists out of the Prohibition
party.[85] Speaking for party men disgusted with League endorsement
of major-party candidates, the Nebraska Party Chairman ridiculed
the "Into-Saloon League."[86]

For many Prohibitionists, however, theory did not square with
practice. The period 1897-1902 saw the first stirrings of Prohibitionist
cooperation with the League, and the evidence indicates that the *New
Voice* did indeed have something to worry about when it counseled
"friendly inactivity." Little data is available on the most important indicators of cooperation: Prohibitionists' money contributions
to the League and support for Anti-Saloon-League-backed major-party
candidates. Among party leaders, however, both active and tacit cooperation seemed to be extensive and spreading.

Some of the party's most influential men were willing to lend the
prestige of their names and sometimes their presence to Anti-Saloon
League conventions and official bodies. They represented both the
narrow- and broad-gauge factions within the party. During 1898-1901
these men included members of state and national committees, one
former and two future presidential candidates, and National Chairman
Samuel Dickie. During the same year six party prohibitionists were
named to the Anti-Saloon League Board of Directors.[87] Other party
leaders moved from the passive lending of their names to active work
with the League on both state and national levels.[88]

The Anti-Saloon League welcomed every addition from the party
ranks. But two incidents during this period indicated that party Prohibitionists, accustomed to the open debate and parliamentary maneuvers
of their own conventions, could pose a threat to the strict discipline
and centralized control aspired to by the leaders of the League. At
the third annual convention of the League (1898), Fred E. Britten,
chairman of the Michigan Prohibition party, nearly upset the arranged
proceedings when he proposed that the Resolutions and Nominations
Committees be filled by election rather than by appointment. Apparently
fearful that such a procedure would take control of important decisions
out of the hands of the hierarchy, the League officers beat back Britten's
upstart resolution. Britten then offered a motion to prohibit League men
from supporting license parties—a truly dangerous proposal tantamount
to endorsement of the Prohibition party. Upon the motion of a less
militant Prohibitionist, the convention tabled Britten's resolution.[89] In

1901 the *New Voice* reported that Prohibitionists in Iowa, incensed at
the endorsement of the antiprohibitionist Republican gubernatorial
candidate by the League Superintendent, attended the state Anti-
Saloon League convention in sufficient force to depose the superintendent
and pass a resolution preventing the League from endorsing major-party
candidates.[90]

The story of cooperation in Wisconsin illustrated both the compelling
need of Prohibitionists to find success and their difficulties in breaking
ties with the old organization. The Wisconsin Anti-Saloon League was
founded in the summer of 1897 after a visit to the state by Anti-Saloon
League leaders from Michigan and Ohio. Wisconsin Prohibitionists were
prominent among its early leaders, and by the summer of 1898 the posts
of president, secretary, and field secretary were occupied respectively
by the Reverend John Faville, T. C. Richmond, and the Reverend T. K.
Thorvildsen, all former Prohibitionists.[91] J. Burritt Smith, who had
denounced the League in 1898, by 1900 divided his reform work between
campaigning as the Prohibition party gubernatorial candidate and serving
as State Attorney for the Anti-Saloon League.[92] Thorvildsen wrote to
Richmond his feelings on making the move:

> Well, I am through with the Prohibition party. I was elected
> delegate to our state convention but refused to go. If I had any
> doubts about the course to pursue before, my work for the
> Anti-Saloon League has dispelled those doubts. The bigotry,
> fanaticism, and narrowmindedness of the prohibitionists,
> manifested towards my present work, have convinced me
> that sticking to that party any longer is detrimental to the
> best interests of temperance and prohibition.[93]

H. A. Miner, editor of the Wisconsin party paper, was at first recep-
tive to cooperation with the League and aided materially in its organiza-
tion in Wisconsin. He consistently maintained, however, that Anti-Saloon
League men must eventually find their way to the Prohibition party.[94]
Miner's paper, the *Northwestern Mail*, became so friendly to the Anti-
Saloon League that a Menomonee Falls Prohibitionist founded the
Wisconsin Agitator in April 1899 in an effort to replace the *Northwestern
Mail* as the party's state organ.[95] The *Agitator* began by professing friend-
ship for the League, but shortly moved to antagonism before folding in
September 1900.[96] In 1899 Miner began to differ with the League

publicly, and by the summer of 1901 he was engaged in a bitter public debate with Anti-Saloon League Superintendent Henry Colman. Apparently, Miner was ready to compromise when doing so brought success, but at that time even the most humiliating compromises accepted by the League accomplished little.[97] By 1900 even T. K. Thorvildsen was securely back within the party fold.[98]

Wisconsin party leaders had found it difficult to work directly with the League when it became embarrassingly obvious that the party derived little or no benefit from the coalition. Yet they could not cut themselves off from efforts in behalf of reforms in which both party and League were interested. Their solution was the creation of a third, umbrella organization through which they could cooperate with the League without the embarrassment of a direct endorsement. Thus, the Wisconsin Federation of Reforms was born at a meeting in Stevens Point, November 17-18, 1898; the midwives included the Reverend Henry Colman of the Anti-Saloon League; Samuel D. Hastings and the Reverend H. A. Miner of the Prohibition party; a representative of the Wisconsin WCTU; and the Reverend Dr. Wilbur F. Crafts of Washington, D.C., founder of the International Reform Bureau and successor to William D. P. Bliss as the nation's ubiquitous universal reformer. The purpose of the Federation was to unite "the moral forces of the state against the saloon and its allied vices, such as Sabbath desecration, impurity, gambling, and the like."[99]

By its next meeting a year later, the Federation counted among its institutional members the major Protestant conferences, associations, and synods of Wisconsin, the Good Templars, the WCTU, the Sunday Rest Day Association, and the Anti-Saloon League, and extended invitations for membership to the Catholic Total Abstinence Union and the Northwestern Purity Association.[100] The Federation functioned as a means of uniting the various groups of moral reformers in petition campaigns and lobbying on behalf of bills concerning the issues enumerated in its statement of purpose. In 1902 the annual convention changed its name to the "Wisconsin Federation of Churches and Christian Workers."[101]

The pattern of relationships between Wisconsin Prohibition party leaders and the Anti-Saloon League embraced cooperation, followed by rejection and then eventual limited, indirect cooperation. Driven by their need for success, Prohibitionists turned to the League in desperation, then rejected it when they found that full cooperation usually required the breaking of bonds to their own organization. A similar pattern appeared in the career of an individual whose influence was considerable in the national party.

William P. F. Ferguson, editor of the prohibition department of the old *Voice,* became disillusioned with the progress of the cause in late 1898 when the Funk & Wagnalls Company altered the paper's character from a straight-out party organ to a general-circulation family journal. For him, "the opening weeks of 1899 were the darkest days that the cause of political Prohibition ever saw." Seeking other means of pursuing the fight, he was attracted by the League's claims of success in Ohio and by "the fact that this organization seemed to be securing a ready hearing for the reform with the people whom the Prohibition party had experienced such difficulty in reaching—the respectable, well-to-do Christian masses." Charmed by a meeting with National Superintendent Howard H. Russell, Ferguson consented to lend his considerable oratorical powers to the work of the League. After delivering a few speeches under League auspices, however, he returned to the party when he found party loyalty and League support of major-party candidates incompatible.[102] Thereafter, he became the Anti-Saloon League's most implacable and formidable opponent within Prohibition party ranks.

THE RISE OF JOHN G. WOOLLEY

The nomination of John G. Woolley for President in 1900 aptly summed up the developments in the Prohibition party during the six years after 1896. Woolley's nomination on a single-issue platform and his campaign for the church vote represented the culmination of the single-issue drive which had helped to split the party in 1896. When Woolley found that under these favorable circumstances the party had failed even to equal its 1892 vote, he began to turn toward the Anti-Saloon League, thus giving the lie to the exclusivist conception of the party which he had helped to create. For some of Woolley's most powerful supporters in 1900, however, the party still filled an important need, and Woolley's move toward cooperation was to shatter the coalition which had elevated him to preeminence.

The coalition was formed in 1899. The first phase included the purchase by Samuel Dickie and Woolley of *The Lever* in February and its combination with the *New Voice* in August. The immediate appointment to the managing editorship of William P. F. Ferguson, the most effective editorialist in the party after E. J. Wheeler's departure, brought a third member to the group. Oliver W. Stewart, Illinois State Chairman, won their favor by promoting the new paper throughout his state, and upon Dickie's resignation from the national chairmanship in December his devoted National Committee selected Stewart as his successor.[103] Thus, the group which was to run the party for the next five years gained control of the national chairmanship and the national organ, the two most powerful levers of the party machinery.

As Ferguson told the story later, Woolley decided in February of the following year that he would like to receive the party's nomination for President. Woolley's friends thought at first that no particular effort would be required to secure his nomination, but a boom for the Reverend Silas C. Swallow by Pennsylvania Prohibitionists changed their minds.[104] Swallow was a strong candidate because he had garnered 132,000 votes in his 1898 race for Governor of Pennsylvania, but in the eyes of those who saw the party as a league of saints he was suspect, for he had campaigned merely as an anticorruption, anti-Quay candidate and had accepted support from independent Republicans.[105] One week before the convention, Ferguson started the Woolley boom through the editorial columns of the *New Voice*. Declaring that prohibition would be the single, dominant issue in the election and assuming that the convention would adopt a single-issue platform, Ferguson nominated Woolley as the best man to stand upon such a platform.[106]

Woolley's strategy became clear when he spoke out in the following issue to accept Ferguson's nomination only on the condition that the convention adopt a single-issue platform directed toward Christian voters.[107] He hoped to use his candidacy as a lever to swing the adoption of a single-issue platform, then use the platform as a means of bringing about his nomination. Swallow, in contrast, stood for a platform including planks opposing monopolies and "imperialism" (but not "expansion") and advocating civil-service and ballot reform, arbitration among nations and between capital and labor, and the submission to the states of a woman-suffrage constitutional amendment.[108] Unlike the fierce conflict over the platform in 1896, then, that of 1900 involved little more than a contest between supporters of the two rival candidates for nomination. A Pennsylvanian made clear the basic agreement between the two sides when he appealed for Swallow's nomination with the argument that, as a Methodist minister, Swallow could make a more effective appeal to the churches than the layman Woolley.[109]

In the convention Woolley's forces won all the battles, but the manner of their victory indicated that their control of the party machinery may well have been the deciding factor. First, the National Committee unanimously selected Samuel Dickie as temporary chairman, and the convention kept the former leader as permanent chairman.[110] Then A. A. Hopkins, leading theoretician of the single-issue wing, produced a platform restating at greater length all the themes of his letter to *The Voice* five years earlier. The Resolutions Committee reported the Hopkins platform to the convention with only the additon of a supplementary resolution advocating woman suffrage.[111]

The Woolley forces played their trump card when National Chairman Stewart personally placed Woolley's name before the convention. This important and precedent-setting favor had been granted, Ferguson later claimed, only after "Mr. Woolley's personal solicitation."[112] The convention then nominated Woolley, but only by a vote of 380-320, making the contest the closest in party history.[113]

Woolley mounted the most determined campaign the party had ever seen. The *New Voice* gave him active support, asserting that, while no possibility existed of electing a Prohibition President, the casting of a million votes for Woolley would mean "the death knell of the liquor traffic."[114] Woolley himself travelled more than 23,000 miles, which Prohibitionists claimed to be more than any other presidential candidate of any party had ever travelled.

In its last issue before the election the *New Voice* confidently stated: "There is at the present moment no cause to doubt that we shall poll a far larger vote than we have ever polled before in all the party's history."[115] Prohibitionists therefore had cause for disappointment when their final total reached only 210,200, or about 60,000 less than the party's high mark in 1892.[116] The distribution of the vote was almost identical to those of 1892 and 1896 (see Table 6, p. 46).

The election results pushed John G. Woolley a little further
on the path to the Anti-Saloon League on which his affinity for
the churches had already set his feet. In 1897, while warning
Prohibitionists not to contribute money to the League, he had
also cautioned against opposing or antagonizing supporters of
the new organization.[117] Speaking in South Dakota in 1899, Woolley
"cordially commended" the work of the League.[118] During the 1900
campaign he spoke against the League in an effort to win support
for the party, but after the election he wrote a significant
editorial which showed the true direction of his thinking.[119]
Arguing against the charge that morality could not be legislated,
Woolley asserted that the mere enactment of a prohibitory law,
even without enforcement, would raise the moral tone of American
society. Almost as an afterthought, he justified the party's existence,
but only as a means for righteous men to maintain their righteousness, and not, significantly, as a necessary enforcer of a prohibition
law.[120] Implicitly, Woolley had thus undermined the party's last
credible defense against the League, for after 1896 the party could
distinguish itself from the League only by the argument that a
prohibition law would be nugatory without the effective enforcement which must be provided by the Prohibition party in power.

Woolley's new conception of the Prohibition party and its task
had thus ironically led him away from the party. Failure had
necessitated the revision of the party's goal from the enactment
and enforcement of prohibition to the triumph of righteousness.
It had motivated the prediction that righteousness could be attained
by the conversion of at least a million church voters to the Prohibition party. When Woolley could admit, as he did in this editorial, that
the triumph of righteousness could also be achieved, or at least
grasped, through enactment of a prohibitory law by anyone, inside
or outside the party, he was thenceforth bound to the party not by
conviction but only by his loyalty to a discredited institution. In
February 1901 he reached the League's side door when he cooperated
with the Chicago Anti-Saloon League superintendent in the reorganization of a local law enforcement organization under League auspices.[121]

NOTES

1. Computed from lists in David Leigh Colvin, *Prohibition in the*

United States: A History of the Prohibition Party and of the Prohibition Movement (New York, 1926), pp. 643-657.

2. *The Voice,* December 1, 1898; *New Voice,* February 4, 11, August 26, 1899, November 29, 1900; *American Issue* (Columbus, Ohio), March, 1899.

3. Minutes of National Executive Committee (NXC) meeting, March 24, 1899, Cincinnati; Minutes of National Committee (NC) meeting, December 13, 1899, Chicago, "Minutes of the National Committees, Conferences and Conventions of the Prohibition Party," vol. 1, pp. 80, 86-88, Michigan Historical Collections (MHC), Ann Arbor; *New Voice,* November 16, 1899; *Northwestern Mail* (Madison, Wis.), February 9, December 21, 1899.

4. *New Voice,* September 14, 1899, p. 5. Ferguson was born at Delhi, New York, in 1861. Taking a theological degree at Drew Theological Seminary (1887) and a bachelor's degree at Texas Wesleyan University (1889), he served during his ministerial career as pastor of Methodist, Presbyterian, and Universalist churches. He was also a renowned prohibition orator. The role in which he became best known, that of prohibition journalist, began in earnest when he joined the *Voice* staff in 1897. He had been a party prohibitionist since 1884. Ernest H. Cherrington et al., eds., *Standard Encyclopedia of the Alcohol Problem,* 6 vols. (Westerville, Ohio, 1924-30), vol. 3, pp. 978-979.

5. *Wisconsin Agitator* (Menomonee Falls), April 19, June 7, July 19, September 13, 1899; *New Voice,* October 19, 1905.

6. *Minutes of the N.W.C.T.U.* (Chicago, 1898), p. 66; Samuel Unger, "A History of the National Woman's Christian Temperance Union" (Ph.D. dissertation, Ohio State University, 1933), pp. 41, 44, 45.

7. J. E. Clayton of Wisconsin, in *Northwestern Mail,* May 2, 1901.

8. Computed from Colvin, *Prohibition in the U.S.,* pp. 643-657.

9. *Northwestern Mail,* January 2, 1902.

10. *New Voice,* May 29, 1902; *Northwestern Mail,* November 3, 1898; James B. Sellers, *The Prohibition Movement in Alabama, 1702 to 1943* (Chapel Hill, 1943), p. 87.

11. See *The Voice,* April-August 1898, and the discussion of cooperation with the Anti-Saloon League, below.

12. *New Voice,* February 7, 1901.

13. *Wisconsin Agitator,* May 10, June 7, 1899; *New Voice,* December 13, 1900.

14. *Northwestern Mail,* April 4, 1901.

15. Ibid., August 15, 1901.

16. Ibid., August 8, 1901.

17. Colvin, *Prohibition in the U.S.,* p. 323.

18. Ibid., pp. 323-326. Interview with Dr. Harry S. Warner, Columbus,

Ohio, August 29, 1970. Warner, the former secretary of the ICPA, reported that Samuel Dickie had provided his salary during the organization's early years.

19. *New Voice,* June 14, 28, 1900.

20. Ibid., September 7, 1900.

21. Ibid., March 8-September 13, 1900.

22. *Northwestern Mail,* June 9, July 7, September 8, 22, 1898; *New Voice,* September 21, 1899, March 8-September 13, 1900, May 16-October 17, 1901, April 3-July 3, 1902.

23. See Chapter 8 below.

24. *New Voice,* August 30, 1900, January 31, December 19, 1901, June 5, 1902; John G. Woolley, "The Prohibition Party," *The Independent* 52 (September 27, 1900): 2326.

25. *The Voice,* March 3, May 19, 1898; *New Voice,* April 1, May 6, December 14, 1899, July 26, August 23, 1900, April 4, September 5, 1901, January 23, April 24, June 19, 1902; *Northwestern Mail,* October 19, 1899, November 15, 1900, May 16, 1902. See also John Sobieski, *The Life-Story and Personal Reminiscences of Col. John Sobieski* (Shelbyville, Ill., 1900), pp. 46, 109.

26. *New Voice,* July 19, September 20, 1900, September 19, December 12, 1901.

27. Ibid., January 21, February 4, 18, March 25, 1899; *Wisconsin Agitator,* April 26, 1899; *Northwestern Mail,* June 8, October 12, 1899, May 24, 1900, June 6, 1901.

28. *New Voice,* January 14, July 8, 1899, August 15, 1901. State Chairman J. E. Clayton, in *Northwestern Mail,* December 5, 1902, reported that many staunch Wisconsin Prohibition party leaders had voted for La Follette that year.

29. *Northwestern Mail,* December 3, 1896, May 25, 1899; Samuel D. Hastings to T. C. Richmond, December 22, 1897, Richmond Papers, State Historical Society of Wisconsin (WHS), Madison; *New Voice,* April 29, August 5, 1899, April 26, 1900; Interview with Dr. Harry S. Warner, August 29, 1970.

30. *New Voice,* July 5, 1900, May 30, 1901.

31. *Northwestern Mail,* September 12, October 3, 1901.

32. *New Voice,* April 5, 1900, May 2, 1901; *Northwestern Mail,* October 25, 1900, December 5, 1901.

33. *New Voice,* September 14, 1899, May 10, November 29, 1900, March 27, April 3, 1902; *Northwestern Mail,* October 3, 1902.

34. *The Voice,* January 14, March 4, April 1, July 1, 1897; *Northwestern Mail,* September 2, October 14, 1897, August 25, 1898; *New Voice,* June 24, 1899, March 29, April 12, 1900.

35. *The Voice,* March 3, 1898; *Northwestern Mail,* April 14, 28,

1898; *New Voice,* March 25, April 1, July 29, September 21, 1899, January 25, September 27, 1900; Unger, "History of the N.W.C.T.U.," p. 170.

36. For evidence to support this statement, see articles, editorials, and letters, too numerous to list, in *The Voice* (1897-1898), *New Voice* (1899-1902), *Wisconsin Agitator* (1899-1900), and *Northwestern Mail* (1897-1902), as well as John G. Woolley, "Prohibition Party," p. 2325.

37. *The Voice,* May 27, 1897; *Northwestern Mail,* August 25, 1898; *New Voice,* September 7, 1899, September 6, 1900.

38. *Northwestern Mail,* July 20, 1899, July 4, 1901; *New Voice,* July 18, November 28, 1901.

39. Editorial, "Decline in Methodism," *Outlook 64* (March 17, 1900): 610-611. Actually, the Presbyterian membership did not decline at all, and the Methodist decline of about 1 percent in 1899 was only temporary (though shocking). U.S. Bureau of the Census, *Historical Statistics of the United States, Colonial Times to 1957* (Washington, 1960), p. 228.

40. *New Voice,* April 12, May 3, 1900.

41. Ibid., May 24, October 18, 1900.

42. Timothy Smith, *Revivalism and Social Reform: American Protestantism on the Eve of the Civil War,* Harper Torchbook edn. (New York, 1965).

43. William G. McLoughlin, Jr., *Modern Revivalism: Charles Grandison Finney to Billy Graham* (New York, 1959), p. 346. McLoughlin notes that, about 1900, the evangelists' advocacy of prohibition obscured their conservatism. But, as we shall see, prohibition sentiments were becoming less and less of an obstacle to conservatism.

44. *The Voice,* January 21-February 25, 1897; *New Voice,* June 24, August 31, 1899, April 4, 1901, January 2, 1902; *Wisconsin Agitator,* September 13, 1899; *Northwestern Mail,* November 21, 1902.

45. *New Voice,* July 12, 1900.

46. Ibid., January 2, 1902.

47. *Wisconsin Agitator,* September 6, 1899.

48. *The Voice,* March 4, 1897.

49. *New Voice,* August 31, September 21, 1899, July 5, December 20, 1900, February 28, March 7, 21, August 8, 1901; *Northwestern Mail,* January 13, 1898, May 10, November 15, 1900; *Wisconsin Agitator,* October 11, 1899.

50. *The Voice,* July 8, 1897.

51. *New Voice,* May 10, 1900.

52. *The Voice,* November 11, 1897; *New Voice,* April 8, October 5, 189

53. See, for example, *Northwestern Mail,* May 11, 1899.

54. *New Voice,* July 10, 1902.

55. Ibid., December 20, 1900; *Northwestern Mail,* August 30, 1900. See also *Northwestern Mail,* August 25, 1898, June 27, 1901.

56. *New Voice,* August 16, 1900.

57. *Northwestern Mail,* January 10, August 8, 1901; *New Voice,* October 26, 1899, February 15, 1900.

58. *New Voice,* January 11, 1900; *Northwestern Mail,* August 25, 1898, August 8, 1901, June 27, 1902.

59. *New Voice,* December 28, 1899, January 3, 1901.

60. *Northwestern Mail,* July 4, 1902.

61. *New Voice,* April 12, 1900.

62. *New Voice,* September 14, December 14, 1899, February 15, 1900.

63. Ibid., May 31, December 27, 1900.

64. *Northwestern Mail,* May 17, 1900; *New Voice,* April 11, 18, 1901.

65. *Northwestern Mail,* August 25, 1898.

66. *New Voice,* December 21, 1899, December 12, 1901.

67. Ibid., December 20, 1900.

68. Ibid., May 10, 1900.

69. Herbert Asbury, *Carry Nation* (New York, 1929), pp. 172, 189; *Baptist Standard,* quoted in *New Voice,* January 31, 1901; *New Voice,* May 2, 1901; *Northwestern Mail,* February 7, 14, 28, 1901, August 8, 1902. Compare Norton Mezvinsky, "The White-Ribbon Reform, 1874-1920" (Ph.D. dissertation, University of Wisconsin, 1959), p. 71.

70. *New Voice,* February 7, 1901.

71. *Northwestern Mail,* February 7, 1901; *New Voice,* January 24, February 7, 14, 1901.

72. Virginius Dabney, *Dry Messiah: The Life of Bishop Cannon* (New York, 1949), p. 38. By making ominous threats, the League hoped to frighten Ohio legislators into adopting moderate temperance legislation in order to pacify the supposedly desperate and frustrated temperance voter. In addition, National Superintendent H. H. Russell travelled to Topeka and helped to arrange bail for Nation. H. H. Russell diary, entries for February 22, 23, 24, 25, 1901, Howard Hyde Russell Papers, MHC.

73. "Superintendent's Report," *Proceedings of the Sixth National Convention of the Anti-Saloon League of America* (hereafter referred to as *ASL Proceedings*), *1901,* pp. 3-4.

74. *Northwestern Mail,* February 3, 1898; *New Voice,* August 31, 1899, February 15, 1900.

75. *Minutes of the N.W.C.T.U.* (Chicago, 1895), p. 24.

76. Unger, "History of the N.W.C.T.U.," p. 72.

77. *New Voice,* November 28, 1901; *ASL Proceedings, 1901,* p. 31.

78. *The Voice,* December 17, 1896, February 3, July 7, 1898; *American Issue,* April, August, 1899; *New Voice,* July 22, 1899; *Northwestern Mail,* July 14, 1898.

79. *New Voice,* September 7, 1899.

80. Ibid., September 28, 1899.

81. Ibid., February 15, 22, April 19, 1900.

82. Ibid., April 26, May 10, 1900.

83. Ibid., March 14, August 1, 1901.

84. Ibid., December 19, 1901. See also letters, articles, and editorials in *New Voice,* January 2-October 9, 1902. Meanwhile, Prohibitionists in Utah and New York joined efforts to win local option laws from state legislatures. *New Voice,* January 21, 1899, December 5, 19, 1901; Norman H. Clark, *The Dry Years* (Seattle, 1965), pp. 41-53.

85. See *Northwestern Mail,* 1896-1901; *New Voice,* August 31-December 14, 1899; *American Issue,* April 19, October 4, 1901; "Local Option," address by the Rev. Barton S. Taylor, n.d., Taylor Family Papers, MHC.

86. Robert E. Wenger, "The Anti-Saloon League in Nebraska Politics, 1898-1910," *Nebraska History* 52 (Fall 1971): 279.

87. *ASL Proceedings, 3d Annual Convention, 1898,* pp. xxv, xxvi, xxviii, xxxiii; *ASL Proceedings, 4th Annual Convention, 1898,* pp. viii, x, xii, xxv, xxvi, xxviii; *ASL Proceedings, 1900,* pp. viii, x, xi, xii, xix; Ibid., *1901,* pp. xxiv, xxvi, xxvii.

88. Ibid., *1913,* p. 329; *American Issue,* January, March, September, 1899, February 8, 1901; *New Voice,* May 20, 1899, March 21, 1901; *Northwestern Mail,* December 15, 1898; George R. Grose, *James W. Bashford, Pastor, Educator, Bishop* (New York, 1922), pp. 81-82.

89. *ASL Proceedings, 3d Annual Convention, 1898,* pp. 63-64, 87-88.

90. *New Voice,* September 5, 1901.

91. *Northwestern Mail,* June 10, July 29, 1897; Rev. T. K. Thorvildsen to T. C. Richmond, August 25, 1898, Richmond Papers.

92. *Northwestern Mail,* August 25, 1898; *American Issue,* November 30, 1900; *Facts and Figures* (Menomonee Falls, Wis.), January, 1901.

93. Thorvildsen to Richmond, August 25, 1898, Richmond Papers.

94. *Northwestern Mail,* November 12, 1896-June 15, 1899.

95. Ibid., April 27, 1899; *American Issue,* May, 1899.

96. *Wisconsin Agitator,* May 17, July 12, August 2, 1899.

97. *Northwestern Mail,* October 26, November 2, 1899, August 23, 30, 1900, August 1, September 26, 1901.

98. Ibid., August 23, 30, 1900, September 26, 1901.

99. Ibid., November 24, 1898.

100. Ibid., November 30, 1899.

101. Ibid., August 16, 1900, May 2, November 21, 1901, November 21, 1902; *American Issue,* September, 1900.

102. *New Voice,* February 15, 1900; H. H. Russell diary, entry for January 13, 1899, Russell Papers.

103. Minutes of NXC meeting, Cincinnati, March 24, 1899, and Minutes of NC meeting, Chicago, December 13, 1899, "Minutes," vol. 1, pp. 80, 86-88.

104. *The Citizen,* February 22, 1905.

105. *New Voice,* April 5, July 5, 1900; E. J. Wheeler, "The Prohibition Party and Its Candidates," *Review of Reviews* 22 (September 1900):'327-328.

106. *New Voice,* June 21, 1900.

107. Ibid., June 28, 1900.

108. Wheeler, "Prohibition Party," pp. 327-328.

109. *New York Times,* June 29, 1900.

110. Minutes of NC meeting, June 26, 1900, Chicago, "Minutes," vol. 1, p. 90; Colvin, *Prohibition in the U.S.,* p. 310.

111. *New Voice,* July 5, 1900; Colvin, *Prohibition in the U.S.,* p. 311.

112. *The Citizen,* February 22, 1905; *New Voice,* July 5, 1900.

113. *New Voice,* July 5, 1900; *New York Times,* June 29, 1900.

114. *New Voice,* September 13, 1900.

115. Ibid., November 1, 1900.

116. Svend Petersen, *A Statistical History of the American Presidential Elections* (New York, 1963), p. 67.

117. *The Voice,* March 4, 1897.

118. *American Issue,* May 1899.

119. Woolley, "The Prohibition Party," p. 2325.

120. *New Voice,* December 20, 1900. The authorship of the editorial was not given. I base my identification of Woolley as the writer upon the similarity of the rhetoric to Woolley's and the dissimilarity of the uncertain logic to Ferguson's usual tight, straightforward arguments.

121. *Northwestern Mail,* February 7, 1901.

6

Early years of the anti-saloon league, 1893-1904

Nonpartisan temperance organizations had functioned sporadically since the Prohibition party's founding in 1869. Until the pressures of the 1890s forced prohibitionists to choose between class allegiance and commitment to reform, the party had always overshadowed such organizations. The leadership vacuum in the prohibition movement created by the decline of the party made both possible and necessary the rise of a national nonpartisan prohibition organization.

The new mood of prohibition's middle-class constituency shaped the new organization's early development in crucial ways. Most important, it required that the Anti-Saloon League steer clear of attempts at drastic social change and of alliance with lower-class groups who would benefit most by such change. The new prohibitionist leadership thus consisted of men and women whose approach to reform was elitist, manipulative, and, ultimately, antidemocratic. The emergence of such an organization represented a revolutionary reversal, not an evolutionary development, of the dominant tendencies in the Prohibition party during the early 1890s.

Policy and structure in the new organization reflected this reversal. The League refused, even after constant rebuffs by the major parties, to consider formation of or inclusion within a third party. While the party had insisted upon immediate national prohibition achieved through majority vote, the League asked only for the longest step toward prohibition which could be supported by a minority holding the balance of power. If the party before 1896 had attacked the churches, the League would court them assiduously. If the party before 1896 depended upon itinerant lecturers paid by day-to-day collections, the League would build a symmetrical structure resting upon salaried workers stationed in a single area and a financial system based upon annual contributions from supporting churches. If party control had rested ultimately in state conventions, the League would bind together its organizations with a tight, highly centralized direction. And so it went. Every aspect of party policy and structure was matched by a corresponding yet exactly opposite tack taken by the League.[1] Above all, by appealing directly to the middle class, standing upon the sole issue of prohibition, working through the major parties, and building upon the churches, the League guaranteed that its triumph would disturb, outside of the liquor industry, none of the institutional arrangements of American society.

The failure of the prohibition movement under the party's leadership pervaded public statements by League leaders since it provided the most convenient justification for the League's existence. The party had seen American society as corrupt but had considered the individual American to be susceptible to appeals for change. As evidence, it pointed to the presumed success of the anti-slavery movement. The evidence of Prohibitionist failure was more convincing to the League. Because of this failure, League leaders argued, the time had come for disaffected Americans to cease utopian efforts to change society and instead devote their energies to self-protection. Just as Booker T. Washington used the failure of Reconstruction to justify redefinition of goals for blacks, League leaders pointed to Prohibition party failure in urging prohibitionists to seek the possible rather than the desirable.

There was some truth in what they said, but the argument was also self-serving, for both the League and the prohibitionist constituency to which it appealed. After all, the party's failure was attributable to the refusal by thousands of prohibitionists to give it their support during the late eighties and early nineties. To argue simply from party failure was to ignore this fact. It was necessary to ignore it, however, if prohibition supporters wished to avoid acknowledging the class bias implicit in their failure to support reform. Refusal to look beyond Prohibition party failure allowed the League to pretend that its single-issue policy had no relation to the larger context of national politics.

The timing of the League's appearance suggests another interpretation. The party's failure to hold its balance-of-power position was evident in the election returns of 1888; yet the League did not begin to organize locally for another five years. The organization of the first two "state" Leagues, in Ohio and the District of Columbia, which took place following the depressing election results of 1892, also followed the party's adoption of its most radical platform. The Anti-Saloon League organized nationally

in the fall of 1895, following the fusionist overtures toward Populism
and one year before the party finally discredited itself by splitting.
The same events seem to have crystallized the single-issue faction within
the Prohibition party and the Anti-Saloon League without. If so, party
radicalism as much as party failure was responsible for the change within
the prohibition movement. And the staying power of the League, in
spite of numerous difficulties and in contrast to the failure of earlier nonpartisan organizations, showed that it provided an appropriate vehicle
for the mood of middle-class supporters of prohibition.

THE STATE OF THE LEAGUE

Most of the men who established the national Anti-Saloon League
and led it during its early years were long-time opponents of the
Prohibition party. Howard Hyde Russell, founder of the Anti-Saloon
League, cast his first vote for Rutherford B. Hayes, supported McKinley
in 1896, and in between demonstrated his party regularity by speaking
in 1884 for James G. Blaine while other temperance men, repelled by
Blaine, were rushing to the Prohibition party. In 1890 Russell fought
Prohibitionists in Missouri over the creation of a nonpartisan temperance
league.[2] Hiram Price of Iowa, the League's first president, had attended
the Prohibition party's founding convention in 1869 to argue vainly
against the launching of a separate party.[3] The Reverend A. J. Kynett of
Pennsylvania, who was instrumental in setting the League upon its national
career, had a long history of nonpartisan work and hostility to the third-
party method.[4] The influential League leaders from Ohio, Purley A. Baker,
Ernest H. Cherrington, and Wayne B. Wheeler, were all "strong" Republicans.
A. E. Carhart, founder of the South Dakota nonpartisan temperance organization, shared mutual hostility with party leaders, as did the Alabama
minister who established the Southern Negro Anti-Saloon Federation.[6]
Leadership always remained in the hands of men who were more than
ready to recognize and proclaim the failure of the Prohibition party.[7]

The League's leadership during its first twenty years shared with
Prohibition party leaders origins in farm families of the East and Midwest
followed by mobility into middle-class occupations in eastern and mid-
western cities. Leaders of the nonpartisan organization, however, were
ten to twelve years younger, on the average, than the party leaders, enjoyed
more formal education, lived in larger cities, moved more often, joined a

TABLE 7: *GROWTH OF THE ANTI-SALOON LEAGUE, 1895-1904*

Date		State or Territorial Organizations
Annual Convention		
1st	Dec. 1895	2
2d	Dec. 1896	6
3d	Jan. 1898	7
4th	Dec. 1898	18
Superintendent's Annual Convention	July 1899	31
5th	May 1900	30
6th	Dec. 1901	36
7th	Dec. 1902	Not reported
8th	Dec. 1903	41
9th	Nov. 1904	42

Source: Proceedings of the Annual Conventions of the Anti-Saloon League of America, 1895-1904. Some discrepancies exist among different official listings for the same conventions. I have counted only those auxiliaries officially recognized as *organizations* rather than those accorded representation on the National Board of Direction. Some of the recognized organizations actually existed only on paper or in the mind of a sole worker. For example, the Virginia Anti-Saloon League was recognized at the 2d Annual Convention (1896) and was represented on the Board of Direction at the 2d and 4th Annual Conventions but was actually not organized until March 1901. See C. C. Pearson and J. Edwin Hendricks, *Liquor and Anti-Liquor in Virginia, 1619-1919* (Durham, 1967), p. 224. The Alabama Anti-Saloon League was recognized in 1903 and 1904 but was not organized until after the latter year. See *American Issue*, December 2, 1904. The same situation may have existed in other states as well.

political prohibition organization later in their lives, included a significantly larger percentage of clergymen, and possessed fewer ties to the abolition movement.

These men oversaw the growth of the League from the two affiliates (in Ohio and the District of Columbia) represented at the 1895 founding convention to the forty-two state and territorial auxiliary organizations of 1904. Table 7 shows the number claimed at each convention.

The League achieved its growth in two ways. The first was the organization of state leagues from the ground up. National League officials usually supervised and sometimes personally conducted this process. In Wisconsin a variant of the process occurred when National Superintendent Howard H. Russell had to effect the reorganization of the League in February 1898 after an unsupervised group, including former Prohibitionists, had made an abortive beginning in 1897. Russell rewrote the constitution of the Wisconsin League, prodded the Prohibitionists' man into resigning from the superintendent's post, and replaced him with the loyal and dependable Reverend Henry Colman.[8] Russell could reorganize the League but he could not give it vitality, and the organization operated more or less under the wing of the Wisconsin Federation of Reforms until 1905, when it held its first separate convention.[9]

Another approach consisted of recognizing existing nonpartisan state temperance organizations as national League affiliates. Of the six auxiliaries recognized in 1896, those of Ohio and the District of Columbia were the founding groups of the national League, Virginia was only a paper organization, Pennsylvania and South Dakota were preexisting groups, and only the Michigan League had been constructed from the ground up.[10] The founding of an Anti-Saloon League in California in 1898 only added a new name and a national affiliation to the conflict between partisan and nonpartisan temperance men which had been raging in that state since 1874.[11] Of the eighteen state leagues recognized in December 1898 after the great leap forward of that year, at least six were preexisting nonpartisan groups.[12] In 1899 the national League took in existing organizations in Kentucky, Maine, and Massachusetts.[13] Absorption of these groups sometimes created problems for the League's leaders when their policies and practices came into conflict with those of the older state groups. In Massachusetts, after two years of cooperation with the Massachusetts Total Abstinence Society, League men seceded and established an antisaloon league which displaced the older organization.[14]

Another thorny and persistent problem for the Anti-Saloon League, as for the Prohibition party, was organizing what was assumed to be the widespread prohibition sentiment of the South. The League established its first southern beachhead in Arkansas in 1899, attempting to make that state a sort of southern Ohio from which it could dispatch trained or at least willing leaders to other southern states. In July 1899 the League claimed southern auxiliaries in Mississippi, Tennessee, Texas, Oklahoma, and the Indian Territory, as well as Arkansas, but the superintendents of all of these listed home addresses in two Arkansas towns.[15] Most of the southern leagues apparently remained paper organizations through 1904, when the new national superintendent, Purley A. Baker, once again mounted a southern effort by holding a poorly attended conference in Atlanta and appointing a successful Kentucky organizer as Assistant General Superintendent for the South.[16] The prohibition work which took place in the South through 1904 went on largely outside the Anti-Saloon League.[17]

The rapid multiplication of state organizations and the claim of one scholar that the League had won the leadership of the prohibition movement by the turn of the century should be weighed against the manifold difficulties encountered by the League throughout its first twelve years.[18] As Gilman M. Ostrander has pointed out, one important source of the League's power was its ability to picture itself as a thoroughgoing success.[19] Aware that they required not the substance so much as the appearance of success, League leaders made a determined effort to keep from the public eye any sign of failure or error.[20] Sufficient evidence exists nevertheless to conclude that, despite rapid expansion in the number of its state affiliates, the national League was unable to demonstrate strength adequate to convince temperance reformers of its preeminence until after the Ohio gubernatorial election of 1905. This election showed that the League could command a large enough balance-of-power vote to unseat an incumbent Republican governor in a Republican state. But until 1905, the League had failed to achieve credible success in local and state elections, had struggled with money problems, had muddled through internal conflicts, and had sought in vain for competent leadership in its rapidly proliferating state organizations.

The lack of success seemed to derive from a wholesale confusion over methods. League leaders blamed faulty methods for early failures of state Leagues in six states.[21] One problem shared by many state Leagues in the years before 1904 was a reluctance to give church bodies sufficient procedural control over League activities to ensure their active cooperation. Following the lead of Illinois under William H. Anderson, most leagues were eventually able to make such concessions, but the reorganization process did not begin until 1903. Another persistent problem followed from overemphasis upon the law-enforcement aspect of League work

and the hiring of League detectives.[22] Wayne Wheeler noted in 1903
that "several state leagues have been practically wrecked" by this practice.[23]
One was New York, where overzealous prosecutions incurred a debt of
$15,000 which crippled the League, required the personal attention of
National Superintendent Russell, and was not liquidated for three years.[24]
The ultimate obstacle lay, of course, in the strength of antiprohibition
sentiment, and in at least the important states of California and Pennsylvania
the League never did overcome it.[25]

In 1903 Purley Baker reported that "the financial department of the
league is not well handled in many states," and *American Issue,* the national
organ, added: "Some have a financial system that is crude, embarrassing
and unsatisfactory. Their books would not stand inspection."[26] In some
states the result was empty treasuries.[27] The national League never got
out of debt during its early years and, despite initiation in 1903 of a
plan whereby the state organizations contributed 2½ percent of their
annual gross cash receipts to the national League, an indebtedness of about
$4,200 remained in November 1904.[28] Russell's diary and personal cor-
respondence during these early years provide abundant testimony to
the "terrible hard times in the league treasury" and to the sacrifices made
by the families of devoted League men.[29]

These "terrible hard times" pushed League leaders into a dependence
upon wealthy supporters that was reinforced by ideological affinity.
As early as 1894, Russell sought out John D. Rockefeller for help and
was rewarded by generous contributions and a friendship which both
continued for many years. Three years later, when Russell turned over
the League reins in Ohio to Purley Baker, one of his first acts was to
take his successor to Cleveland for an introduction to Rockefeller.[30]

Although the League took pains to insist that all was harmony within its ranks, it appears that some of the trouble with incorrect methods
may have been the result of factional fights within state organizations.
Discord among its leaders, combined with defeat in its first election
campaign, made the Nebraska League's methods suspect "even in the
eyes of friends."[31] Factional squabbles, too, were involved in the disaster
within the New York League which forced Russell to take over the superintendency in 1902.[32] Russell blamed the repeal of Vermont's statewide
prohibition law in 1903 upon a conflict over methods.[33] William H.
Anderson, one of the more influential state superintendents, ascribed
his resignation in 1905 from the Illinois superintendency to intraorganiza-
tional squabbling.[34] In 1905 a majority of Oregon League workers rose

in revolt against their President over a question of tactics to be used in defending their state's local option law.[35]

The most persistent and perhaps most debilitating difficulty during the early years was the inability to procure sufficient competent leadership for the all-important state organizations. Part of the difficulty undoubtedly stemmed from the meager salaries the League was able to offer its full-time workers (contrary to the charges of party men). In some states the League came to resemble the picture of it which William H. Anderson found in the minds of some clergymen: "a . . . dumping ground for ecclesiastical misfits and ministerial odds and ends." The result was "a damaging number of mistakes" admitted by *American Issue* in 1903 and the discrediting of the League in the eyes of temperance men. From 1898 to 1904 ministers occupied an average 81.5 percent of the state superintendencies, and in 1903 Purley Baker appealed for leaders from other occupations: "There is no good reason why ministers should be the only class expected to do Christian work on small salaries." In 1903 the national convention finally acted on Russell's recommendation of two years before and adopted procedures for firing incompetent, immoral, or dishonest state superintendents.[36] The rate of annual turnover in state superintendencies averaged 32.0 percent during the years 1899-1904, compared to 22.5 percent per year for the Prohibition party's state chairmanships during the same period.[37]

The circulation of *American Issue,* the sometime official national organ, provided another indicator of the League's uneven career during these early years. Edited by the Reverend John C. (Jesse) Jackson and beginning as the organ of the Ohio League, by February 1904 *American Issue* had become the official paper of state leagues in Ohio, Illinois, Michigan, Indiana, New York, and Wisconsin.[38] From a total circulation of 33,000 in March 1899, it dropped to 20,000 by January 1903, then rose again to 23,000 in December 1903, and to 60,000 one year later.[39]

The difficulties of the early years affected the composure of even such dedicated men as Russell, despite his outward show of optimism. Russell's letters to his wife reveal alternating moods of hope and despair, with depression probably the dominant tone.[40] In 1894 he confessed: "I am very blue this morning about this League work. . : . I feel almost sometimes as though I would let go and get back to the regular ministry in a quiet place somewhere and get the comfort of home and family"[41] As late as 1902 he was exploring opportunities in Idaho for ranching and pastoral work.[42]

THE POLICIES OF OPPORTUNISM

Recognition of the failure of the prohibition movement stood behind every policy of the League. While this recognition left the League spokesmen obsessed by the need for success, no matter how insignificant, it also cleared from their minds the conviction that only the discovery of the proper key was necessary to unlock the door behind which lay the grand triumph of the cause. League leaders were thus much more realistic than Prohibitionists in assessing the strength of both their friends and their enemies.

The balance-of-power policy which lay at the heart of League strategy necessarily implied a downward revision in the expectations of Prohibitionist leaders. The success of a party, at the least, required the conversion of majorities in each state as well as the nation to the policy and the party of prohibition. The balance-of-power strategy of the League, however, demanded no such conversion of majorities. As one League writer put it, " 'Balance of power' may not represent a majority sentiment, but it *controls* it."[43] League men claimed that they supported at any given time only the most advanced liquor-control legislation which could win the support of "public opinion" at that place and time. Their actual practice of seeking to influence the election of officials by swinging the weight of the "church vote" for or against them indicated, however, that "public opinion" could include the views of only a very small fraction of the electorate. The League thus conceded without a murmur the hope of representing a broad spectrum of American opinion and defined itself instead as "the church in action against the saloon."

A League vision of its constituency and the means of its triumph appeared in a 1902 article in *American Issue*. The writer predicted a great forward movement for the cause in the four states of Ohio, Indiana, Illinois, and Michigan. Three significant characteristics made these states amenable to League work. First, "the population is homogenous. There are no such large blocks of almost exclusively un-American inhabitants as in parts of the northwest. The descendants of those immigrants who came into this region three generations ago are largely assimilated to American ideas." Second, "Ten millions of the 14,000,000 population of these states is . . . in the country, and in small villages and towns and cities that are amenable to temperance local option work and influence." Finally, "The church is perhaps relatively stronger in members, wealth and influence in this central four-state section than anywhere else in the United States. Church ideas, wishes and votes can dominate the election." Because all four states had local option laws, the entire region could be dried up, and then "this great federated temperance movement . . . can control the future in the heart of the Union and so throughout the United States."[44] This was truly balance-of-power politics on a grand scale.

From the same recognition of the weakness of the prohibition forces which produced the balance-of-power strategy came the League's emphasis upon the need for propaganda. League leaders realized that a vast amount of "education" was a prerequisite for victory and thus downplayed the Prohibitionists' belief in the existence of extensive temperance sentiment. Discussing the 1901 activities of the Ohio League, *American Issue* claimed that "fully three fourths of the work and money of the League are expended in the creation of public temperance sentiment." League histories are replete with breathless enumerations of the millions of pages turned out by its presses. Wisconsin Superintendent Henry Colman made the connection explicit in 1902 when he pointed out: "Not one-fourth of the voters of the state to-day are opposed to the saloon. We must do a vast amount of education before we win."[45]

Once the League leaders had perceived the weakness of their own forces, it was easy to see that the liquor interests on the other side did not possess the overwhelming strength attributed to them by Prohibitionists, who were wont to see the machinations of their enemies behind every adverse event. Jackson made this clear as early as 1900, confessing, "It is largely the creation of our imaginations that we have feared."[46] Such an admission was never possible for party prohibitionists.

The League's attitude toward local option, its chief weapon during these early years, also illustrated its assessment of the situation. Tactical reasons forced some states to claim that they would not go beyond local option to a demand for statewide prohibition. National League opinion held, however, that local option constituted little more than a compromise necessitated by adverse conditions and was useful primarily as a means of educating voters on the desirability of prohibition. In 1901 the Maryland superintendent admitted publicly the truth of the Prohibition party's charge that the attainment of dry status under local option allowed many temperance voters to ignore the need for prohibition on a larger scale.[47]

Seeing the havoc wrought by Prohibitionist quarrelsomeness,

League leaders resolved at the beginning to present a united front. Wayne Wheeler's biographer later quoted one leader as saying, "It is better to be united in a bad fight than divided in a good one."[48] During 1898-1901, the League's Executive Committee adopted as the official motto, "Let Us Emphasize Points on Which We Agree, and Avoid Subjects as to Which We Differ."[49] Their spokesmen followed this policy inconsistently with respect to the Prohibition party, but within the League, and especially at national conventions, they found it easy to maintain an appearance of harmony.

Professions of willingness to cooperate with other organizations co-existed uneasily in League rhetoric with declarations that the League represented the only possible method.[50] These declarations became especially heated whenever someone proposed a federation of church forces outside or above the League.[51] Acting upon an assumption of supremacy which was at that time quite unjustified, the League's Executive Committee in 1898 discontinued the sending of fraternal delegates to the conventions of allied groups, a practice by which reformers had traditionally exchanged courtesies.[52]

The Prohibition party, sometimes willing to compromise in practice, was uncompromising in its rhetoric. The League, in contrast, always accepted the necessity for compromise and thereby embroiled itself in the tangled and ever-recurring question of how much compromise was permissible in any given situation. Consequently, leaders in the field sometimes involved their organizations in compromises which turned out to be embarrassing. Such situations provided hostile Prohibitionists with opportunities to pillory the entire League unmercifully for its abandonment of principle.[53] While League men occasionally acknowledged mistakes arising out of their willingness to compromise, they refused to accept the charges of complicity with evil provoked by their cooperation with the major parties.[54] League theoreticians answered such charges by postulating the existence of two conflicting wings in each party: in the Republican party the "liberal" wing stood opposed to "the people who care for religion and morality, the conservative and constructive forces of a Christian civilization"; the "immoral end" of the Democratic party, based largely in the North, fought "the religious elements" controlling the party in the South.[55] The true strategy lay not in bringing the "moral elements" out of their parties and concentrating them in a third party, even if that were possible, for "if they were all to gather in one party, the indifferent and the hostile in other parties would outnumber them, and good men could accomplish less than they do now when holding the balance of power in many places." Rather, the League should keep its followers within their parties where they could influence party nominations and policy. Therefore, as an official statement put it in 1903: "The League does not seek the disintegration of any political party. . . . It avoids all efforts that would tend to destroy party integrity or effect the overthrow of any political organization." "There will never be," said the Reverend John C. Jackson in 1901, "but two great parties in this country, as there never have been."[56]

The purpose of the Anti-Saloon League's opportunistic policies was the enlistment of church voters in the prohibition cause through support of the League. Support was needed at the collection plate as well as the ballot box, for the League came to depend financially upon pledges made during the annual appearances of its workers in the pulpits of cooperating pastors. From the beginning the League, like the Prohibition party after 1896, saw church voters as its special constituency and directed every effort into lines thought to be most appealing to them. Nor was their appeal exclusively Protestant, as their spokesmen welcomed eagerly every evidence of support for temperance among both Catholics and Jews.[57]

The League's direct tactics in this appeal were quite similar in kind, though not in degree or effectiveness, to those of the Prohibition party. On the one hand, League men made constant rhetorical appeals for church support and worked within church conferences, synods, and associations to gain influence and secure the passage of favorable resolutions.[58] On the other, they mounted attacks upon ministers and church voters who failed to espouse the cause (at the same time that they chided Prohibitionists for doing precisely the same thing) and threatened uncooperative churches with decline and "dry-rot." In 1901, Illinois Superintendent William H. Anderson told the International Epworth League Conference, "The church will never again have a genuine, widespread revival of religion until it gets right on the liquor question."[59] Like the Prohibition party, the League showed its frustration with its slow progress in its denunciations of clerical and congregational apathy, although League men never went as far as the Prohibitionists of the 1890s who had called for withdrawal from the churches.

League spokesmen based their claims to church allegiance on the assertion, shared by the Prohibition party and Social Gospel leaders, that the church's duty lay in improving the conditions of this world as well as in preparing men's souls for the next.[60] The League received support from Social Gospellers Washington Gladden, Josiah Strong, and Louis Albert Banks.[61] On one of the very few occasions when *American Issue* addressed the argument that the church's support of the prohibition movement led to union of church and state, Jackson simply ignored the danger of such a possibility and concluded that the church could and should involve itself in political activities directly connected with its role as society's moral instructor.[62]

Despite their overriding need to attract the support of the churches and all their rhetoric directed toward that end, League men did not put into action until 1903 an effective plan to bring it about. Before then, the national Anti-Saloon League saw itself as the representative of all temperance organizations and thus included on its Board of Direction representatives from every organization endorsing the League. In 1902, however, Illinois Superintendent Anderson put into effect in his state a reorganization designed to elicit full support from the churches. He placed ultimate control of the League in the hands of representatives selected by each of the denominational ruling bodies.[63] Anderson had recognized what other leaders had refused to acknowledge and what the Prohibition party never saw, that the churches would assume substantial responsibility for the movement's support only when they felt that they held a meaningful share of control over its activities. Once formal control had been invested in official church representatives, of course, the League's full-time workers could do pretty much as they pleased in the intervals between meetings of the control group, as Wayne Wheeler demonstrated in Washington, D.C., during the 1920s; but the formal procedural recognition of church control was the essential step which, once taken, guaranteed the permanent support, if not the ultimate success, of the Anti-Saloon League.

THE MYTH OF CONSENSUS

The League leaders who, like the Prohibitionists, were seeking cultural supremacy within the middle class, ended their quest by postulating the existence of an "Americanism" whose possession separated them from their enemies. When the League spokesmen attempted to make distinctions within society, however, it became evident that the most important quality of their "Americanism" was a willingness to vote for prohibition or for whatever step toward prohibition the League happened to be advocating at the time. Their need to secure approval for their brand of

"Americanism" from a largely hostile or indifferent society led them
to blend it with an Americanism defined as loyalty to every aspect
of the status quo but the liquor traffic.

While Prohibitionists had maintained a healthy skepticism toward
claims for the inherent virtue of the Angle-Saxon "race," League spokesmen leaped at every opportunity to identify their cause as an indispensa-
ble part of the national creed and readily embraced the popular nativism
of the day.[64] Discarding the contention of party editorialists that the
saloon was primarily an American problem with its roots in the greed
and hypocrisy of American society, the League sought to identify prohibitionism with Americanism and to picture the recent immigrant as the
major obstacle to its success.[65] Easily captivated by current estimates of
the power of heredity, the League explained native American opposition to
prohibition as a product of "moral and physical decline."[66] These attitudes
provided an appropriate context for the prediction of a Chicago minister
whom *American Issue* quoted in 1903:

> Yes, deliverance will come, but it will be from the sober and
> august Anglo-Saxon south, unspoiled and unpoisoned by the
> wine-tinted, beer-sodden, whiskey-crazed, sabbath-desecrating,
> God-defying and anarchy-breeding and practicing minions
> from over the sea and from the vast and virile countrysides
> where the bible is not yet effete, nor Christ a myth.[67]

For Prohibitionists, the black man in America provided an opportunity
to demonstrate their idealism and their ties to the abolition movement; for
the Anti-Saloon League, blacks were an active factor in the battle over
liquor control, to be cursed or congratulated according to their vote. On the
rare occasion when black voters sided with the drys, the Reverend Mr.
Jackson was moved to express egalitarian sentiments.[68] However, on the
more common occasions when they allegedly sold their votes to saloon-
keepers or merely voted for the wet side, he thundered threats of the peni-
tentiary and disfranchisement.[69] It was in fact the mass disfranchisement
of blacks in Virginia, North Carolina, and Alabama which paved the way
for prohibition progress in those states.[70] The national League in 1902
selected as one of its honorary vice-presidents the black Professor E. W.
B. Curry of Urbana, Ohio, who had asked the Ohio League shortly before
"to tip your hat to the patriotism of the unbleached American. We are
whitening within."[71]

Another difference between League and party was evident in their respective views of morality and its reward, respectability. For the party, at least before 1896, morality seemed to be synonymous with Prohibition party membership. For the League, which sought to work through rather than against existing institutions, the matter was not quite so simple. While party men verged upon setting themselves up as sole judges of morality, League men took refuge behind the legal limits of behavior, glorifying law and order and seeking to identify themselves with those who made laws, claiming, "The enforcement of proper laws makes for morality."[72] Apparently, lawfulness did not constitute as effective a badge of respectability as membership in the Prohibition party, for President Hiram Price and Editor J. C. Jackson both urged the preservation of virtue through social ostracism of liquor-men and their families, a step never advocated by party leaders.[73]

The Anti-Saloon League model of reform was thus "coercive" in the sense used by Joseph R. Gusfield: it offered an insecure middle class an opportunity to validate its standing by forcing upon the rest of society a symbol of middle-class cultural style.[74] But prohibition could become an appropriate symbol for the middle class only in the event that its members were convinced of the value of self-restraint, an event which was becoming progressively less likely. If it occurred, conversion was likely to be temporary. Many middle-class men and women were frightened by even a single-issue prohibition movement's confiscatory thrust; a growing number simply liked their drinks and felt justified in having them.[75] The Anti-Saloon League never solved this crucial problem, although its attempts at "education," its leaders' blasts at the churches, and its pathetic appeals to "Americanism" showed that it recognized the problem's existence. Instead, the League sought to subdue its enemies outside the middle class, thus trading the hope of victory in the temperance movement's long war for the promise of winning a single battle.

LEAGUE AND PARTY

The methods of the Prohibition party and the Anti-Saloon League stood, as Professor Ostrander has pointed out, in direct opposition.[76] Given the Prohibition party's poor chances for success, the League could not consistently endorse party men running against major-party candidates who were even slightly sympathetic to the temperance cause.

The League did not in fact endorse very many Prohibition party candidates, and the consequence during its early years was a running conflict with the party. This antagonism, however, did not preclude cooperation in situations where Prohibition party integrity was not in danger, and the cooperation which took place at such times provided the foundations for the bridges which John G. Woolley began to build between party and League in 1902.

The League always claimed that no inevitable conflict existed between its methods and those of the party, and proclaimed from the first a policy of cooperation with all other temperance organizations.[77] Implicit in all these declarations was insistence upon recognition of the League as supreme in political activity. League spokesmen smoothed over this unpalatable fact by acknowledging the party's preeminence in exhortation while the League itself took over the leadership in day-to-day political combat.[78] The role in which League men thus placed the party was in fact the same role which the party was then assuming in response to its political failure, but party spokesmen could hardly admit that fact when it involved surrendering to the League the political leadership of the movement.

Some party leaders and editorialists thus followed the lead of the *New Voice* after August 1899 and launched bitter attacks upon the League. *American Issue* editor J. C. Jackson and other League leaders replied in kind, punctuating their counterarguments against the party with pious claims that the League refused to participate in intramovement debate.[79] League attacks upon the party followed two themes. In the first place, those who attacked the League from within the prohibition movement ranged themselves, in effect, upon the same side as declared liquor advocates. *American Issue* was quick to point out, for example, that the Ohio Prohibition party paper and the Ohio liquor organ borrowed from each other's attacks upon the League. Those who sowed dissension among the temperance ranks, according to the Reverend Mr. Jackson, were Satan's "left-hand agents" (the saloons, of course, were his "right-hand agents").[80] In the second place, the party's distrust of established institutions represented a "cloistered style of piety that can only preserve its purity by withdrawing from the world, and the cloistered theory of politics that withdraws itself as soon as something goes wrong in the old organization." Furthermore, it was unsuccessful in furthering the cause. In contrast, the League claimed "pre-eminently to be going out into the field in a hand-to-hand fight with the saloon as no other organization does." The Anti-Saloon League "takes the heaviest of the enemy's blows, and strikes the heaviest blows in return."[81]

As in the case of the party, cooperation in practice counterpointed rhetorical antagonism. During 1898-1901 League leaders joined Prohibitionists in advocating and defending the anticanteen law as well as a host of other limited liquor-control measures on the national level.[82] League endorsements for Prohibition party candidates seem to have been few in number and weak in conviction until after 1902, when O. W. Stewart, by securing his own election to the Illinois legislature, showed that Prohibitionists could be successful. Stewart had won election under a system by which voters in each legislative district cast three votes to elect three candidates. When he had built a coalition of reform-minded major-party men together with Prohibitionists, many of his supporters had "plumped" all three of their votes for him. Under this system, Illinois Superintendent Anderson was able to recommend in 1904 the election of nineteen Prohibitionists candidates to the legislature, suggesting the casting by League supporters of from one to three votes for each of them, depending on the positions taken by their major-party opponents.[83] This halfway cooperation, using Prohibitionist candidates primarily to punish the major parties, was as far as the League was able to go in extending the hand of fellowship to the party.

Genuine cooperation, as the League saw it, would obviously entail the surrender by Prohibitionists of their party method. When John G. Woolley in 1902 began to move openly toward just this sort of cooperative policy, League leaders gleefully welcomed him. Eagerly, the League seized upon Woolley's growing enchantment with its claims of success, using his cooperative attitude as a club to beat party members who still maintained their faith in the logic and righteousness of the party method.[84] By doing so, the League threw wood upon the fires of conflict which blazed fiercely within the party after 1902.

NOTES

1. The shape of League policy has been capably outlined in Peter H. Odegard, *Pressure Politics: The Story of the Anti-Saloon League* (New York, 1928).
2. "Howard H. Russell Chronology"; H. H. Russell Diary, entry for

November 3, 1896; H. H. Russell to Lillian D. Russell, August 13, 1890;
all in Russell Papers, Michigan Historical Collections (MHC).
    3. John Sobieski, *Life-Story and Personal Reminiscences of Col.
John Sobieski* (Shelbyville, Ill., 1900), pp. 175, 176. Sobieski had been
a delegate to the 1869 convention.
    4. Earl C. Kaylor, Jr., "The Prohibition Movement in Pennsylvania,
1865-1920," 2 vols. (Ph.D. dissertation, Pennsylvania State University,
1963), vol. 2, p. 315.
    5. *Bishop Cannon's Own Story: Life as I Have Seen It,* ed. Richard L.
Watson, Jr. (Durham, 1955), p. 168.
    6. Albert E. Carhart, *A Partial Life Story, How Booze Was Beaten
in a Mid-Western State* (n.p., 1931), pp. 30, 31, 32; B. F. Riley to Ernest
H. Cherrington, June 1, 1909, Cherrington Papers, Temperance Education
Foundation (TEF), Westerville, Ohio; James B. Sellers, *The Prohibition
Movement in Alabama, 1702 to 1943* (Chapel Hill, N.C., 1943), p. 80.
    7. See, for example, the address of Ohio Superintendent Baker at the
Ohio Anti-Saloon League Congress, 1902, in *American Issue* (Columbus,
Ohio), December 9, 1902.
    8. *Northwestern Mail,* February 17, March 3, June 9, 1898; *Anti-
Saloon League Proceedings* (hereafter referred to as *ASL Proceedings),
4th Annual Convention, 1898,* p. 10; *Wisconsin Issue* (Madison), November
1905. Howard H. Russell was born in Stillwater, Minnesota, in 1855.
After education at home and in public and preparatory schools, he spent
three years driving cattle across the plains from Iowa, then pursued
brief careers in schoolteaching and journalism before studying law and
setting up practice in Corning, Iowa, in 1878. His revival conversion in
1883 led to abandonment of his law career and enrollment in the theological department at Oberlin, from which he graduated as a Congregational minister in 1888. After holding pastorates and doing mission work in
Kansas City, Mo., and Chicago, Russell turned to full-time temperance
work in 1893 with his appointment as first Superintendent of the Ohio
Anti-Saloon League. Ernest H. Cherrington et al., eds., *Standard Encyclopedia of the Alcohol Problem,* 6 vols. (Westerville, Ohio, 1924-30), vol. 5,
pp. 2324-2326.
    9. *Northwestern Mail,* May 26, 1905.
    10. *ASL Proceedings, 1896,* pp. 16, 19; Kaylor, "Prohibition Move-
ment in Pennsylvania," vol. 2, p. 318; Carhart, *Partial Life Story,* p. 36.
    11. Gilman M. Ostrander, *The Prohibition Movement in California,
1848-1933* (Berkeley, 1957), pp. 54, 86.
    12. *ASL Proceedings, 4th Annual Convention, 1898,* pp. 9-10; *American
Issue,* December 2, 1904.

13. *Program* of Superintendent's Convention, Lake Bluff, Illinois, July 18-27, 1899; *American Issue,* May 13, 1904.

14. H. M. Chalfant to Howard Hyde Russell, June 23, 1931, Russell Papers.

15. *Program* of Superintendent's Convention, Lake Bluff, Illinois, July 18-27, 1899.

16. *American Issue,* March 11, May 13, October 21, December 2, 1904. Purley A. Baker was born in Jackson County, Ohio, in 1858, and entered the Methodist ministry in 1883 after education in local and normal schools and two years of school-teaching. After thirteen years occupying various Ohio pulpits and fighting saloons, he became Superintendent of the Cleveland District of the Ohio Anti-Saloon League. In 1897 he was elevated to the Ohio State superintendency and in 1903, upon Howard H. Russell's decision to lead personally the League work in New York, Baker succeeded him as National Superintendent. Cherrington et al., eds., *Standard Encyclopedia,* vol. 1, p. 258-260.

17. Ernest H. Cherrington, *History of the Anti-Saloon League* (Westerville, Ohio, 1913), p. 100; Daniel J. Whitener, *Prohibition in North Carolina, 1715-1945* (Chapel Hill, 1945), p. 186.

18. Frederick W. Adrian, "The Political Significance of the Prohibition Party" (Ph.D. dissertation, Ohio State University, 1942), p. 166.

19. Gilman M. Ostrander, *Prohibition Movement in California,* p. 85.

20. See, for example, *American Issue,* May 26, 1905.

21. *ASL Proceedings, 1901,* pp. 60-61; *ASL Proceedings, 1904,* pp. 29, 47-48, 55; *American Issue,* November 6, 1903, January 13, 1905.

22. *American Issue,* April 17, 1903.

23. Ibid., May 29, 1903. See also *ASL Proceedings, 1901,* pp. 60-61.

24. Address by Howard H. Russell at the First Methodist Episcopal Church, Wellsville, New York, June 7, 1904; Superintendent's Report, 1902, Russell Papers.

25. Ostrander, *Prohibition Movement in California,* p. 85; Kaylor, "Prohibition Movement in Pennsylvania," vol. 2, p. 395.

26. *American Issue,* April 17, November 27, 1903.

27. *ASL Proceedings, 1904,* pp. 29, 47, 48.

28. *ASL Proceedings, 1903,* pp. 40-41; *American Issue,* December 25, 1903; *ASL Proceedings, 1904,* p. 43.

29. See, for example, H. H. Russell Diary, entries for October 5-14, 1897, February 5, 1901; H. H. Russell to Lillian D. Russell, August 3, 1895, July 28, 1901, May 13, 1903; all in Russell Papers.

30. H. H. Russell Diary, entries for September 7 and 12, 1897, and January 14, and April 30, 1903; "John D. Rockefeller Approves the League in September 1894," draft chapter of unpublished autobiography; all in Russell Papers.

31. Robert E. Wenger, "The Anti-Saloon League in Nebraska Politics, 1898-1910," *Nebraska History* 52 (Fall 1971): 279.

32. Annual Report, 1902; H. H. Russell to Lillian D. Russell, July 28, 1901; both in Russell Papers.

33. *ASL Proceedings, 1903*, pp. 24-25.

34. *American Issue*, November 24, 1905.

35. John E. Caswell, "The Prohibition Movement in Oregon, Part 2, 1904-1915," *Oregon Historical Quarterly* 40 (1939): 68.

36. Justin Steuart, *Wayne Wheeler, Dry Boss* (New York, 1928), p. 60; *American Issue*, April 26, 1901, April 17, July 31, November 27, December 25, 1903; *ASL Proceedings, 1904*, pp. 29, 97; W. M. Burke, "The Anti-Saloon League as a Political Force," *Annals of the American Academy* 32 (November 1908): 500. For the period 1893-1913, clergymen comprised 60 percent of the entire League leadership. See also *ASL Proceedings, 1901*, pp. 5-6.

37. These figures, computed from lists of leaders in the various *ASL Proceedings* for every year but 1902 and from David L. Colvin, *Prohibition in the United States: A History of the Prohibition Party and of the Prohibition Movement* (New York, 1926), pp. 643-657, include only changes in established positions and not new entries, thus discounting to some degree the factor of rapid Anti-Saloon League expansion. See also A. E. Carhart's recital of leadership changes and difficulties in *Partial Life Story*, pp. 44, 48, 49, 50-51; *American Issue*, August 7, 1903; *Northwestern Mail*, August 7, 1903.

38. *American Issue*, January, 1899, July 17, August 21, 1903, February 19, 1904. J. C. Jackson was born on a farm near Lancaster, Ohio, in 1847. After service in the Civil War he earned a bachelor's degree from Ohio University, Athens, then entered the Methodist ministry in 1874. He served pastorates in Ohio, Wisconsin, and New Jersey before joining the Anti-Saloon League in Ohio in 1897, immediately becoming editor of its journal. Jackson died in 1909. Cherrington et al., eds., *Standard Encyclopedia*, vol. 3, pp. 1371-1372.

39. *American Issue*, March, 1899, January 9, December 11, 1903, December 23, 1904.

40. H. H. Russell to Lillian D. Russell, December 7, 1893, June 28, 1896, February 9, 1898, Russell Papers.

41. H. H. Russell to Lillian D. Russell, July 4, 1894, Russell Papers.

42. G. C. Gray to H. H. Russell, September 19, 1902, Russell Papers.

43. *American Issue*, November, 1899.

44. Ibid., August 29, 1902.

45. Ibid., February 22, 1901, March 14, 1902.

46. Ibid., November 30, 1900. See also *Facts and Figures* (Menomonee Falls, Wis.), January 1901.

47. Virginius Dabney, *Dry Messiah: The Life of Bishop Cannon* (New York, 1949), pp. 56, 57; *American Issue,* July 5, 1901, January 17, 1902; *ASL Proceedings, 1901,* p. 68.

48. Steuart, *Wheeler,* p. 188.

49. *ASL Proceedings, 3d Annual Convention 1898,* p. ii; *ASL Proceedings, 4th Annual Convention, 1898,* p. ii; *ASL Proceedings, 1900,* p. ii.

50. Cherrington, *History of the Anti-Saloon League,* p. 61.

51. *New Voice,* February 2, 1905.

52. *ASL Proceedings, 4th Annual Convention, 1898,* p. 5.

53. *American Issue,* December 21, 1900, March 14, 28, September 19, 1902, March 27, September 4, 1903, February 26, 1904.

54. Ibid., July 19, 1901.

55. Ibid., August 2, 1901. Note the similarity of this analysis to that of the single-issue wing of the Prohibition party, which sought to unite conservative northern and southern church voters by dropping platform planks repellent to either.

56. Ibid., December 28, 1900, August 2, September 27, 1901; *ASL Proceedings, 1903,* pp. 21-22; *Northwestern Mail,* August 7, 1903.

57. *ASL Proceedings, 3d Annual Convention, 1898,* p. 24; *Facts and Figures,* July 1901; *American Issue,* April 1900, August 9, 1901, August 12, 1904; Norman H. Dohn, "The History of the Anti-Saloon League" (Ph.D. dissertation, Ohio State University, 1959), p. 75.

58. *American Issue,* May 27, June 17, 1904; Odegard, *Pressure Politics,* pp. 5, 18.

59. *American Issue,* November 23, December 28, 1900, July 19, August 9, 1901, February 14, 28, March 14, 21, April 25, October 17, 1902, September 25, November 20, 1903, March 4, August 12, 1904.

60. Ibid., November 30, 1900, January 25, 1901, March 18, 1904.

61. Dohn, "History of the Anti-Saloon League," pp. 91-92; *American Issue,* December, 1899, October 9, 30, 1903; Charles H. Hopkins, *The Rise of the Social Gospel in American Protestantism, 1865-1915* (New Haven, 1940), p. 158.

62. *American Issue,* June 26, 1903.

63. Ibid., December 19, 1902, July 31, 1903.

64. See, for example, *New Voice,* February 19, 1903.

65. *American Issue,* November 30, 1900, February 21, May 16, August 1, 1902, February 27, March 6, June 12, August 7, 1903, August 5, 1904. In Wisconsin the League employed workers able to speak the German and Scandinavian languages, but I have found no evidence of League workers in any state able to speak any of the southern European tongues. *Northwestern Mail,* January 1, November 11, 1904, February 10, 1905; Wenger, "Anti-Saloon League in Nebraska Politics," p. 276.

66. *American Issue,* June 5, 1903.

67. Ibid., June 26, 1903; see also October 23, 1903.

68. Ibid., June 10, 1904.

69. Ibid., December 20, 1901, June 13, September 19, 1902.

70. Pearson and Hendricks, *Liquor and Anti-Liquor in Virginia*, p. 230; Whitener, *Prohibition in North Carolina*, pp. 133, 134; Sellers, *Prohibition Movement in Alabama*, pp. 101-102.

71. *American Issue*, October 24, December 9, 26, 1902.

72. Ibid., February, November 16, 1900, December 1, 1905; *ASL Proceedings, 1901*, pp. 27-28.

73. *ASL Proceedings, 3d Annual Convention, 1898*, p. 26; *American Issue*, October 9, 1903, March 25, 1904.

74. Joseph R. Gusfield, *Symbolic Crusade: Status Politics and the American Temperance Movement* (Urbana, Ill., 1963), p. 111.

75. Apparent liquor consumption reached its post-Civil War peak during the years 1906-1915. Raymond G. McCarthy, ed., *Drinking and Intoxication: Selected Readings in Social Attitudes and Controls* (New Haven, 1959), p. 180.

76. Gilman M. Ostrander, *Prohibition Movement in California*, p. 92.

77. *American Issue*, January, 1899, November 2, 1900, October 18, 1901, May 2, October 17, 1902, May 20, 1904; Dohn, "History of the Anti-Saloon League," pp. 131-132.

78. *American Issue*, August, 1899, December 26, 1902, August 19, October 7, 1904.

79. See, for example, *American Issue*, April, October, November 23, 1900, July-September 1901; *Northwestern Mail*, August 29, 1901.

80. *American Issue*, June, July, 1899, September 26, 1902.

81. Ibid., March, November 2, 1900, October 4, 1901.

82. *The Voice*, July 7, August 4, 1898; *New Voice*, July 22, 1899, March 21, 1901; *American Issue*, April, August, 1899, August 23, 1901.

83. *American Issue*, March 15, December 27, 1901, October 10, November 28, 1902, January 30, 1903, November 4, 1904; *New Voice*, July 3, 1902.

84. *ASL Proceedings, 1902*, p. xxi; *ASL Proceedings, 1904*, pp. 21-22, 41; *American Issue*, January 2, February 13, March 6, August 28, November 20, 1903; August 19, November 25, 1904, April 7, May 5, 1905; *New Voice*, November 24, 1904.

7

Cooperation and conflict, 1902-1908

*T*he history of the Prohibition party in the years after 1896 is the story of a political movement in decline. After 1902 Prohibitionists' responses to decline filled out the patterns which had appeared following the split of 1896. Following the lead of John G. Woolley, many party men now devoted as much energy to building up the Anti-Saloon League as they did to attempts at rejuvenating their old organization. Those who found the League an unsatisfactory vehicle for prohibition reform offered no credible alternative, for their social outlook had become virtually indistinguishable from that held by Woolley and the League leadership. As long as they managed to maintain the Prohibition party, it would present an alternative to the League whose plausibility would vary only in inverse proportion to the League's success.

COOPERATION, 1902-1903

Cooperation between party men and the Anti-Saloon League was widespread during 1902-1903. Party leaders continued to serve on both the Board of Direction and the National Executive Committee of the League.[1] Party leaders in California, Nebraska, and New York accepted leadership positions in the leagues of their states. In Mississippi, Ohio, Wisconsin, Oregon, and Illinois, cooperation between party and League went forward on a more or less official basis. Throughout the Prohibition party, the need for success seemed to be undermining doctrinaire insistence upon a no-compromise policy. Despite occasional attacks upon the League from the party ranks, in practice, cooperation gained during these years.[2] The most important hold-out from this policy was the *New Voice*, from whose editorial chair William P. F. Ferguson continued to denounce the League. By September 1902, however, John G. Woolley had forced Ferguson out.[3]

On September 18 Woolley announced his personal assumption of control over the *New Voice* editorial pen and inaugurated a new policy of cooperation. Before, party spokesmen had argued that the general sentiment of the country was in favor of prohibition and that consequently only the failure of Prohibitionists to strike the proper chord in their appeals had prevented Americans from expressing their true hostility to the liquor traffic. Now, Woolley argued that the prohibition forces were indeed on the right track and moreover were prevented by no significant differences from achieving unity of action, while the general population still remained unconvinced of the true value of the reform. Harmonious cooperation among the like-minded was now both the goal and the guarantee of success. It was time to unite the moral elements. "It is spring," Woolley said during January, "in the Great Reform."[4]

In November 1902 Woolley modified his plea for cooperation with insistence upon the party's leadership of the movement. But before then he had formulated a conception of the party's leadership role which could be used to rationalize its abdication of active political leadership.[5] Actually, this conception was no more than the old showcase image of the party as the container and protector of moral virtue. Up to this point it had functioned only as a part of the appeal to Christian voters; now Woolley began to use it to justify a cooperative policy which amounted to surrendering the realm of political activity to the League. In December Woolley hinted at the role he would now begin to assign the party by delineating what the League could not accomplish:

> The Anti-saloon league has and can have on its present thesis
> no great inspirational value. It never did and never will set
> a patriotic heart pounding the martyr blood into the brain un-
> til it fairly staggered. It never did and never will bring an audi-
> ence to its feet in an instant reaching as with one right hand
> for the gullet of the liquor traffic.[6]

The superheated rhetoric concealed, and perhaps was meant to compensate for, the essentially passive nonpolitical role left for the party: providing "inspirational value."

Woolley took hold of the party's rationale in January 1903. Justifying the existence of the party, he defined its function as the badge of virtue: "If an honest youth at his majority decide to cast his lot for *morality*—straight, uncompromising, unremitting, unequivocally—he has to join the Prohibition party." The "honest youth" could not, however, expect his vote to have any other than symbolic effect: "It is the strong, comprehensive extreme position that marks leadership. The compromisers and traders and diplomatists and politicians do most of the business of the world, but they do not *lead.*"[7] One month later he announced that "THE PURPOSE OF THIS NEWSPAPER IS TO KEEP CALLING ATTENTION TO PERSONAL IDEALS IN POLITICAL LIFE."[8] Woolley then gave the rationale its final wrench when he asserted that "the Prohibition party battle argument is dangerous to a local skirmish. It is too big."[9] In November he followed the new doctrine by urging Prohibitionists who would deliver sermons on Temperance Sunday to refrain from preaching party doctrine so as not to alienate those in sympathy with the cause but not the party.[10]

Woolley's finished statement of the new nonpolitical role of the Prohibition party came in an editorial early in 1904. "Primarily," he said, the party's "work is not to carry Prohibition, but to acknowledge and proclaim the long looked for and talked of type of legislation whose kernel and motive power shall be *righteousness,* and thus inaugurate an era which in theory, nature and logic of it will involve the Prohibition of organized evil as naturally as an apple tree bears apples." This did not, however, mean that the party should work for righteous legislation. That department belonged exclusively to the Anti-Saloon League, for Prohibitionists' righteous extremism precluded the compromises necessary to legislative activity. Nor was normal political activity appropriate, for by winning a large vote for the Prohibition party "without . . . an adoption [by the voters] of cleanness and conscience and conviction as the basis of suffrage, . . . we should be as bad off as we are now,—worse off by far than we are now." "Absolutely all that we can do as a party," Woolley concluded, is to *"move up the accent from the local to general, from material to moral, from partizan to CHRISTIAN."*[11]

John G. Woolley thus formulated a perfect theory to match the practice of party Prohibitionists during this period. They could now cooperate as individuals in all the expedient compromises of the League's work while collectively maintaining their stand on the loftiest ground of principle.

CONFLICT, 1904-1905

In 1903 and 1904 John G. Woolley advocated cooperation with the Anti-Saloon League, defining the party as the moral vanguard of the prohibition movement in order to justify its relegation to the political rear. In 1903 an opposition faction began to form around William P. F. Ferguson, the party's most vigorous and eloquent opponent of the Anti-Saloon League. Ferguson, supported by National Chairman O. W. Stewart, conducted his vendetta against Woolley through the pages of *The Citizen,* a new party organ published in the model dry community of Harriman, Tennessee. Woolley was supported throughout the conflict by William E. Johnson, managing editor of the *New Voice.*

Ferguson made *The Citizen* into the kind of forum for attacks upon the Anti-Saloon League which the *New Voice* had provided under his editorship from 1899 to 1902. For the most part, these attacks followed well-charted paths, denying the League's claims of success and denouncing it as an obstacle to the party's triumph.[12] Ferguson also began a retreat from his earlier sanction of local-option laws and now contended that support of halfway measures was dangerous insofar as it impeded party progress.[13]

Ferguson combined his attacks on the Anti-Saloon League with an attempt to find a political role for the party apart from the passive banner-bearing visualized by Woolley. Ferguson, however, had been one of the single-issue men of 1896 and had helped Woolley during 1899-1902 to turn the party away from the hostility toward counting-house and church and the openness toward outcasts which had been the most significant difference between party and League. Unwilling to revive the divisions of the early nineties by advising a return to serious social criticism, Ferguson found his usually tight arguments becoming flabby and labored under the strain of trying to find a political role for a political failure.[14]

Not all of Woolley's opponents shared Ferguson's difficulty. In February 1903 Dan R. Sheen, a Peoria, Illinois, lawyer, attempted to revive broad-gauge sentiment and direct it into an effort to align the party once again with critics of the dominant institutions of American society. In a provocative speech delivered before a conference of Illinois Prohibitionists, Sheen resurrected the party's pre-1896 analysis of the situation. He noted that "years ago," 3,000,000 voters had favored prohibition, but that the party had never been able to attract as much as one-tenth of this number: "This fact proves that there is something wrong with Prohibitionists, or with their party." For Sheen, what was wrong

was the single-issue platform. Attacking it, he neatly applied to the
Prohibition party the same logic used against the major parties concerning the liquor traffic, that silence in the face of wrong constituted acquiescence in the existence of that wrong. If the party acknowledged the
existence of wrongs other than those of the liquor traffic (and it did),
did its silence square with its beliefs?[15]

"Nor is it striving," Sheen said of the party, "for supremacy in the
state. It may be striving to get ready to strive, but its present policy
is to establish the glory of the church, and to create individual righteousness, rather than to promote public weal and governmental justice by
deposing the party in power." Not only was the present goal a task impossible for a political party, it was also the wrong task for a reform party.
"Temperance will be fought out on the field of reason, justice and humanity, instead of upon biblical grounds in the churches." The true constituency for the party, Sheen concluded, did not consist of those whose
only quarrel with the saloon was a moral one. "Go out into the high-
ways, and byways, and among the hedges," he directed, "and do as
Christ did[:] turn from the phylacteried people who thank God that
they are not as other men are, and ask the poor to help you get the
power to help them." Unlike Ferguson, Sheen had presented a real
alternative to the party's current policy, and the Prohibitionists who
heard him realized it. "The discussion on Mr. Sheen's address," the
New Voice reported, "was the most interesting feature of the whole
conference."[16]

Realizing the importance of Sheen's challenge, Woolley replied immediately through the *New Voice*. He must have felt that Sheen's ideas
commanded some support within the party, for he conceded that expansion of the platform in 1904 might be necessary. But Woolley refused
to accede to Sheen's basic demand that the party turn away from the
middle-class church voter. Woolley insisted, therefore, that nothing
be included in the platform which would violate the conscience of any
of its members. For example, the inclusion of a woman suffrage plank
would offend such men as the Texan J. B. Cranfill.[17] The chasm between
these two views of the party was evident when Woolley fell back three
weeks later upon his conception of the party as preacher. "The function
of such a party as ours," he claimed, "is logically and imperatively educational, and in the largest sense religious. The order of our legitimate aspi-
ration is moral independence, moral union, political power."[18]

Sheen soon became exasperated, as T. C. Richmond had in the platform debate of 1895-1896, by the self-satisfied intransigence of the single-issue spokesmen. Pleading for a woman suffrage plank, he raged, "Half of our people are disfranchised, and are helplessly seeing their husbands murdered, their homes destroyed, and their children beggared by a bribe-purchased, vote-established traffic, and this conscience party remains silent concerning the disfranchisement for fear of disturbing Mr. Cranfill's conscience!"[19] Single-issue men nevertheless continued to join Woolley in proclaiming their policy both a spiritual and a political success.[20]

State Prohibition party platforms in 1902 and 1904 showed how little support existed for the single-issue policy. Of eleven known state platforms in 1902, only four limited themselves to a prohibition plank; two others added only endorsement of woman suffrage; three went beyond prohibition and woman suffrage while declaring the former to be the dominant issue; and in Nebraska and California, Prohibitionists adopted broad platforms without apology, in California including a demand for public ownership of public utilities. Also in 1902, Oliver W. Stewart ran successfully for the Illinois legislature on a personal platform which included demands for the initiative and referendum, municipal ownership of public utilities, civil-service reform, and economy and consolidation in Chicago city government.[21]

In 1904 support for broad platforms increased. Of the thirteen known platforms adopted before the national convention met, only three held to the single issue; two others were broad but dominant-issue declarations; while platforms in eight states, including six of the party's eight best states in 1900, were uncompromisingly broad. In Illinois, Robert H. Patton, the delegate who had moved the adoption of the 1896 single-issue national platform, ran for governor on a broad platform.[22]

A close reading of these broad state platforms of 1904 indicates, however, that their adoption derived more from the mere frustration of failure with a single issue and from a recognition that the middle class would now tolerate strict measures for control of big business than from a willingness to forge an alliance with the lower-class groups who were hurt most by business rapacity. The Michigan plank on labor and capital, typical of the other four state planks on the same subject, "commended the enterprise of laboring men in organizing to protect their rights as against the unjust usurpation of capital, but condemned all interference with the rights of fellow laborers who do not choose to unite with them in their organizations."[23] While some state parties advocated equal suffrage upon the natural rights basis proclaimed by the national party in 1876 and 1892, others reverted to the national party position of the 1880s by declaring for educational qualifications for the franchise.[24]

Three weeks before the opening of the 1904 national convention, Sheen once again tried to place the party in the front rank of reform. Writing in the *New Voice,* Sheen proposed a thirteen-plank national platform which combined some of the most generous reforms of the Progressive period with avoidance of the intolerant and nativist impulses frequently associated with them. He broadened the woman suffrage demand to the principle that "no citizen should be discriminated against on account of race, sex, or color." He coupled support for national and international arbitration with a demand for the reduction of armies and navies. Unafraid to tackle economic issues, Sheen demanded government control of the issue and volume of currency, collective ownership of public utilities, abolition of trusts and combines, the fixing of reasonable interest rates, and an income tax. While he supported setting aside one day's rest each week, he did not insist that it be any particular day. Sheen argued for the abolition of "child-labor, the sweat-shop system, sale of convict labor, lynch law, and the inhuman torture of negroes suspected of crime." He was careful in his discussion of immigration to avoid restrictions based on nativism and advocated an open door for all but "known paupers, criminals, or lunatics." Finally, he proposed independence as soon as possible for America's new colonies and supported the popular election of "all important officers."[25]

Sheen's proposals pointed to a conception of the party different from that of the dominant group. He would broaden its thrust to include stands on economic and political issues; he would appeal to those outside the circle of native, white, primarily Protestant middle-class voters courted by the League and by the party since 1896. Like the broadgauge fusionists of the early 1890s, Sheen saw the Prohibition party as a potential bridge between middle-class and lower-class elements dissatisfied with the workings of American society. Since his ideas included all these factors, they have been accorded more importance here than they actually held in the minds of Prohibitionists in 1903 and 1904. The party debates in 1904 concerned not policies but personalities; for serious discussion of the party's role, Prohibitionists substituted a petty squabble among the ruling single-issue clique. Meaningful questions of platform, purpose, and policy toward the Anti-Saloon League became little more than weapons to be used by the factions in attempts to read their opponents out of the party.

The making of the national platform illustrated the deterioration of the party's willingness to take a stand on issues other than prohibition. The adoption of a broad platform of some sort was assured when John G. Woolley, the most influential single-issue leader, declared for a platform including opposition to colonialism and support for direct legislation, a stand which he took in order to secure the nomination of General Nelson A. Miles.[26] Most of the platform draft eventually adopted was the product of William P. F. Ferguson's pen. The remainder, added by Woolley's forces, included nothing which offended Ferguson or anyone else in the convention, judging from the enthusiastic response and unanimous approval which the document received.[27]

The platform was a masterful example of how to avoid controversy through a process of careful abstraction. It was obviously calculated to appeal to all Prohibitionists and to offend no one who shared their backgrounds and prejudices. For example, it was not even clear whether it was a single-issue, dominant issue, or broad-gauge platform. Of the seven planks, the first six concerned prohibition of the liquor traffic. The sixth declared "that there is . . . no other issue of equal importance before the American people today." The seventh plank conceded "that the intelligent [!] voters of the country may properly ask our attitude on other questions of public concern" and went on to make eleven statements in answer.[28]

On economic questions, the platform declared that the making of tariff schedules should be in the hands of an "omnipartisan commission" and managed to take everyone's side at once by advocating "the safeguarding of the people's rights by a rigid application of the principles of justice to all combinations and organizations of capital and labor." As the *New Voice* noted, this was "sufficiently general to meet the approval of J. Pierpont Morgan and Eugene V. Debs." Another statement demanded suffrage restricted by "mental and moral qualifications." This was clearly understood to mean the enfranchisement of educated women and the accompanying disfranchisement of poorly educated men and women, and thus endorsed the various literacy tests by which southern states were taking the vote from black citizens. With the exception of a demand for direct election of senators and an omnibus plank on divorce-law reform, "the final extirpation of polygamy," and prostitution, the rest of the platform either avoided firm positions by the use of qualifiers or took such lofty ground as to be meaningless. As the *New Voice* noted, "There certainly are no divisive issues in it."[29]

The main business of the convention, as in 1900, was not the making of a platform but the nomination of a presidential candidate. On March 31,

1904, Woolley had proposed the nomination of General Nelson A. Miles.[30] Apparently, Woolley hoped to capitalize upon the public standing that Miles had achieved through his criticism of adulterated army rations, his feud with President Roosevelt, and his opposition to colonialist policies. Woolley was also willing to endorse Miles if, as seemed possible, he was nominated by the Democrats.[31] Miles received support from many prominent Prohibitionists. The movement for Miles's nomination marked an important step in the formation of the warring factions which were to plague the party for nine years thereafter. The opposing faction, occupying what had formerly been Woolley's ground, claimed that the purity of the party would be defiled by the nomination of a non-Prohibitionist.[32]

In the midst of the convention maneuvers, Miles withdrew his name from consideration.[33] The two factions settled upon the Reverend Silas C. Swallow as the party's candidate, but the conflict left wounds on both sides.

Those wounds began bleeding profusely soon after the election when Woolley, through the *New Voice*, and Ferguson, through *The Citizen,* published spectacular charges against each other.[34] During the campaign, O. W. Stewart had secretly channelled over $13,000 in party funds to Ferguson in order to send *The Citizen* to 115,000 party supporters.[35] Woolley, enraged by what he considered "machine politics," had retaliated by sabotaging Stewart's campaign for reelection to the Illinois legislature.[36] The factional quarrel came to a head in December when the National Committee deposed Stewart from the national chairmanship and forced the resignation of the entire Executive Committee, which included antagonists from from both sides. In January, the reconstituted Executive Committee elected Charles R. Jones, a Woolley partisan, to the national chairmanship.[37]

This bitter, extended conflict had little to do with party policy. While Ferguson and others of his faction sought to discredit the *New Voice*'s party loyalty by pointing to Woolley's defense of cooperation with the League, their hostility probably derived more from personal rancor than from ideological or tactical differences. Even Ferguson's accusations of disloyalty were based more upon the alleged presence of non-Prohibitionists on the *New Voice*'s governing board than upon Woolley's cooperative policy.[38] From the other side, Johnson and Woolley rested their attacks for the most part upon moral grounds.[39]

The reason for this paucity of conflict over policy toward the League was simply the lack of significant difference between the two factions on the question. Woolley and Johnson, of course, spoke strongly throughout 1904 for cooperation and participation in local-option campaigns.[40] Ferguson continued to be an outspoken opponent of cooperation. He seemed, however, to have compromised his insistence upon the necessity of party enforcement by serving in 1903 as secretary of a nonpartisan enforcement agency in a dry Chicago suburb.[41] Dan R. Sheen, who participated in the anti-Miles movement and served as Stewart's attorney before the National Committee, had welcomed Anti-Saloon League support in his successful campaign for the Illinois legislature.[42] Perhaps the most important factor in keeping the cooperative policy out of the debate was Oliver W. Stewart's cooperation with the Illinois League, which had begun in 1902 and continued through 1904. In July 1904 Stewart was elected a vice-president of the Illinois Anti-Saloon League.[43]

An important result of the conflict was John G. Woolley's movement closer to the Anti-Saloon League. The signal came with his appearance as a featured speaker before the Anti-Saloon League national convention on November 17, 1904. There he proclaimed, "I have come to this convention on purpose to take off my hat to the Anti-Saloon League as the most sane, safe, and successful application of Prohibition doctrine the world has ever known."[44] The convention responded with a resolution giving thanks for the "rapidly growing spirit of fraternity among all temperance workers" and rejoicing especially in the cooperative attitude of the *New Voice.*[45]

The Reverend Henry A. Miner returned from the convention to Madison, Wisconsin, to write in the *Northwestern Mail* of the "growing harmony of spirit and work" between prohibitionists of party and League.[46] William P. F. Ferguson, however, used Woolley's speech to mount renewed attacks on both of his old enemies, Woolley and the League. He struck at the League by denying that it represented in fact an "application of Prohibition doctrine," and he renewed his charges of Woolley's disloyalty to the party. Woolley's speech, he raged, was "practically a surrender or an offer to surrender the Prohibition party's position—a running up of the white flag."[47]

POLARIZATION, 1905-1908

Disagreement over cooperation with the League had underlain the 1902 split between Woolley and Ferguson which represented the first crack in the coalition ruling the Prohibition party since 1899. Their dispute had divided the party by 1904, but the issue of cooperation had become a subsidiary theme in the largely personal conflict. After Woolley's endorsement of the League at its national convention in November 1904, the Anti-Saloon League became an obsessive concern for Prohibitionists as Ferguson made party integrity the spearhead of his attacks upon Woolley and the *New Voice*. The personalized conflict of 1904, even though it did not primarily concern party policy, ensured the party's survival by spawning a faction bitterly opposed to any action taken by John G. Woolley. When Woolley moved to the Anti-Saloon League, the only course left to his opponents was unceasing defense of the party, even as some of them bowed to the need for success and themselves flirted occasionally with the League.

By the end of March 1905, Woolley had become exhausted by the conflict and by his efforts in behalf of an abortive merger between the *New Voice* and *American Issue*. On his doctor's advice, he left on a year-long recuperative trip to New Zealand. Meanwhile, Samuel Dickie and A. A. Stevens rescued the *New Voice* from its financial difficulties, which had been aggravated by Woolley's premature investment in new equipment to effect the proposed merger. They took over ultimate control of the paper in Woolley's absence, but left William E. Johnson in editorial charge.[48]

Undismayed by the failure of the proposed merger of the papers, Johnson continued Woolley's cooperative policy. His arguments followed the same lines that Woolley had laid down in an editorial in January 1905: "Now the Prohibition movement is a great church on the frontier of Christian democracy. The party is preacher. . . . The League is a hustling business man who 'belongs.' " Both organizations performed necessary functions in the work of the movement; they should provide mutual support and refrain from antagonizing each other in the progress toward their common goal.[49]

An impressive number of party leaders shared the *New Voice*'s cooperative attitude toward the League. All four of its living presidential nominees supported cooperation.[50] John P. St. John invoked his old cry of aiding "the common people" but failed to show how cooperation with the League could accomplish such an end.[51] State Chairmen in eight states, as well as National Chairman Jones, either expressed themselves in favor of cooperation or actively worked in its behalf during 1904-1908.[52] In 1906 Samuel Dickie, while confessing that he had "not the strongest faith in its method of work," advocated cooperation with the

League when it moved toward suppression of the liquor traffic.[53] Cooperation conferences with League workers were held in Iowa (1905), California (1905), Indiana (1908), and Texas (1908).[54] After his return from New Zealand in 1906, Woolley advocated withdrawal of Prohibition party candidates in order to endorse major-party men sympathetic to prohibition, and in Maryland (1903), Illinois (1905), Iowa (1906), Pennsylvania (1906), and Massachusetts (1906), Prohibitionists demonstrated their willingness to do so, with indifferent success.[55] Even Oliver W. Stewart and Ferguson admitted in 1905 that they could conceive of a situation in which the Prohibition party could unite with the national Democratic party if its southern, prohibitionist wing should gain control.[56] All this openness toward cooperation stemmed more from the utter bleakness of the Prohibition party's future than from the demonstrated triumph of the League. Woolley himself revealed this fact implicitly in 1906 when he admitted that despite the League's activity, "it is true that enforcement limps somewhat and that the total number of saloons is not much, if any, diminished."[57] There was, however, no choice. "The Prohibition party is no longer the Prohibition movement, or even a major part of it."[58]

For Woolley, the League's slow progress seemed less important than the party's failure. Although Ferguson and others hostile to Woolley denounced the League as a failure, the point to which they invariably returned in their denunciations was its success in damaging the Prohibition party. *The Citizen* had collapsed in 1905, but by November 1907, Ferguson had built from its ruins and those of several other party papers a new Prohibition weekly which he called the *National Prohibitionist*. The *New Voice* had gone under late in 1906, and Ferguson's new paper served as the party's national organ from 1907 to 1911. Throughout this period, Ferguson maintained a consistent and vociferous antagonism toward the Anti-Saloon League and its principal weapon, local option.[59]

Thus, the party now existed primarily as a haven for those who, for one reason or another, could not agree to accept the League. While this function left it with little significance outside the prohibition movement, within the movement the party still represented a threat to League supremacy, especially at moments when the League's claims of success began to appear illusory. The nature of the threat was illustrated by the career of the Reverend Michael J. Fanning, who had been a professional prohibition worker since the 1880s. In 1899 Fanning had abandoned the party for the League and immediately secured appointment as superintendent of the New Hampshire organization.[60] The League regarded

his work there as "very successful," but in 1902 he resigned to work for
the New York Anti-Saloon League. He then became superintendent of the
Massachusetts League.[61] After three years in that position, he worked
for a short time as a field secretary for the national League. Finally,
deciding that the League's method was unavailing, Fanning left League
work altogether and by 1906 he was back with the Prohibition party,
denouncing the League for its lack of success.[62] Here again was the pattern—acceptance and then rejection of the League—which had first appeared
in the earliest days of relationships between Prohibitionists and the Anti-
Saloon League.

The most severe test of party prohibitionists' willingness to cooperate
with the Anti-Saloon League came in Ohio in 1905. The League in Ohio
supported the Democratic nominee, James Pattison, in order to punish
the Republican Governor Myron T. Herrick, who had personally emasculated
the League's local-option bill in 1904. Ohio Prohibitionists had been drawing
gradually nearer to the League. They were thus torn between the need
to maintain their party and the desire to present a unified front of the
temperance forces against Herrick. After a heated convention debate,
they produced a compromise which probably pleased no one. Having
failed to secure from Pattison sufficiently strong assurance of his hostility to the saloon, they nominated their own gubernatorial candidate,
Aaron S. Watkins, who had been noted for his cooperation with the Anti-
Saloon League.[63] They declared their loyalty to prohibition and to their
party, but also advocated cooperation at all levels with other organizations. They dodged issues other than prohibition by advocating the use
of the initiative and referendum to decide questions such as the granting
of public franchises and municipal ownership of public utilities or natural
monopolies, and promised the submission of a woman-suffrage constitutional amendment to the states.[64]

The Ohio Prohibitionists reflected accurately both the confusion and
the growing conservatism of the national party. As their sense of failure
became more and more acute, Prohibitionists drew further away from
the commitment to social change which had marked their party before
1896. The same influences that nourished the League and turned it toward
an exclusive reliance upon an insecure middle class were operating on the
party, and the results were similar. Failure gave rise to pessimism; pessimism
encouraged withdrawal from exposed positions; and its hostility toward
established institutions represented the Prohibition party's most exposed
position.

Hostility toward the churches, which had been a distinctly minor theme in the party press during 1896-1902, virtually disappeared after 1902. It was replaced by frequent appeals to the churches, unaccompanied for the most part by threats of withdrawals or predictions of ecclesiastical debility.[65] Opposition to the major parties became less strident and less automatic as Prohibitionists more and more often left blank places on their tickets in favor of major-party candidates or cooperated with old-party men through the Anti-Saloon League.[66] A diffused hostility toward the economic system remained, but it was accompanied by no willingness to ally with other critics to effect changes. Instead, Prohibitionists clung ever more tightly to their places in the middle class and sought to build walls rather than bridges between themselves and those below them.

The need to defend the middle class, a need that lay at the center of these changes, was expressed in a speech in 1906 by a Pennsylvanian who had been a single-issue leader at the 1896 convention. He pointed to the evils of big business (who could avoid them in 1906?), but saw as their most serious result the impending destruction of "the great middle class of the comfortably fixed." He proposed a "paternalism" which amounted, however, only to "rigid investigation and control by government with publicity of their conduct" of "at least the public utility corporations." The object was to guarantee "a fair chance for all." The agent of such a policy would of course be the Prohibition party, which had distinguished itself since its founding by preserving "the thought of political virtue," much as "the monasteries of old" had "safely locked and kept the grain of learning and piety, while the dark ages of sin, vice and ignorance stalked abroad."[67]

Other Prohibitionist spokesmen also sought to identify themselves with the middle class and to claim for it a special virtue or intelligence.[68] Henry A. Miner began to refer to beer as "a coarse, plebeian beverage."[69] Presidential candidate Eugene W. Chafin claimed in 1908 that "we represent more thoroughly than any other political party the Christian conscience, the intelligence, the morality and the business interests."[70] A Prohibitionist minister referred to class, not color, when he asserted, "Prohibitionists do not believe that either vicious men or women have any right to vote and if we make any deliverance on the franchise it ought to be in favor of the disfranchisement of ignorant and vicious men and of the enfranchisement of intelligent and worthy women."[71] The Prohibition national platform of 1904 verified this claim, and the 1908 platform followed suit, declaring for "legislation basing suffrage only upon intelligence and

ability to read and write the English language."[72] Prohibition parties in
at least eleven states adopted similar suffrage planks between 1904 and
1908.[73] In 1908, Ferguson linked the claim to special virtue with approval
of elitist, conservative reform: "We must all agree (1) that if the present
order is right, society ought intelligently and unitedly to rally itself for
its preservation; (2) if a change ought to come, the brain power and educated ability of the world ought to so carry itself that it shall be in position
to direct the change."[74]

While some Prohibitionists, like Sheen and Ferguson, refused to blame
the immigrant for America's troubles, others, like A. A. Hopkins and
Henry A. Miner, screamed of "foreign conquest" and urged support for
educational restrictions upon immigration.[75] The abolitionist tradition
continued to survive in Prohibitionist denunciations of lynchings, and
the high point of the 1908 campaign occurred when presidential candidate Chafin, speaking in Springfield, Illinois, risked his life to save a black
man from a lynching mob.[76] Yet even here a shift was apparent. As John
G. Woolley drew closer to the Anti-Saloon League, he became the most
obvious offender against the antislavery tradition. In 1904 he published
the only justification for lynching I have found in Prohibition party papers
when he claimed that the lynching of a black man in Springfield, Ohio,
meted out the justice that would probably have been unrealized if a
clever criminal lawyer had been allowed to secure his acquittal through
"cunning expedients." "*Every man in town knew he was guilty,*" Woolley
asserted.[77]

The old friendliness toward socialism still survived in the party, as
did a willingness among former broad-gaugers at least to support major-
party politicians identified as "Progressives."[78] Chafin's 1908 invocation
of identity with the business interests, however, seemed to represent more
accurately the prevailing orientation of party attitudes.[79] The 1912 national platform provided the party's classic statement of its position: "We
favor . . . absolute protection of the rights of labor, without impairment
of the rights of capital."[80]

The continuing control of the Prohibition party by those friendly to
business and the churches was reflected in two incidents in 1905 and
1906. During Woolley's absence from the country after March 1905,
William E. Johnson assumed editorial direction of the *New Voice,*
under the ultimate control of Samuel Dickie and A. A. Stevens. On
April 13, 1905, Johnson placed the union label on the *New Voice*'s masthead for the first time in its history and wrote a notice of the fact which

left no doubt that he was responsible for conversion to a union printing shop.[81] Apparently, some Prohibitionists protested the move vehemently, and Johnson, never one to avoid controversy, replied with the same vigor which he had shown in the less ideological intraparty debate of the previous year. Characterizing his detractors as "obese loafers, who live and feed on money earned or stolen by somebody else," Johnson unhesitatingly and uncompromisingly defended labor, claimed identity between the ultimate goals of Socialists and Prohibitionists, and even pointed to recent grand-jury indictments against leading capitalists, "trust magnates who were also leading lights in the church."[82] The conflict culminated in a published debate over labor unions between Johnson and James B. Cranfill at the end of August 1905.[83] On September 14 the union label disappeared without explanation from the *New Voice*'s masthead, and in November Dickie and Stevens fired Johnson because of his pro-union position, replacing him with George M. Hammell of Cincinnati.[84]

The choice of Hammell was unfortunate for Dickie and Stevens, for he turned out to share Johnson's sympathy for the working class and socialism. He also revealed an antipathy toward the Anti-Saloon League which Johnson had lacked. The *New Voice*'s first issue under Hammell's editorship dropped from the masthead the Anti-Saloon League motto which had headed it since 1905. Hammell's opposition to the League apparently derived from his personal experience with the League's 1905 campaign in Ohio. He criticized it for endorsing the Democrat Pattison rather than the Prohibition party gubernatorial candidate, and he questioned the good for the cause which the League claimed had resulted from its action.[85] Hammell soon proved to be just the sort of radical from whose clutches Dickie and Stevens had rescued the party in 1896. He published a letter suggesting that Prohibitionists withdraw from the churches and claimed that the goals of prohibition, socialism, and anarchism were the same.[86] In March 1906 Hammell proposed a party platform which advocated socialization of industrial life, support of artists by the state, a single tax, dissolution of the army and navy, abolition of prostitution through "the development of a social system which shall make it possible for a woman to secure honorable work in the service of the commonwealth on terms equal with those of man," and many other demands which must have horrified Dickie and Stevens.[87] "Business is hell," Hammell proclaimed.[88] Even worse, he began to print attacks on the Anti-Saloon League.[89] When Woolley returned in May 1906, he immediately fired Hammell, retracted the attack on the Anti-Saloon

League and Hammell's suggestion that anarchists blow up saloons, and returned the *New Voice* to the policy of cooperation with the Anti-Saloon League and inoffensiveness toward established institutions which it followed until its death in December 1906.[90] In 1907 Woolley accepted appointment as superintendent of the Anti-Saloon League in the Hawaiian Islands.[91]

The ease with which Woolley transferred his allegiance revealed how narrow the gap had become between the social outlooks of party and League. For the Prohibition party to cooperate fully with the League, however, two further developments were required: success in obtaining statewide prohibition by the nonpartisan method and a commitment by the League to the attainment of national prohibition. The way in which those conditions were fulfilled was to show the bankruptcy of the prohibition movement as a force for reform in anyone's interests but its own.

James H. Timberlake has argued that prohibitionism and Progressivism had much in common. Middle-class prohibitionists and Progressives shared a belief in moral law, a commitment to material progress, faith in science, opposition to the corrupting influence of plutocracy, humanitarian impulses, and a desire to uplift the lower classes.[92] Timberlake draws these conclusions from an examination of the prohibitionists' ideology as it was revealed in the arguments prohibitionists directed toward those outside their movement. Analysis of what prohibitionists said and did to one another shows that Timberlake's conclusions form only part of the picture of prohibition and Progressivism, and a misleading part at that.

Our picture of Progressivism itself has changed recently as scholars have looked beyond what the Progressives said to what they actually did. The most radical advocates of social change were to be found, of course, not among middle-class Progressives but in the Socialist Party and the Industrial Workers of the World. And a good many businessmen supported reform.[93] In fact, the plutocracy whose corrupting influence was supposedly curbed turns out to have been the moving force behind many Progressive reforms.[94] Somewhere between Big Bill Haywood and George Perkins stood the middle-class Progressives, a diverse group and ineffectual even in some of their most celebrated accomplisments.[95] Why was it that the business magnates, and not they, dominated the actual reforms of the Progressive era?

The crucial question in defining middle-class Progressivism, as well as Progressivism in general, is not whether Progressives advocated social change, but what sort of change they worked for, and got. Who was to benefit in fact? All Progressives, for example, wanted humanitarian measures to uplift the lower classes. The National Civic Federation wanted the state to provide workmen's compensation—so that workers could no longer hold employers responsible for industrial accidents.[96] Municipal reformers wanted more efficient city governments—run by municipal reformers and other rising professionals.[97] Railroad reformers in Wisconsin wanted regulation—to serve the interests of Milwaukee grain merchants.[98] Even the big meat-packers wanted state inspection—to facilitate penetration of European markets.[99] Robert Moses, in many ways an archetypal Progressive reformer, built hundreds of parks and miles of parkways—but did everything he could to prevent the lower orders, especially blacks and Puerto Ricans, from using them.[100] Obviously, any analysis of reformers based upon their public rationale is likely to be biased in favor of the reformers' own descriptions of their actions.

What then do the actions and private arguments of the prohibitionists tell us about their Progressivism? As we have seen, prohibitionists in the 1890s realized that the composition of their movement and the constituency to which they chose to appeal had a profound influence upon their movement's public stance and ideology. The debates over platforms, fusion, and the churches were actually disputes over the proper prohibition constituency. Likewise, in the Progressive era prohibitionists thought first of the middle-class, dry, Protestant voters whom their decisions of a decade before had led them to accept as their primary source of support. Within this group there undoubtedly existed some support for radical measures, stemming from continuing and widespread dissatisfaction with the dominant institutions of American society. Much greater support existed for reforms which would give the appearance of change—to fulfill humanitarian impulses, curb the corrupting influence of plutocracy, and uplift the lower classes. Prohibitionists after 1900 thus made their platforms broad. But, given a choice between cooperating with their social inferiors to achieve these ends and joining with their social betters to ensure that change would not disturb their own stake in society, prohibitionists chose the more conservative course. They believed that their constituency would do the same. And so the party and the League tailored their reformism to suit their constituency, ignoring or suppressing the proposals of Sheen, Johnson, and Hammell for a rapprochement with the lower classes.

Thus, I have no quarrel with calling prohibitionists "Progressive."

Many of them, in both party and League, undoubtedly thought themselves so. The crucial point is the content of their Progressivism. It was a Progressivism which sought to restrain the lower orders without compensating them by a fair distribution of American affluence or even by a voice in running their society. Like most other Progressives, prohibitionists were profoundly conservative. That Progressives were conservative should not surprise us; it did not surprise them.[101]

NOTES

1. *Proceedings of the Seventh National Convention of the Anti-Saloon League of America* (hereafter referred to as *ASL Proceedings*), *1902*, pp. 4-13, 42-43; *ASL Proceedings, 1903*, pp. 38, 93-104; *American Issue*, December 25, 1903.

2. *ASL Proceedings, 1902*, p. 16; *American Issue*, May 10, June 21, 1901, September 19, 26, November 14, December 9, 26, 1902, January 23, February 6, 13, June 5, July 31, September 4, October 9, 23, November 13, 27, 1903, July 17, 1904; *New Voice*, December 11, 1902, February 26, March 12, December 31, 1903, February 11, April 14, 1904; *Northwestern Mail*, July 25, 1901, January 30, 1902, February 6, 20, March 6, 20, May 15, 29, July 3, November 6, 1903; John E. Caswell, "The Prohibition Movement in Oregon, Part 2, 1904-1915," *Oregon Historical Quarterly* 40 (1939): 65.

3. The story of the Woolley-Ferguson conflict and its aftermath may be found in: *The Citizen* (Harriman, Tenn.), November 2, December 28, 1904, January 4, 1905; *New Voice*, November 17, 1904, June 28, 1906; W. E. Johnson to H. H. Russell, August 12, 1931, Russell Papers, Michigan Historical Collections (MHC), Ann Arbor.

4. *New Voice*, September 18, October 30, November 6, 13, December 11, 1902, January 1, March 26, 1903.

5. Ibid., October 23, November 13, 1902.

6. Ibid., December 18, 1902.

7. Ibid., January 1, 1903.

8. Ibid., February 5, 1903.

9. Ibid., February 12, 1903.

10. Ibid., November 19, 1903.

11. Ibid., April 7, 1904.

12. *The Citizen*, March 2, April 6, May 11, 25, 1904.

13. Ibid., March 30, 1904.

14. Ibid., March 16, April 20, 1904.

15. Or would it be forced, as Sheen could have added, to avoid

complicity by making the untenable claim that prohibition would cure all social ills?

16. *New Voice*, February 12, 1903. Daniel R. Sheen was born in Peoria County in 1852 and made only one permanent move in his life, into the city of Peoria. After an education in the local public schools and business college, he studied law and was admitted to the bar in 1874. He was a Democrat until 1878 when he joined the Prohibition party, and in 1904 was elected as a Prohibitionist to the Illinois legislature with Anti-Saloon League support. I have found no indication of Sheen's religious affiliation. Ernest H. Cherrington et al., eds., *Standard Encyclopedia of the Alcohol Problem*, 6 vols. (Westerville, Ohio, 1924-30), vol. 5, p. 2429.

17. *New Voice*, February 19, 1903. Woolley seemed to think that planks advocating direct legislation, popular election of Senators, and international arbitration were "getting pretty clear as . . . conscience questions."

18. Ibid., March 12, 1903.

19. Ibid., March 12, 1903.

20. Ibid., February 19, March 19, April 9, 1903.

21. Ibid., July 10-October 2, 1902.

22. Ibid., April 14-June 23, 1904.

23. Ibid., June 9, 1904.

24. Ibid., June 9, July 7, 1904.

25. Ibid., June 9, 1904.

26. Ibid., June 23, 1904.

27. *The Citizen*, July 6, 13, 1904; *New Voice*, July 7, 1904.

28. The text of the platform is printed in *New Voice*, July 7, 1904.

29. *New Voice*, July 7, 1904; Elkhorn (Wis.) *Blade*, July 5, 1904.

30. *New Voice*, March 31, 1904. I have been unable to locate any evidence from the general's side bearing on Prohibitionist attempts to nominate Miles. See Virginia W. Johnson, *The Unregimented General: A Biography of Nelson A. Miles* (Boston, 1962), and Newton F. Tolman, *The Search for General Miles* (New York, 1968).

31. *New Voice*, May 5, 1904.

32. See *The Citizen*, March 23-June 29, 1904.

33. Whether his action was in response to the squabbling over his nomination or merely in recognition of the Prohibition party's futility, it is impossible to say.

34. *The Citizen*, November 2, 1904; *New Voice*, November 17, 1904.

35. *The Citizen*, November 2, December 28, 1904; Minutes of National Executive Committee (NXC) meeting, July 22, 1904, Indianapolis, "Minutes," vol. 1, pp. 118-119; Minutes of NXC meeting, October 15, 1904, "Minutes," vol. 1, p. 120.

36. *New Voice*, November 24, 1904.

37. Minutes of NC meeting, December 15-16, 1904, Chicago, "Minutes," vol. 1, pp. 121-127; *New Voice,* December 22, 1904; Minutes of NXC meeting, January 6, 1905, Chicago, "Minutes," vol. 1, pp. 134-135.
    38. *The Citizen,* November 2, December 7, 28, 1904. Accusations of disloyalty through cooperation with the Anti-Saloon League constituted a rarely used weapon in Ferguson's arsenal during the debate. Also, of twelve published letters from party leaders congratulating Ferguson on his purchase of *The Citizen,* which might have been expected to distinguish between Ferguson and Woolley on the grounds of party policy, only one did so. *The Citizen,* November 2 and 9, 1904.
    39. *New Voice,* July 7, 1904; *The Citizen,* May 25, June 1, 8, 15, October 12, November 16, 1904.
    40. See the *New Voice* throughout 1904, but especially August 25, September 22, December 22, 1904.
    41. *The Citizen,* January 27, 1904; *American Issue,* February 19, October 21, 1904.
    42. *American Issue,* November 18, 1904.
    43. Ibid., July 22, 1904.
    44. *New Voice,* November 24, 1904; *ASL Proceedings, 1904,* pp. 21-22.
    45. *ASL Proceedings, 1904,* p. 41.
    46. *Northwestern Mail,* November 18, 1904.
    47. *The Citizen,* December 7, 1904.
    48. *New Voice,* April 20, 1905; *American Issue,* April 7, 1905.
    49. *New Voice,* January 12, March 23-November 23, 1905.
    50. They were John P. St. John, Joshua Levering, Silas C. Swallow, and, of course, John G. Woolley. *New Voice,* August 9, 16, September 27, October 18, 1906.
    51. Ibid., October 18, 1906.
    52. *ASL Proceedings, 1904,* p. 117; *ASL Proceedings, 1905,* p. 99; *New Voice,* January 26, March 2, October 12, 19, 1905, May 10, August 16, October 18, 1906.
    53. *New Voice,* September 27, 1906.
    54. Ibid., October 12, 19, 1905; *American Issue,* Wisconsin Edition, January, March, 1908.
    55. *New Voice,* April 27, 1905, May 17, 31, July 5, 12, August 2, 1906; *The Citizen,* September 2, 1903.
    56. *The Citizen,* March 8, 1905.
    57. *New Voice,* August 30, 1906.
    58. Ibid., August 16, 1906.
    59. *The Citizen,* March 15, 1905; *National Prohibitionist,* March 12, 1908
    60. *Northwestern Mail,* June 15, 1899; *American Issue,* December 1899; *ASL Proceedings, 1900,* pp. 57-58.

61. *American Issue*, March 28, 1902; *New Voice*, December 18, 1902.
62. *New Voice*, April 27, 1905, June 7, August 9, 1906; *ASL Proceedings*, *1905*, p. 20.
63. *American Issue*, September 30, 1904, August 11, 1905.
64. *New Voice*, August 10, 1905; *American Issue*, August 11, 1905.
65. See, for example, *The Citizen*, December 16, 1903, January 6, March 9, 1904; Silas C. Swallow, "The Prohibition Party's Appeal," *The Independent* 57 (October 13, 1904): 834-835; *National Prohibitionist*, October 22, 1908.
66. See, for example, *New Voice*, November 23, 1905. Compare the proclamation of Ohio Prohibitionists in *New Voice*, August 16, 1906.
67. *New Voice*, March 15, 1906. For a similar version, see *New Voice*, January 21, 1904.
68. *Northwestern Mail*, July 31, 1903; *New Voice*, January 7, 1904; *National Prohibitionist*, January 23, 1908.
69. *Northwestern Mail*, October 16, 1903.
70. Eugene W. Chafin, "The Prohibition Party's Appeal," *The Independent* 65 (October 15, 1908): 882.
71. *New Voice*, March 12, 1903.
72. David L. Colvin, *Prohibition in the United States: A History of the Prohibition Party and of the Prohibition Movement* (New York, 1926), p. 338.
73. *New Voice*, March 31, 1904, March 9, August 17, 31, October 19, 1905, May 31, October 4, 1906; *National Prohibitionist*, June 4, 18, September 3, 10, 1908; *Chicago Record-Herald*, July 15, 1908.
74. *National Prohibitionist*, April 2, 1908.
75. Ibid., April 2, May 14, 21, 1908; A. A. Hopkins, *Profit and Loss in Man* (New York, 1908), pp. 234-235; *Northwestern Mail*, December 12, 1902.
76. *The Citizen*, March 16, 1904; *National Prohibitionist*, August 20, 1908.
77. *New Voice*, March 24, 1904. For Ferguson's denunciation of the same incident, see *The Citizen*, March 16, 1904.
78. *New Voice*, June 15, August 10, 17, 1905, October 4, 1906; *National Prohibitionist*, May 21, 1908.
79. E. W. Chafin, "The Prohibition Party's Appeal," *The Independent* 65 (October 15, 1908): 882; *The Citizen*, September 9, 30, 1903; *National Prohibitionist*, May 14, 1908.
80. Colvin, *Prohibition in the U.S.*, p. 350.
81. *New Voice*, April 13, 1905.
82. Ibid., August 3, 1905. Johnson himself, incidentally, was never noted for his slender build.
83. Ibid., August 31, 1905.

84. Ibid., November 23, 1905. Johnson's biographer, Frederick A. McKenzie, in *"Pussyfoot" Johnson, Crusader—Reformer—A Man among Men* (New York, 1920), pp. 63-64, probably repeated Johnson's version of the incident, tying the latter's departure from the paper to the conflict over labor unions, although he claimed the precipitant was an antiunion advertisement accepted by Dickie and Stevens. I have not been able to locate either the advertisement or the answering editorial which McKenzie claimed Johnson had written.

85. *New Voice,* December 7, 1905.

86. Ibid., February 1, 8, 1906.

87. Ibid., March 15, 1906.

88. Ibid., May 3, 1906.

89. Ibid., April 19, 1906.

90. Ibid., May 10, 1906.

91. *National Prohibitionist,* May 14, 1908.

92. James H. Timberlake, *Prohibition and the Progressive Movement, 1900-1920* (Cambridge, Mass., 1963), p. 2.

93. Robert H. Wiebe, *Businessmen and Reform: A Study of the Progressive Movement* (Cambridge, Mass., 1962).

94. Gabriel Kolko, *The Triumph of Conservatism: A Reinterpretation of American History, 1900-1916* (Glencoe, 1963); James Weinstein, *The Corporate Ideal in the Liberal State, 1900-1918* (Boston, 1968).

95. Diversity: Peter G. Filene, "An Obituary for the 'Progressive Movement,' " *American Quarterly* 22 (Spring 1970): 20-34; Lawrence W. Levine, *Defender of the Faith. William Jennings Bryan: The Last Decade, 1915-1925* (New York, 1965). Ineffectuality: Stanley P. Caine, *The Myth of a Progressive Reform: Railroad Regulation in Wisconsin, 1903-1910* (Madison, Wis., 1970).

96. Weinstein, *Corporate Ideal,* pp. 40-61.

97. Samuel P. Hays, "The Politics of Reform in Municipal Government in the Progressive Era," *Pacific Northwest Quarterly* 55 (October 1964): 157-169; Weinstein, *Corporate Ideal,* pp. 92-116.

98. Caine, *Myth of a Progressive Reform.*

99. Kolko, *Triumph of Conservatism,* pp. 99-108.

100. Robert A. Caro, *The Power Broker: Robert Moses and the Fall of New York* (New York, 1974).

101. *American Issue,* June 30, 1905.

8

The anti-saloon league succeeds, 1905-1909

The Anti-Saloon League won the leadership of the prohibition movement in 1905 and for the next four years held a solid grip on its position by successfully claiming credit for the upsurge of dry sentiment which appeared during that time. Adoption of statewide prohibition in five southern states and Oklahoma seemed adequate testimony to the power of its nonpartisan method. Endorsements by the Presbyterian General Assembly and the Congregational National Council in 1907 and by the Methodist Episcopal General Conference in 1908 served both to consolidate the League's position and to strengthen it for future battles.

Accompanying the League's success, however, were four factors which indicated that its triumph might yet turn out to be a hollow and short-lived one. First, while the southern victories had indeed been won through the nonpartisan method, in most cases they were not the work of prohibitionists affiliated with the national Anti-Saloon League. Since the League nevertheless claimed a share in their glory, it could also be held responsible for all the defeats of the prohibition cause, whether or not it was to blame. Second, church endorsements of the League were accompanied by a growing movement for a church temperance federation outside the League, a movement which represented an extremely dangerous threat from the quarter in which the nonpartisan organization was most vulnerable. Third, although the rate of turnover among state superintendents was reduced and stabilized during 1905-1909, personnel problems continued to plague the League. Fourth, the Prohibition party, which should have collapsed with the rise of the League, continued to survive and to present an alternative leadership should the League ever falter.

For these reasons the League closed the period of its greatest success to date not by sounding the call to advance but rather by correctly predicting a retreat.

TRIUMPH

On November 7, 1905, Howard Hyde Russell returned to his New York home to record in his diary, "Election Day," and added hopefully, "The Lord reigns in Ohio." At one o'clock the next morning, he received a telegram from National Superintendent Purley A. Baker confirming that the League had indeed won a crucial battle.[1] Since prohibitionists had long considered Ohio to be the main testing ground of the League's method, its victory over the antiprohibitionist Republican governor, Myron T. Herrick, was widely interpreted as a clear indication of the power which could be exercised by rigorous application of the nonpartisan balance-of-power tactic. As Purley A. Baker announced, "It marks an era in Anti-Saloon League history."[2] Even better for the League, the Democrat James Pattison, whom it had elected, died in office in June 1906, thus conveniently obviating the need for demonstration of beneficial legislative results accruing from his election.

One of the most significant dimensions of the League's victory for the middle-class constituency of the Prohibition movement lay in the composition of the opposing sides. Success followed the organization of middle-class church voters behind the temperance issue and against lower-class elements who were identified with the saloon and with urban machine boss George B. Cox of Cincinnati. This characteristic conflict of the Progressive era informed the League's rhetoric setting "good government" in opposition to "bossism."[3]

The League's activities in Virginia four years later showed that it had no antipathy to political machines as such. There, League officials welcomed alliance with Senator Thomas Martin's dominant machine, undeterred even by the fact that it included a significant portion of the state's liquor dealers.[4] The vital difference between the Virginia and Ohio situations seemed to be that the Virginia machine was based upon local politicians in both rural and urban areas rather than the urban lower class, the class which gave its support to Cox in Cincinnati.[5]

Whatever else might be said of it, the defeat of Herrick did constitute an unmistakable demonstration of the power of the Anti-Saloon League.

Unfortunately, the same could not be said of the passage of statewide prohibition laws in all of the six states which went dry during 1907-1909. In Oklahoma, which became a state in 1907 and had a prohibition clause in its constitution adopted by referendum, the League's claim to effectiveness was at least plausible, for its workers had been active there since 1898.[6] Likewise Tennessee, which went dry in 1909, had seen continuous League activity since 1898.[7]

Adoption of statewide prohibition in Georgia (1907), Alabama (1907), Mississippi (1908), and North Carolina (1908), however, served to illustrate the League's failure rather than its success in the South. In 1904 Baker had appointed the Reverend George W. Young as Assistant General Superintendent to organize in the South, but early in 1906 Young was "compelled," Baker reported, "owing to a lack of funds, to give up his work in the general field, and become Superintendent of the Kentucky League, very much to the detriment of our work in the southern states."[8] Even in 1904 and 1905, while Young was actively at work in the South, Baker could find no substantial progress in that region.[9] The Alabama League, established in 1904, directed the campaign for a local-option law which reached fruition early in 1907. But the ensuing movement for a statewide prohibition law originated among enthusiastic prohibitionists outside the League. Once the bandwagon got rolling, of course the League climbed on board.[10] The Superintendent of the Georgia League announced that his state had not been "fully organized" until January 1906. Yet in November of that year he admitted that "we have practically organized in 45 counties" out of 146.[11] Consequently, Baker omitted both Alabama and Georgia from his list of states considered "already ripe" for statewide prohibition by the end of 1906.[12] Nevertheless, both states would adopt statewide prohibition laws within the next year. Such a performance by leaders who normally leaped at every opportunity to claim results for their cause indicates either that they had wrought better than they knew—and thus were out of touch with the situation; or that they were not in fact responsible for the remarkable upsurge in dry politics. The Mississippi League was not organized until 1911, and in North Carolina the antisaloon league had no ties with the national organization.[13]

American Issue claimed in 1908, however, that "every inch of dry territory . . . was secured by the omni-partisan methods of the Anti-Saloon League."[14] While this claim was strictly correct, it had the additional effect of identifying the success of statewide prohibition not only with the methods but also with the organization which pictured itself as the exemplar of those methods. When success turned to failure, it would be the organization as well as the methods which took the blame.

Of greater long-run importance for the League than the spread of state-wide prohibition were the endorsements it received from the ruling bodies of the Methodist Episcopal and Presbyterian churches. Party prohibitionists had gloried in the resolution adopted by the Methodist Episcopal General Conference in 1892, "that no political party has a right to expect, nor ought it to receive, the support of Christian men so long as it stands committed to the license policy, or refuses to put itself on record in an attitude of open hostility to the saloon."[15] The General Conference of 1904 renewed Methodist support for this position.[16] But in 1908, after strenuous lobbying by League men had overcome Prohibitionist opposition, the General Conference for the first time endorsed local option and commended the Anti-Saloon League by name; it also revised the famous declaration, replacing "political party" with "candidate for any office which in any way may have to do with the liquor traffic" and changing "license policy" to "liquor interests."[17] Perhaps the unkindest cut of all came when Bishop James W. Bashford, a former Prohibitionist, delivered an address favoring local option.[18] The League claimed that "no stronger statement has ever been made by the General Conference of the Methodist Episcopal Church on temperance and the prohibition of the liquor traffic"; William P. F. Ferguson called it "the saddest case of taking a brave flag back to a cowardly regiment to be found in all history."[19]

Nearly as important to the League as the endorsement by the Methodist General Conference was the decision of the Presbyterian General Assembly in 1907 to put an end to its aloofness toward the Anti-Saloon League. The Presbyterians, unlike the Methodists, were barred by their church constitution from establishing official relations with nonecclesiastical organizations. Thus they had been, and continued to be, the largest Protestant group to refuse to send delegates to Anti-Saloon League conventions or appoint Anti-Saloon League trustees.[20] In 1907, however, the General Assembly commended the Anti-Saloon League as a "sane, safe and effective" organization and pledged to it "the fullest co-operation consistent with the constitution of our church."[21] The actions of the General Assembly removed, in spirit if not in letter, the obstacles standing in the path of Presbyterian cooperation with the League.

In 1906 and 1907 the Presbyterian General Assembly took other steps less helpful to the League's drive for supremacy. The Assembly approved in 1907 a recommendation presented the year before by its Permanent Committee on Temperance, suggesting the formation of an interchurch federation for temperance work.[22] Such a federation would avoid the primary objection to the League from the standpoint of Presbyterians and other denominations: that it was an "outside" organization free from complete control by the churches which supported it. The Prohibitionist Charles Scanlon, an influential member of the Presbyterian Permanent Committee on Temperance, made clear in an article in the *New Voice* that this proposal was aimed directly at the objectionable features of the League.

> . . . we think the League might be so modified as to retain all
> of its strong features, eliminate most of its weak ones, broaden
> its platform, emphasize more equally the important phases of
> the work, become less oligarchical in its government, less imper-
> ious in spirit, more just to other organizations, audit its accounts
> more fully, place more emphasis upon the underlying principles
> of the reform and less upon raising money, select its representa-
> tives with greater discrimination, teach that total abstinence and
> Prohibition are two wings of the same bird, refuse to compro-
> mise for the sake of expediency or temporary advantage, claim
> credit only for what it does and is, exercise more modesty and
> courtesy toward other valuable agencies which are its seniors in
> this work, such as the National Temperance Society, the W.C.T.U.,
> the Prohibition party and others, and accept merited criticism
> in a spirit which will increase and not diminish its usefulness.[23]

League spokesmen not surprisingly reacted with dismay to Scanlon's proposal, pointing out, "Could such a federation be formed it would du-plicate the organization and work of the American Anti-Saloon League."[24] The League had itself been attempting to answer the complaints of the churches by reorganizing state leagues so as to place them under the ulti-mate procedural control of their supporting churches.[25] The Presbyterian proposal gave considerable urgency to this process, which became a sort of race by the League to satisfy the churches with representation on its Boards of Direction before the churches decided to pursue the idea of an interchurch temperance federation to the point of supplanting the League.

While the League was securing endorsements from Protestant ruling bodies, it was bringing into its leadership ranks, as Baker had suggested in 1903, men from occupations other than the clergy. The number of clergymen who were state superintendents dropped from an average 81.5 percent during 1899-1904 to an average of 76.4 percent during 1905-1909.[26] More important was the decline in the rate of turnover each year on the organization's second level of leadership, the state superintendents. During the years 1899-1904 the League had changed about one-third of its state superintendents each year, while the Prohibition party was experiencing turnover among about one-fourth of its state chairmen. During the period 1904-1909 the relative positions of the two organizations were reversed: the party's rate of turnover averaged 33.0 percent per year, while the League's averaged only 26.7 percent.[27]

This meant that a state league superintendent could normally be expected to serve four years, but it did not guarantee complete stability. In Illinois, for example, the resignation of Superintendent William H. Anderson in 1905 was accompanied by changes in practically the entire paid staff and in nearly the entire voluntary Headquarters Committee.[28] The Washington (state) League frequently experienced the same problem through 1909.[29] In Washington in 1905 and Missouri in 1908 the League was embarrassed by the dishonesty of state superintendents.[30]

Insufficient funds made strict economies a continuing fact of life for League workers. The Oregon Superintendent, having received only $227 for his 1906 work, turned to spare-time short-story writing to supplement his income. As late as 1909, Howard Russell was writing to his wife: "For the first time in several months only ½ salaries are forthcoming for [January] to the National workmen. It will come in late but makes the situation a little puzzling to me about meeting necessary bills."[31]

Conflict over methods continued behind the scenes, as in the District of Columbia League, which had been instrumental in launching the national organization: when reorganization to effect church control came about in 1909, a minority faction challenged the move.[32] At the 1909 national convention Baker was still lecturing the League on the need for selection of honest, competent leadership. "As a rule," he said, "the most of the difficulty we have encountered from within comes from men whose Christian characters are clouded by a spirit of selfishness and self-seeking, the possession of which utterly unfits any man for high grade Christian work." Baker's remarks also revealed the distance the League had come since its early days when he pointed out that "the League has reached a place in public favor where it can choose its employees. The time was when it was compelled to take only those who offered themselves."[33]

LEAGUE AND PARTY

Cooperation by Prohibition party men with the Anti-Saloon League was widespread during the years 1905-1909. The League welcomed this cooperation, although its spokesmen often could not resist the temptation to use it as an argument against those Prohibitionists who still clung to the party.[34] In 1906, Baker explained why the League considered itself to have no rivals in temperance work. The League, he claimed, with its "sane, practical and pre-eminently successful warfare against the . . . liquor traffic . . . is the federation of 'other organizations,' some of which have worn themselves out and destroyed their usefulness in the rival business." While the leaders of such organizations might still war upon the League, "their constituency, more interested in doing things, than in serving a fretful, faultfind[ing] leadership, have already federated themselves."[35]

Baker thus stated as uncompromising an attitude toward the party as William P. F. Ferguson maintained toward the League. Despite the soothing rhetoric about cooperation, the methods of party and League remained opposed. There could be only one "federation" of the temperance forces, only one "church in action against the saloon," and the League's insistence upon this point appeared not only in Baker's claim that the League could have no rivals but also in the attacks by League men upon the proposal for an interchurch temperance federation. Even those Prohibitionists who cooperated with the League recognized implicitly the irreconcilable contradiction between the two methods when they pleaded with their new allies to adopt a less antagonistic tone toward their old comrades.[36]

THE NEW PROHIBITIONISTS

The Prohibition party's belief that prohibition was the inevitable next step in the progressive betterment of American society after the abolition of slavery implied an optimistic world-view in which evil represented less a threat than a measure of individual and social virtue. Thus, Prohibitionists could see their reform activity both as a demonstration of the reformer's virtue and as a means of supplanting the institutions which obstructed man's path toward perfection. It was this optimism which had made possible the party's social criticism, flirtation with radicalism, and

abortive efforts toward a Populist-Prohibitionist coalition in the 1890s.
While it is difficult to find a pattern among the frequently contradictory
utterances of League leaders, their vision of the world, like their estimate
of the political situation, seems to have been darker than that of their
predecessors and rivals.

Prohibition party leaders had, after all, come from a pre-Civil War
generation which could perceive in its own experience unlimited possibilities for reform. Editing out of their memories the bloody, shattering
effects of the war, Prohibitionists agreed upon an interpretation emphasizing mass idealism, collective self-sacrifice—and success. Anti-Saloon
League leaders, however, came to maturity well after the war, in an age
of recurrent depression and emergent class conflict. More specifically,
the movement which represented their first model of reform—the late-
nineteenth-century prohibition movement—was an undeniable failure.
Upon the pessimism arising from this background, the optimism that
Clyde Griffen sees as the key to the Progressive ethos made little impres-
sion.[37] The Anti-Saloon League, of course, may have simply formed the
most conservative and most pessimistic wing of that amorphous bird,
Progressivism. On the other hand, League leaders were not the only
Progressives who grew up in the Gilded Age. Thus, their pessimism may
have been shared with other Progressives; they may also have shared a
new conception of the reformer which flowed from their pessimism.

Party prohibitionists before 1896 had been able to identify themselves not only as prohibitionists but also in the established role of reformers: social critics, firmly placed in the social order, serving their own
moral interests as well as the interests of the object of reform, the lower
class. In justifying their own activities, they felt no need to look beyond
the ideal of disinterested benevolence. The attempt of those damaged
by the social system to achieve reform themselves, manifesting itself
in the Populist revolt, struck a killing blow to this conception of the
reformer. This is the reason why Populism became, as Robert H. Wiebe
has called it, "reform's precipitant" in the 1890s.[38] After Populism,
it was impossible to pose as a disinterested reformer. Specifically, the
Populists, by their very existence and early success, had brought Prohibition party men face to face with the need for crossing class lines
(as the Prohibitionists saw it) in order to bring about the social change
which the Prohibitionist critique demanded. This the Prohibitionists as
a party had refused to do, and after 1896 the party led the prohibition
movement in a retreat from hostility toward middle-class institutions.

Finding it difficult in the polarized nineties to think in terms of the whole society, Prohibitionists could justify their decision only as serving the interests of a specific group, namely, middle-class Protestants.

The Anti-Saloon League, taking its cue from the refusal of middle-class Protestants to support reform in the nineties, posited the existence of a unified constituency closely associated with the churches, the major political parties, and the free-enterprise system. Thus, it abandoned the role of social critic once claimed by party prohibitionists. With it the League rejected not only the alliance with social outcasts which had tempted the party but also the commitment to reform in the interests of the lower class, now impossible to conceive of seriously without such an alliance. The League (and now the party as well) searched for a new justification of prohibition activity and found it in immediate threats to the middle class. In this new conception, the reformer was no longer the social critic of the nineteenth century, himself disinterested in every way but morally; now the reformer was a strenuous fighter for his own interests and those of his class in a world that threatened him at every point.

In 1891 *The Voice* had distinguished Prohibitionists from Populists by asserting that "the Prohibitionists have been seeking for legislation, not in behalf of themselves, but in behalf of the nation—legislation for which they *least of all men* feel any personal need or from which they would receive personal advantage."[39] In contrast, Ernest H. Cherrington's history of the League in 1913 took pains in its biographical sketches to point to the personal injuries suffered directly or indirectly by Howard H. Russell and Purley A. Baker at the hands of the liquor traffic.[40] At Russell's behest, another Anti-Saloon League writer printed the following explanation of the founder's motivation:

> While yet a lad he saw near and dear relatives brought to a premature death through strong drink. It became evident to him that for several generations this habit had been a family weakness. When visiting in Staffordshire, England, Russell found that at least fourteen relatives not far removed, bright young men, several of them trained in the English universities, had all died before reaching forty years of age, and that the drink habit was the assassin in every case.[41]

James Cannon, Jr., felt the same need, and traced his hostility to the

saloon to three events in his early life: (1) scenes of poverty and degra-
dation caused by drunkenness; (2) the indignities suffered by his mother
as she pleaded with saloon-keepers to close their establishments; and
(3) the death of an uncle caused by the bite of a fierce dog let loose by
a drunken man.[42]

The Reverend T. M. Hare, superintendent of the Wisconsin League
(1903-1907), reflected the League's pessimistic view of social progress
and justified the prohibition movement in 1903 in an address titled
"The Decadence of Manhood." "As a people," Hare was reported to
have warned, "we were breaking down in morals and character and at
such a pace that it was a menace to our future." For a remedy, however,
Hare could suggest nothing more than prohibition, for he rejected the
social criticism represented by the Prohibition party. Prohibitionists had
been known to accept the extremist label attached by their critics and
sometimes emphasized the point by waving cranks at appropriate moments
during convention proceedings. Reporting the Anti-Saloon League national convention of 1905, Hare noted: "There is something in the Anti-Saloon
League that appeals to manly men. . . . Looking over the delegates, . . . one is
impressed with the fact that they are men of a superior grade. They are
not long-haired, wild-eyed, squeaky-voiced cranks." He added, "A marked
feature of the convention was . . . the absence of the extreme and visionary element usually so prominent in reform gatherings."[43]

Hare's invocation of virility merely echoed similar pronouncements
by other League leaders—and other Progressives.[44] In 1900 the Reverend
J. C. Jackson had helped to establish the genre in League literature when
he denounced noncooperative churches: "If any congregation is constructed on too fragile lines for this hard, sword fighting, bloody sea-sailing
service, let it stop singing, 'Am I a soldier of the cross?' and, frankly admitting it is too much of the 'O-to-be-nothing,' gelatinous type of piety
to be worth keeping alive, evaporate, and be replaced by something with
a spine and red blood."[45] Wayne Wheeler incorporated it into his wel-
come to delegates at the 1904 national convention:

> We welcome you too as warriors. The whole world loves a man
> that fights when he has justification for it. The timid good may
> have virtues, but the man who fights, the man who enters the
> arena and risks his future, his fortune and his life for others,
> such a one is dear to the hearts of his countrymen. To overthrow
> the liquor traffic means a terrific struggle, it means fighting,

constantly, persistently and relentlessly, and you are sacrific-
ing your time, your means, and it may be your very life blood
to further this great cause. You are fighting at the point where
the battle is on. You are not standard bearers so far ahead of
the line of march that no bullet or shell should put you in danger, but you are at the fighting point, at the place where the
battle is on, at the primary, at the caucus, the polls, in the courts,
in short contesting every inch of ground and favoring everything
that opposes the saloon.[46]

The inability of League men to agree upon a definition of their enemy
illustrated the difficulty of their presenting themselves as reformers while
admitting the lack of need for reform. How, for example, could the admitted weakness of the liquor interests require the fabulous expenditures
of money and energy upon which League leaders insisted? One writer held
simultaneously that the enemy was man himself, who could only achieve
goodness when it was "beaten into him by authority," and that the temperance victories were the result of the American conscience declaring itself against wrong.[47] League President Hiram Price thought that "the grog-
selling class" represented a wickedness that was irretrievably doomed to hell,
but another leader contradicted him by declaring love for the liquor men
and placing the blame for their wickedness upon the "bad business" in
which they were engaged.[48] The Reverend J. C. Jackson shifted erratically
between positive and negative views of human nature.[49]

One might argue that League men and women believed that attainment of their ultimate goal would be beneficial to the lower class, and
of course they did portray it in those terms. Yet their own words betrayed
the self-interest mixed with their paternalism. In 1902 Russell initiated
what might have been a direct approach to the lower class, a total-abstin-
ence pledge-signing campaign in New York. He justified the campaign to
his followers "as a means of agitation and public sentiment making against
both the habit and the traffic in drink," a pre-local-option stage of progress.
It was necessary because "a special time of crisis in our League work is
upon us just now."[50]

Anxious for success, the League cut itself off from social criticism
and defined itself as a defense agency of the middle class. The League's
commitment to Christian reform naturally aligned it, of course, with the
moderate social criticism voiced by Social Gospellers. Normally, this did
not trouble League spokesmen, although they found more use for the

Social Gospel's activism than for its criticism.[51] When the Social Gospel
alliance threatened to alienate more conventional ministers, however, the
League drew back.[52] If one wished to pursue the Social Gospel into Christian Socialism, he would have to leave the League in order to realize his
commitment, as at least one minister did in 1907.[53]

This disavowal of social criticism would contribute to the movement's
success when Americans required a symbol of their mythical common
identity. But when economic collapse made social criticism once more
imperative, prohibitionists had nothing to offer.

Prohibitionists as reformers were to be impotent in the face of the
Depression for another reason involved in the change from party to
League. As the birth of Populism had made disinterestedness incredible
as a motive for reform, the death of Populism signalled the beginning of
the end for reform as mass politics. This development, too, was reflected
in the prohibition movement. Unlike the Prohibition party, the League
was not, and did not aspire to be, a mass organization; instead, it became
the first successful reform lobby.[54]

Progressives, as Michael Rogin points out, "bureaucratized the reform
impulse."[55] So, also, the League bureaucratized the prohibition impulse,
striving to bend government to its will in response to the party's failure
to organize a mass constituency capable of capturing the reins of power.
In doing so, the League sought to create a channel to power for its constituency, thus removing the prohibition issue from the influence of the
lower class. (The new claim that the middle class was deprived, reflected
in the recitals of injuries suffered from the liquor traffic by League men,
served as rationalization for this change.) When middle-class concern
shifted to economic deprivation, the League, as a single-issue lobby, was
left stranded. But its model of reform as lobbying has, of course, survived.

The period 1905-1909 was a time of triumph for the League, but its
leaders recognized the insubstantial nature of its gains. Unlike Ferguson's
National Prohibitionist, American Issue did not pursue the practice of
constantly threatening its readers with ever-recurring crises for the movement. In July 1908, however, *American Issue* warned: "We are appre-
hensive of the future of the temperance reform in the United States.
There will be a reaction, as sure as the sun rises and sets."[56] In December
it found pessimism justified: "It is evident that another crisal [sic] period
in temperance reform is approaching."[57] When defeats replaced victories,
the League began to fear that the decline of the Prohibition party which
had followed the lapsing of temperance sentiment in the 1890s might
now become its fate as well. The response was a significant change in strategy.

NOTES

1. H. H. Russell Diary, entries for November 7 and 8, 1905, Russell Papers, Michigan Historical Collections (MHC), Ann Arbor.

2. *Proceedings of the Tenth National Convention of the Anti-Saloon League of America* (hereafter referred to as *ASL Proceedings*), 1905, pp. 21-22.

3. *American Issue*, September 8, 1905; Norman H. Dohn, "The History of the Anti-Saloon League" (Ph.D. dissertation, Ohio State University, 1959), pp. 117-118.

4. Robert A. Hohner, "Prohibition and Virginia Politics: William Hodges Mann Versus Henry St. George Tucker, 1909," *Virginia Magazine of History and Biography* 74 (1966): 88-107.

5. C. C. Pearson and J. Edwin Hendricks, *Liquor and Anti-Liquor in Virginia, 1619-1919* (Durham, 1967), chs. xii-xiv.

6. Jimmie L. Franklin, *Born Sober: Prohibition in Oklahoma, 1907-1959* (Norman, Okla., 1971), pp. 3-35.

7. *ASL Proceedings, 4th Annual Convention, 1898*, p. vi.

8. *ASL Proceedings, 1906*, p. 40.

9. *ASL Proceedings, 1904*, p. 26; *ASL Proceedings, 1906*, p. 19.

10. James B. Sellers, *The Prohibition Movement in Alabama, 1702 to 1943* (Chapel Hill, 1943), pp. 101-121.

11. *ASL Proceedings, 1906*, pp. 76-78.

12. Ibid., p. 46.

13. *ASL Proceedings, 1911*, p. 125; *ASL Proceedings, 1909*, p. 140; Daniel J. Whitener, *Prohibition in North Carolina, 1715-1945* (Chapel Hill, 1945), p. 186; R. L. Davis (Superintendent, North Carolina Anti-Saloon League) to E. H. Cherrington, September 4, 1909, Cherrington Papers, Temperance Education Foundation (TEF). Compare Hohner, "Prohibition and Virginia Politics," p. 89.

14. *American Issue*, Wisconsin edition, September 1908.

15. They ignored the qualifying statement, "this report shall not be construed as an indorsement of any political party." *Journal of the 21st Delegated General Conference of the Methodist Episcopal Church* (New York, 1892), p. 494.

16. *Journal of the 24th Delegated General Conference of the Methodist Episcopal Church* (New York, 1904), p. 480.

17. *Journal of the 25th Delegated General Conference . . .* (New York, 1908), pp. 551-552.

18. Silas C. Swallow, *III Score & X, or Selections, Collections, Recollections of Seventy Busy Years* (Harrisburg, Pa., n.d.), pp. 181-182.

19. *American Issue*, Wisconsin edition, June 1908; *National Prohibitionist*, June 4, 1908.

20. *Minutes of the General Assembly of the Presbyterian Church in the United States of America* (Philadelphia, 1906), p. 80.

21. *Minutes of the General Assembly of the Presbyterian Church* (1970), p. 138; *Wisconsin Issue* (Madison), July 1907. The Congregational National Council also commended the Anti-Saloon League in 1907. *The National Council of the Congregational Churches of the United States* (Boston, 1907), pp. 414-415; Permanent Temperance Committee, National Council of Congregational Churches, to Secretaries of State and Local Associations, February 1908, Henry A. Miner Papers, State Historical Society of Wisconsin (WHS), Madison.

22. *Minutes of the General Assembly of the Presbyterian Church* (1906), pp. 175-177, and (1907), p. 138.

23. *New Voice*, June 28, 1906.

24. *Wisconsin Issue*, August 1906.

25. See Chapter 6 above; Earl C. Kaylor, Jr., "The Prohibition Movement in Pennsylvania, 1865-1920," 2 vols. (Ph.D. dissertation, Pennsylvania State University, 1963), vol. 2, pp. 320-321.

26. See Chapter 6 above; computed from lists in *ASL Proceedings*, 1905, 1906, 1907, 1909.

27. Computed from lists in *ASL Proceedings*, 1905, 1906, 1907, 1909, and lists in David Leigh Colvin, *Prohibition in the United States: A History of the Prohibition Party and of the Prohibition Movement* (New York, 1926), pp. 643-657.

28. *ASL Proceedings, 1906*, pp. 79-80.

29. *ASL Proceedings, 1909*, p. 164.

30. *ASL Proceedings, 1905*, pp. 20-21; *ASL Proceedings, 1909*, pp. 72-73, 120-122; Frederick A. McKenzie, *"Pussyfoot" Johnson—Crusader—Reformer—A Man among Men* (New York, 1920), pp. 128-129; Peter Odegard, *Pressure Politics: The Story of the Anti-Saloon League* (New York, 1928), pp. 220-222.

31. P. A. Baker to H. H. Russell, May 22, 1907, H. H. Russell to Lillian D. Russell, February 3, 1909, Russell Papers; Rev. Paul Rader to P. A. Baker, February 22, 1907, copy in Ernest H. Cherrington Papers.

32. *American Issue*, Wisconsin edition, February 1909.

33. *ASL Proceedings, 1909*, pp. 47-48. See also *ASL Proceedings, 1906*, p. 40.

34. *American Issue*, June 23, 1905; *Wisconsin Issue*, November 1905, June 1906, *New Voice*, November 8, 1906, *American Issue*, Wisconsin edition, May 1908, February 1909; Frederick W. Adrian, "The Political Significance of the Prohibition Party" (Ph.D. dissertation, Ohio State University, 1942), p. 112.

35. *ASL Proceedings, 1906*, p. 44.

36. Ibid., pp. 55-56; H. A. Larson to Henry A. Miner, October 21, 1907, Miner Papers.

37. Clyde Griffen, "The Progressive Ethos," in Stanley Coben and Lorman Ratner, eds., *The Development of an American Culture* (Englewood Cliffs, N.J., 1970), pp. 120-149.

38. Robert H. Wiebe, *The Search for Order, 1877-1920* (New York, 1967), pp. 89-90.

39. *The Voice*, January 8, 1891. Italics in original.

40. Ernest H. Cherrington, *History of the Anti-Saloon League* (Westerville, Ohio, 1913).

41. Louis Albert Banks, "The Anti-Saloon League, Origin and Personnel," in George M. Hammell, ed., *The Passing of the Saloon* (Cincinnati, 1908), pp. 186-187.

42. James Cannon, Jr., *Bishop Cannon's Own Story: Life As I Have Seen It*, ed. Richard L. Watson, Jr. (Durham, 1955), pp. 12, 15-17.

43. *Northwestern Mail*, December 4, 1903; *Wisconsin Issue*, December, 1905.

44. James R. McGovern, "David Graham Phillips and the Virility Impulse of Progressives," *New England Quarterly* 39 (September 1966): 334-355.

45. *American Issue*, April 1900.

46. *ASL Proceedings, 1904*, pp. 13-14.

47. F. C. Iglehart, "The Nation's Anti-Drink Crusade," *Review of Reviews* 37 (April 1908): 475, 476.

48. *ASL Proceedings, 3d Annual Convention, 1898*, p. 38; *ASL Proceedings, 1909*, p. 16.

49. *American Issue*, February 1900, May 24, October 11, 1901, January 24, June 20, 1902.

50. Howard H. Russell to Lillian D. Russell, March 16, 1902, Russell Papers.

51. *ASL Proceedings, 1907*, p. 20; *ASL Proceedings, 1909*, p. 12.

52. *American Issue*, March 18, 1904.

53. Charles H. Hopkins, *The Rise of the Social Gospel in American Protestantism, 1865-1915* (New Haven, 1940), p. 236.

54. Odegard, *Pressure Politics.*

55. Michael P. Rogin, *The Intellectuals and McCarthy: The Radical Specter* (Cambridge, Mass., 1967), pp. 193-194.

56. *American Issue*, Wisconsin edition, July 1908.

57. Ibid., December 1908.

9

The progressive pattern, 1909-1913

At its twentieth-anniversary national convention in November 1913, the Anti-Saloon League began the drive for national prohibition which culminated in adoption of the Eighteenth Amendment. Historians have noted that the Amendment's passage by Congress and ratification by the states came at the crest of a surge of dry sentiment which had placed twenty-six states under state prohibition by April 1917 and seven more by the time of ratification less than two years later. But they have failed to notice that the League's decision to initiate the national effort came not on the upward slope of that surge but rather during a lull between two crests, at a time when defeats in statewide prohibition contests came more often than victories, when the churches showed signs of restiveness under the League's leadership, and when Prohibitionists who had cooperated with the League during its early days deserted its banner to seek rejuvenation of their old organization.

During the years 1909-1913 League leaders began to fear that their supremacy within the prohibition movement was at stake and accordingly started to search for a means of rallying their disheartened supporters. The passage of the Webb-Kenyon Act in March 1913 directed their attention toward the national Congress and aimed their plans toward a national campaign. Such a drive might serve at one and the same time to focus the nation's attention upon the prohibition issue, give fresh impetus to efforts for prohibition in the states, convince Prohibitionists of the League's sincerity, and retain the League's position at the head of the dry forces. Thus, a sense of impending failure as well as recognition of past success produced the resolution calling for a national prohibition constitutional amendment which 3,000 prohibitionists presented at the steps of the Capitol on December 13, 1913. The final drive for national prohibition was now launched in earnest; but the circumstances surrounding its inception and the character of the movement behind it ensured that its attainment would not bring about the cultural change—within the middle class or among the society at large—required to sustain political victory. Nor would national prohibition be accompanied by the broader changes in American life for which some of its proponents in the 1890s had hoped.

THE LEAGUE STUMBLES

Seeking to justify the decision to move for national prohibition, Superintendent Purley A. Baker told the Anti-Saloon League national convention in 1913, "Reforms cannot move in a circle—they must progress or die speedily."[1] The historian James H. Timberlake has used the figure of a "plateau" to describe the state of the prohibition movement during the five years before Baker's address.[2] Baker's "circle" appears to be a more accurate representation of both the picture in the minds of League leaders and the actual situation. The rising arc of success for statewide prohibition during the years 1907-1909 was at least matched and perhaps exceeded by a falling curve in statewide contests during the next four years. Even Ernest H. Cherrington, in his official history of the Anti-Saloon League in 1913, admitted the existence of "a decided reaction" in the year 1911, although he tried to balance it with a "revival" in 1912-1913.[3]

The principal reason for the string of losses in statewide prohibition contests during 1909-1913 seems to have been the shifting of the battleground from legislative chambers to ballot boxes through increasing use of the initiative and referendum. The League's balance-of-power tactics were best suited to bringing pressure upon individual politicians in contested districts. When the prohibition question was the sole issue to be voted upon by citizens of an entire state, the League's voting bloc wielded no power greater than its actual numbers, which usually constituted a decided minority. In Ohio, for example, Superintendent Wayne B. Wheeler claimed to control only about 400,000 votes among Ohio's total voting population of about 1,250,000. He was thus able to obtain desirable legislation only so long as he could use his minority bloc as a lever upon the legislature. When statewide contests on temperance issues were decided by referendum, Wheeler and the League suffered crushing defeats in 1912 and 1914.[4] The defeat of 1912, when Ohio voters replaced the no-license clause of the state constitution with a provision allowing license, threatened to cancel out the benefits which had accrued to the League from its defeat of Herrick seven years earlier.

Four of the six states which had gone dry during 1907-1909 had done so by action of their legislatures. In contrast, eight states rejected statewide prohibition during 1909-1913, all through referendum votes. Included among their number was Alabama, whose voters defeated a prohibitory constitutional amendment in 1909 and whose legislature followed suit in 1911 by repeal of the four-year-old prohibition law. A referendum victory in West Virginia in 1912 offset the loss of Alabama, but the League could find little but this sole gain to set beside the dreary string of rejections in Florida, Oregon, and Missouri in 1910, Texas in 1911, and Arkansas, Ohio, and Colorado in 1912.[5] Little encouragement could be found in Oklahoma's decision to retain prohibition or in the hairbreadth defeat of resubmission in Maine in 1911, in a vote so close that prohibition leaders predicted defeat and for some time after the election believed they had lost.[6]

Some of these defeats were not entirely the fault of the Anti-Saloon League. In Missouri, for example, League leaders claimed to have advised against the initiative petition for a vote on statewide prohibition, although they joined in the campaign once the necessary signatures had been secured.[7] The Prohibitionists who had led the campaign from the beginning had thus succeeded in pushing the League into a position more advanced than it wished to occupy. Nevertheless, as the self-proclaimed leader of the prohibition forces, the League could not escape the blame and loss of prestige which attended the defeat.

In Oregon, the referendum defeat of 1910 "largely nullified" the gains made by prohibitionists in the three previous general elections.[8] In states which did not hold referenda on statewide prohibition, decline was also evident. The California League seemed to have reached the limit of its possibilities by 1910 and rejuvenated itself thereafter only through an alliance with the onrushing Progressives.[9] The newly appointed Arizona Superintendent reported in 1913 that "nothing, practically, has been done by the League in the last two years."[10] "The situation in New York state," Baker confessed as early as 1908, "is critical. The feeling that they are not doing anything or getting anything over there has become quite formidable indeed."[11] In Virginia the stagnation of the local option drive by 1910 led to predictions of defeat and in turn to consideration of a shift toward statewide prohibition.[12] Sending the results of 1910 local option elections to the *Anti-Saloon League Yearbook*, the New Hampshire Superintendent reported discouraging news:

> I dare not give the returns of 1908 in the towns to compare with 1910 as it would make a bad showing. We *lost* in the campaign a good deal more than we gained. The cities and towns we lost were larger than [those] we gained. We reached the limit of success under local option in 1908. Now we can only fluctuate between a small lose *[sic]* and gain.[13]

The number of Wisconsin towns voting dry in no-license elections suffered a sharp drop during 1908-1911 and rose significantly only in 1915, when the campaign for national prohibition was in full swing.[14] The Wisconsin League had always been financially insecure, but the sharp drop during the period May 1911 to May 1912, to an income of $9,480.07, less than half of the amount gathered during a similar period two years earlier, forced it to announce, "We are crippled for want of money." The financial crisis went unalleviated until the national League came to Wisconsin's rescue in 1915.[15]

In 1911, however, the national League had difficulty in keeping its own still-meager accounts in the black. During the period November 1, 1910 to October 31, 1911, the national League showed a deficit of $545.65 in total expenditures of $12,805.74.[16] This total was slightly less than the national League's disbursements during 1903 and less than half the amount spent by the Prohibition party National Committee during the year 1910.[17] The national League's income dropped still further in 1912 and 1913.[18]

Frustration reappeared in the prohibition press. *American Issue* tried to interpret defeat as victory, claiming in 1910 that merely to have held the ground gained during 1908-1909 would have been "a real victory for the moral forces."[19] When that tactic wore thin, the editors soberly reminded League workers that every successful war had its lost battles.[20] In 1911 a Prohibitionist writing in *American Advance* concluded that recent electoral defeats and the increase in consumption of liquor during 1910 added up to a serious crisis confronting the movement.[21] In June 1913 the newly elected superintendent of the Wisconsin Anti-Saloon League acknowledged the growing pessimism of League men:

There are doubtless many sincere, honest people, people who
have given of their means in the past to help on this cause, who
really believe that the Anti-Saloon League has lived out its day,
and its usefulness, if it ever had any, is all in the past. Like some
other societies, it promised well for a time, grew rapidly and was
in great favor, but now it has become a salary raising institution,
its workers have no message with which to inspire the hosts of
the Lord, no ringing call to battle against the forces of evil and
the powers of this world.[22]

The most significant indicator of the sense of impending failure appeared
in the angry, frustrated report delivered by National Superintendent Purley
A. Baker to the 1911 national convention. Baker's report contained the
first serious unalloyed criticism of League activities ever made by its chief
executive before a national convention.[23] Fear and hostility set the tone
of the report. The fear reflected both the League's specific defeats and
the generalized insecurity of the League's middle-class constituency.
The hostility revealed a new willingness to accept polarization rather
than accommodation as the basis of League strategy.

Noting a growing strength among the liquor interests, Baker reserved
his sharpest thrusts for those whose class standing should have aligned
them with the League. He denounced businessmen, preachers, politicians,
and newspaper owners who gave aid and encouragement to the saloon,
and fervidly urged the organization of Anti-Saloon League boycotts.
against members of "Business Men's Associations" formed to fight prohibition. Attacking temperance folk who refused to support the League,
Baker pictured them "meaninglessly mumbling the ritual of reform until
they have lost not only their moral muscle, but their moral bearings,
and stand flabby and helpless while the battle rages."

Crisis led Baker to cling tightly to the vested interests with which
the League had always tried to ally itself, and this reaction led him
to deepen and broaden his denunciation of those suspect elements to
which the League could appeal in better days. Commenting gratuitously
upon alleged egalitarian and anti-ecclesiastical remarks by Ohio Socialists,
Baker claimed: "Men who will make such utterances and men who will
applaud them when they are made, need only slight provocation and a
reasonably safe opportunity to apply the torch, or pistol, or bludgeon.
The initiative, referendum and recall in the hands of *that kind* of people
are serious things."[24] He departed from the League's official single-issue

position to advocate woman suffrage, which he thought would provide a moral balance for the "coming pure democracy unsupported." Baker also appealed for large contributors to the League's work.

Finally, Baker implicitly admitted the Prohibition party's position when he asserted that prohibition laws "must be placed in the hands of friends of the law for execution, if they are to be effective." But he maintained that the League was still the leader of the temperance forces, pleaded for a united front, and denounced both independent and denominational temperance societies which refused to put themselves under the League's command. These statements reflected the League's concern with the threat of expansion by denominational temperance societies into areas of work claimed by the League; League men fought out this issue in numerous church councils during these years.[25] Besides revealing the League's recognition of the impending failure facing both the organization and the movement, the report indicated that the League was casting about, like the Prohibition party in the early 1890s, for other issues with which to attract support for prohibition. The issues chosen, it was clear, would be those that would align the organization not with the rising tide of social criticism but rather with the threatened middle class which felt that its interests could be served only by suppressing the clamor of the outcast.

Thus, despite continued claims of adherence to the single-issue policy, the League swung its support behind "moral issues" other than prohibition.[26] In California in 1908 the League backed a WCTU campaign against race-track gambling; in Rhode Island it attacked gambling, prostitution, and Sabbath-breaking; in Wisconsin the League continued to cooperate, through the Wisconsin Federation of Churches and Christian Workers, with movements for "purity" and Sabbath protection.[27] The Texas League supported a movement in 1911 to disfranchise blacks and Mexicans.[28] Although *American Issue* went under the union label in 1911, the switch seemed to reflect no change in the League's attitudes.[29] The Wisconsin League spoke out in 1911 for new immigration laws which would halt "the yearly importation of hundreds of thousands of drunkards and drunkard-makers from other lands."[30]

During 1909-1913 the League continued to be plagued by attacks from its former workers. The Reverend U. G. Robinson, discharged superintendent of the Missouri League, kept up a running fire of scandalous criticism of the League's national leadership until in 1912

William E. Johnson exposed his ties with the liquor interests.[31] The
Reverend W. C. Helt, former superintendent of the Indiana Anti-Saloon
League, turned not only against the League but also against prohibition.[32]
The most serious, although temporary, defection was that of Edwin C.
Dinwiddie, the first party man to turn to the League, superintendent
of leagues in Pennsylvania (1896-1899) and Oklahoma (1905-1907),
and first legislative superintendent for the national League (1899-1905).[33]
In 1910-1911 Dinwiddie represented the National Inter-Church Temperance Federation in Washington, D.C., and threw a scare into League
leaders by attempting to discredit his former colleagues and place the
national legislative leadership of the prohibition movement in the hands
of his new organization.[34]

The most dangerous threat to the League's hegemony came indirectly
from its most persistent critics, Prohibition party men. The League in
1909 had staked its existence upon continued support from the churches,
and the interchurch temperance federation promoted by Prohibitionists
struck at precisely this vulnerable point. Only valiant efforts to restrict
to "educational" work the role of the denominational temperance societies which would make up such a federation maintained the League's
predominant role in political activity.

The League's enemies proceeded nevertheless to found the Inter-
Church Temperance Federation at Pittsburgh on January 30-31, 1907.[35]
By 1912 the Federation claimed affiliation with the temperance agencies
of nine denominations representing twelve million members.[36] Charles
Scanlon, general secretary of the Presbyterian Temperance Committee
and a Prohibitionist, was the leader of this movement. In June 1911 he
joined with other current and former party men to bring about the
creation of the National Church Temperance Council by uniting the
National Inter-Church Temperance Federation with the Temperance
Committee of the Federal Council of the Churches of Christ in America.[37]

Support of the denominational temperance societies by Prohibitionists hostile to the League led to bitter intradenominational fights over
the jurisdictions of the societies and the League. At the Methodist
Episcopal General Conference of 1912, three delegates, including a
WCTU leader sympathetic to the party, demanded and got a chance
to examine the financial reports of the national League but were unable
to find evidence to support charges of either the League's unmerited
affluence or the dishonesty of its leaders. At the same General Confer-

ence, a Prohibitionist produced a minority report of the Committee on Temperance and Prohibition, refusing to endorse the Anti-Saloon League. The report was rejected after a brief debate, and Prohibitionists savagely denounced Baker's political maneuvers at the conference.[38]

In Wisconsin, at least, the amount of cooperation that the League received from the churches was not impressive. In 1910-1911 the League was "heard and helped" by the following percentages of Wisconsin churches in the four largest cooperating denominations: Methodist, 29.2 percent (178 of 609); Congregational, 11.3 percent (53 of 467); Presbyterian, 21.4 percent (43 of 201); and Baptist, 20.8 percent (37 of 178).[39] Perhaps in frustration at this record, the General Superintendent of the Wisconsin Congregational churches, a League leader, began to adopt the old Prohibitionist equation between piety and prohibitionism. "Every true church of Christ," he said, "is against the saloon."[40]

With the slowing of its forward progress, the League's confidence eroded, and that erosion manifested itself in an increasing hostility toward the Prohibition party. League spokesmen had once conceded the party a place in the prohibition movement, but they now began to hope that the party would disappear so as to clear the path for the League. Actual cooperation had been frequent during those early days, but after 1909 it seemed to become more difficult. The League still found it possible to cooperate with the party in 1910 in Pennsylvania and Minnesota, and in 1911 in Nebraska. But in Illinois by 1909 acrimony had replaced the friendly relations established by Superintendent W. H. Anderson and O. W. Stewart, and the alliance between the two organizations in Oregon broke down by 1910.[41]

On September 1, 1911, John G. Woolley became superintendent of the Wisconsin Anti-Saloon League. During the four months which he spent in that position, he seems to have devoted his efforts to winning Prohibitionists over to the League. He argued no longer, as he had done in the early days of his romance with the League, that the two organizations could work together harmoniously, the party providing "inspiration" and the League taking the lead in political work. Now, he said, conditions had changed. The Prohibition party had won its victory: "partyism" was dead. Now the task of winning the final battles for prohibition could be completed only through the practical methods of the League. Not that the population had been convinced of the need for prohibition; Woolley believed that it had not, but he found the liquor traffic consolidating.

He argued, therefore, that the order of the day was an attack upon the weakest point of the enemy's lines, an attack only the League was capable of leading. The Prohibition party's day, in short, was over.[42]

Other League leaders frequently denounced the Prohibition party. More and more, the League came to depend on the simple fact of party failure, justifying itself as a success, no matter how limited, in contrast to the party's complete ineptitude.[43] The culmination of League attacks upon the party came in Baker's report to the 1913 national convention. Charitably acknowledging the contribution of the party in temperance education and in demonstrating the impracticality of its method, Baker requested that it now quietly pass away: "There comes a time when the best service an individual or organization can render is to so live and die as to reproduce themselves in other individuals and other organizations that can carry forward on an improved plan the very thing for which they lived and wrought."[44]

THE PARTY RECOILS

During the period 1909-1912, the pattern of cooperation followed by rejection, which had characterized the careers of leaders like Ferguson and Fanning, appeared among many more party men as the triumphs of the nonpartisan approach began to seem hollow. Seeing the difficulties of enforcement both locally and on the state level, they returned to the belief that only a national party, elected for the purpose, could enact and enforce prohibition laws. Their return to full party allegiance did not rejuvenate the Prohibition party, but it represented to the League another sign of its faltering leadership.

J. Burritt Smith, a Madison, Wisconsin, lawyer, began to separate himself from his League affiliation after his election as Prohibition party state chairman in 1909. Smith had provided legal advice to the Wisconsin League at least since 1900; he claimed to have drawn up every county option bill which the League had presented to the state legislature.[45] Continuing his friendship for the League through September 1909, he made a drastic change in his thinking by July 1910, when he came out against the League even more strongly than Ferguson. "Every makeshift, every halfway measure for dealing with a wrong," he declared of local option, "only perpetuates, protects and increases it."[46] The point of difference between Ferguson and Smith lay in Ferguson's willingness to support campaigns for statewide prohibition. Smith, the first Prohibitionist to carry the logic of party devotion to its conclusion, refused to approve any activity not directly connected with building the party.[47] Ferguson himself had argued abstractly that prohibition without a party was ineffective, but he had never faced the exclusivist implications of his theory. Smith's statement of those implications was logically correct and politically absurd at the same time, but, together with the perception of Anti-Saloon League failure, it could and did serve as a justification for party men to break their ties with the League. At Smith's urging, in January 1911 the National Committee expelled from its ranks a former Wisconsin party chairman who had become a paid official of the League, although it refused to take the same action in the case of a higher party leader who had aligned himself with the League in Nebraska.[48]

For the Reverend Silas C. Swallow, who had supported cooperation in 1906, the failure of its method and the League's continued drain upon church resources justified rejection by early 1911.[49] The Illinois State Chairman, who had cooperated at least tacitly with the League since 1898, decided in 1911 that "our non-partisan friends have failed after ten years of hard work and the expenditure of more than a half million dollars. We believe their method has been wrong." Inviting League men to the Prohibition party, he offered perceptive advice: "We feel assured that the quickest way to obtain the county [option] law is to ask for something better. You must strike for State and National prohibition before you can get any more advance [d] legislation in Illinois."[50]

A more important defector from the ranks of the cooperators was the Illinois lawyer Robert H. Patton. Patton, like Smith, had provided invaluable aid to the Anti-Saloon League in drafting option bills and in 1905 he had been rewarded with election to a vice-presidency in the Illinois League. But by July 1911 he seemed to have been repelled both by the League's failure and by the expedient compromises which it had been forced to accept.[51] By April 1912 he was insisting that further cooperation between League and party men could take place only within the Prohibition party.[52]

If the League's future looked dim during the defeats of 1909-1913, the party's outlook remained an inky black. After increases in the national vote in 1900 and 1904, its total dropped slightly in 1908 and then plunged further in 1912. In the latter year, only a doubling of the party vote in California saved it from dropping below 200,000

votes nationally for the first time since 1896.[53] Party work languished
on all levels, and brave claims for the party's value to the prohibition
movement found immediate contradiction in confessions of the dismal
state of its organization.[54] Its organs of communication suffered, too,
from the general decline of the dry forces.[55] The Prohibition party
maintained a spark of life through this dark period only because of the
survival of Ferguson's faction. Furthermore, the League, beset by its
own troubles, was unable to offer Prohibitionists a convincing alternative to the party. Because the party did manage to survive, it continued
to represent an alternative to the League's leadership of the Prohibition
movement.

Although a few Prohibitionists of Ferguson's faction attempted to
distinguish themselves within the party by picturing themselves as
more hostile to the League than their opponents, the differences between
Prohibitionists on the question of cooperation were differences more of
tone than of substance. At the high tide of the League's apparent triumph
in 1909, Ferguson has asserted that the local-option movement "is clearly
and wholly a Prohibition movement," and said of the League that
"No intelligent man for a moment doubts the honesty of purpose
and the devotion of the men who make up its rank and file, fill its
coffers and win its fights at the polls."[56] He had also moved toward
the Anti-Saloon League's view of the saloon as an alien institution
when he claimed that the public sentiment which supported the liquor
traffic was "a manufactured, counterfeited, disloyal, un-American
thing that in no way represents the real thought of the American people."[57]
By mid-1910, however, partly under Smith's prodding, Ferguson had
returned to a strict "middle-of-the-road" position from which he saw
the Anti-Saloon League as the principal obstacle in the path of the
Prohibition party and condemned local option as a movement which
not only diverted Prohibitionists' efforts from the task of party-building
but also set back the public's progress toward true, national Prohibition.[58]
"The worst enemy of the best," Ferguson told Wisconsin Prohibitionists,
"is the good."[59]

In order to gain official status for their middle-of-the-road policy,
Ferguson and Smith during 1910 agitated for the calling of a national
congress of the Prohibition party. On December 29, 1910, they issued
a call for such a meeting in Chicago on January 26, 1911. The call
stated, among other things, that "men can no longer be non-partizan,
if they would; and it is wrong to be non-partizan, if they could." It

carried the endorsement of thirty-four National Committeemen and the State Chairmen of twenty-two states.[60] Unfortunately for Smith and Ferguson's hopes of leading the party, the congress lost some of its effectiveness when it became involved in a factional dispute then being fought out in the National Committee. Nevertheless, it still demonstrated the thinking of a sizeable body of party leaders by adopting a resolution along the lines suggested by Smith:

> The policy of the Prohibition party . . . is that a Prohibition party for the enactment and enforcement of state and national prohibitory law is necessary. Therefore, Resolved, that we declare it our conviction that the party organization EVERYWHERE should conduct ALL its affairs in harmony with this policy.[61]

Smith claimed that the congress had decided "to cut out all platform declarations for local or county option, and quit spending time, work or money on them."[62]

American Advance, the organ of the opposing faction, began its career with a tentative endorsement of cooperation, then moved quickly to hostility toward the League, claiming that its arguments with the nonpartisan organization would be conducted with logic rather than abuse so as to win League men to the party.[63] By late 1911 *American Advance* was denouncing the Anti-Saloon League for failing to provide adequate enforcement for the laws it secured and for failing to halt the increase in liquor consumption.[64] In December 1911 the party held a conference in Chicago, ostensibly to arrange the "union" of prohibition forces, but it was actually designed to draw League men into the party ranks by a phony show of compromise.[65] Throughout 1911 *American Advance* carried denunciations of the League, nonpartisanism, and local option which were authored by party leaders in seven states, as well as by National Chairman Jones.[66]

In 1912 *American Advance* reported public debates in Minnesota and Oregon between party and League leaders, and gloated over successful Prohibitionist efforts to engineer the withdrawal of Anti-Saloon League endorsements by various church bodies.[67] Its editor called Purley Baker an "exploiter" of "church and people," claimed that the League was "becoming more a mere auxiliary to license party politics, consciously or unconsciously manipulated by politicians for their own interests," and referred to support of the League as a "pitiful, childish

spectacle."[68] At the 1912 national convention, the party renominated
for president and vice-president two candidates who stood uncompromisingly for the middle-of-the road policy.[69]

It was not only organizational debility which made the middle-of-
the-road policy ring hollow. More important, by refusing to criticize
established institutions, the party avoided distinguishing itself from the
League. It even abandoned the last vestiges of economic radicalism which
still tinged some of its pronouncements. The party claimed to be "progressive" and took its stand with those business elements which sought reform as a means of heading off the growing Socialist threat.

William P. F. Ferguson continued to look to the mid-nineteenth
century for models. He still denounced lynchings, but now found analo-
gies for Prohibitionists in the Civil War rather than in the abolition movement. He took his inspiration from the ostensible prohibitionist Lincoln
rather than the reformer Garrison.[70] State parties customarily adopted
woman suffrage planks which conditioned voting privileges upon intelligence or education.[71] In 1909 Ferguson's concern over slavery led only
to war on the "white slave trade."[72]

The success of major-party politicians who called themselves "Progressives" made the Progressive label and rhetoric attractive to the Prohibition
party during the years 1909-1913.[73] The success of the Socialist party
at the same time, in contrast, led Prohibitionists to portray their party
as an alternative to Socialism.[74] A significant exponent of this policy
was Dan R. Sheen, who had vainly urged the party in 1904 to turn its
attention to the poor and to adopt a broad platform which included
advanced economic demands. By 1908 Sheen joined Ferguson in denouncing the Socialist attack upon "the institutions which our fathers
established and which we hold dear" and in supporting "our government
which, without its evil methods of administration, is the best government
under the sun."[75] Three years later, Sheen suggested that the Prohibition
party change its name to "Progressive Party" and adopt a platform including "Prohibition, Woman Suffrage, the Iniative, Referendum and
Recall" but apparently omitting the economic planks he had proposed
in 1904.[76] Isolated socialists such as George M. Hammell still remained
Prohibitionists, but *American Advance* now gloried in the fact that some
of the party's leaders were "counted among the most substantial business men."[77]

Church support of the Anti-Saloon League frustrated Prohibitionists
and brought about their effort to wean the churches from the League.[78]

The frustration emerged in occasional criticism of the churches and, more concretely, in an abortive attempt led by National Committmen from Maryland and Minnesota to turn the party away from its cultivation of the church voter. The dissidents' program, like that of Ferguson, however, included no suggestions of an alternative constituency.[79] The party refused to heed their pleas and continued to compete with the League for the support of church voters.[80]

The fragility of the Prohibition party's alternative to the Anti-Saloon League was evident in its instantaneous collapse when Baker, after the passage of the Webb-Kenyon Act in March 1913, proclaimed the drive for national prohibition to be the "logical next step." At a party conference in January 1913, even middle-of-the-road Prohibitionists such as Ferguson had begun to hint that they were ready to adopt a more cooperative attitude toward the League. After Baker's announcement, party leaders, with near unanimity, hastily assumed a cooperative stance, even though for some of them the position must have been embarrassing.[81] In October 1913 the Council of One Hundred, a figurehead group of prohibition leaders formed to promote national prohibition, included thirty luminaries of the Prohibition party along with all of the important leaders of the League.[82] At a meeting following the Anti-Saloon League national convention in November 1913, a group of party leaders including Ferguson passed a resolution endorsing cooperation. The group rejected another statement which sought support for the party on the grounds that it might be considered antagonistic to other organizations.[83] Thus, although it still maintained that national prohibition could be enforced only by a party elected for that purpose, the Prohibition party in effect surrendered to the League the leadership of the movement. It thereby put a temporary end to the conflict which had raged off and on between the two organizations for the past twenty years. By any standards important outside the prohibition movement, however, it would have mattered little if the party had made the same decision at any other point after 1896. The fact that the decision came in 1913 was less a tribute to the strength of the League than it was an indication of weakness in the entire movement.

THE DECISION FOR NATIONAL PROHIBITION

The leaders of the Anti-Saloon League were not men who customarily overestimated the extent of their own success. Although the League press always claimed every development in the temperance situation to be a triumph for the League or its methods, when it came to making the hard decisions concerning future strategy and tactics, League leaders normally took the smallest possible step which their standing at the head of the prohibition movement would allow. This trait was evident both in their reluctance to accept campaigns for statewide prohibition before 1913 and in their discomfiture after 1913 in the face of more far-reaching state and national measures than they thought feasible.[84]

During the years 1909-1913 League leaders did in fact recognize the crisis confronting the prohibition movement, despite official claims to the contrary.[85] Baker's files bulged with letters from state superintendents reporting little or no progress.[86] Some League leaders believed that a prohibition amendment should not be presented to Congress until after a majority of the states had adopted statewide prohibition.[87] Why then did they choose in 1913 to build the movement for national prohibition upon the shell of their crusade for statewide prohibition, thereby violating their claim of perfect accord with public sentiment?[88]

The answer seems to be that they had no other choice. Having won the leadership of the prohibition movement by portraying itself as unfailingly successful, the League could not retain its primacy by leading the forces into battles already once lost; instead it had to seek new battlefields. This conclusion appeared in Anderson's prediction in 1909 that the fight in the states would be won only by success on the national level and in the Virginia League's 1908 threat to move for statewide prohibition as a result of the failure of local option.[89] Twenty-seven years afterward, Ernest H. Cherrington still believed that in 1913 the League had stood "at the forks of the road." Had the leadership not been "equal to the emergency which we faced as an organization," the Eighteenth Amendment would not have been adopted.[90]

Furthermore, League leaders saw in the estrangement of Prohibition party men a threat disproportionate to its actual size.[91] In his report to the 1913 national convention, Baker claimed that the initiation of the drive for national prohibition made further hostility toward the League untenable. The convention's featured speaker, John G. Woolley, made his keynote speech an eloquent plea for cooperation, taking as his text, "Make a chain; for the land is full of bloody crimes and the city is full of violence."[92]

Finally, the passage of the Webb-Kenyon Act had clearly demonstrated the potential power of the League over Congress, as the defeats of 1909-1913 had indicated its weakness in statewide referenda. In this as in so many other ways, prohibitionists replicated a Progressive pattern. Defeated locally, they turned to statewide contests. Frustrated there, they went national. Successive retreats from electoral conflict were justified by the righteousness of the cause and by the ability of corrupt interests to prevent the people from expressing their will. The League differed from other Progressive groups only in its control over balance-of-power blocs in many states and congressional districts. If these were effective, its only enemy in the halls of Congress would be a weak and divided liquor lobby.

If success for the Prohibition movement could be defined merely as the passage of a prohibitory constitutional amendment by Congress and its ratification by the states—and most leaders of the League did define it in this way—then why worry about whether public sentiment had demanded prohibition?[93] And if the Prohibition party had now reached the point where it added nothing to this definition of success but enforcement by the party, why should it refuse to support such a movement? Why indeed?

NOTES

1. *Proceedings of the Fifteenth National Convention of the Anti-Saloon League of America* (hereafter referred to as *ASL Proceedings*) *1913*, p. 62.

2. James H. Timberlake, *Prohibition and the Progressive Movement, 1900-1920* (Cambridge, Mass., 1963), pp. 158-159.

3. Ernest H. Cherrington, *History of the Anti-Saloon League* (Westerville, Ohio, 1913), pp. 123,127,134-136.

4. Justin Steuart, *Wayne Wheeler, Dry Boss* (New York, 1928), pp. 76-77.

5. Ernest H. Cherrington, *The Evolution of Prohibition in the United States of America* (Westerville, Ohio, 1920), pp. 293-315; Ferdinand C. Iglehart, "The Campaign against the Saloon," *Review of Reviews* 48 (July 1913): 80-81; *ASL Proceedings, 1913,* pp. 278-279.

6. *American Issue,* Wisconsin edition, September 1911; *American Advance* (Chicago), September 16, 1911. The pattern of the statewide

contests of 1907-1913 reappeared in the legislative ratification and repeal by convention of the Eighteenth Amendment.

7. *ASL Proceedings, 1911*, p. 126; *American Issue*, Wisconsin edition, November 29, 1910.

8. John E. Caswell, "The Prohibition Movement in Oregon, Part 2, 1904-1915," *Oregon Historical Quarterly* 40 (1939):73.

9. Gilman M. Ostrander, *The Prohibition Movement in California, 1848-1933* (Berkeley, 1957), p. 85.

10. W. D. Cox to P. A. Baker, September 2, 1913, E. H. Cherrington Papers, Temperance Education Foundation (TEF).

11. P. A. Baker to S. E. Nicholson, October 13, 1908, Cherrington Papers.

12. Robert A. Hohner, "Prohibition and Virginia Politics, 1901-1916" (Ph.D. dissertation, Duke University, 1965), p. 108.

13. J. H. Robbins to E. H. Cherrington, November 29, 1910, Cherrington Papers. Emphasis in original. The *Anti-Saloon League Yearbook* for 1911 (pp. 64-65) magically turned this report into a picture of progress.

14. Peter R. Weisensel, "The Wisconsin Temperance Crusade to 1919" (M.S. thesis, University of Wisconsin, 1965), p. 142; *American Issue*, Wisconsin edition, May 16, 1911.

15. *American Issue*, Wisconsin edition, June 1910, May, September 1912; Weisensel, "Wisconsin Temperance Crusade," p. 35.

16. *ASL Proceedings, 1911*, p. 158. League leaders claimed that the reduced total (down about $10,000 from 1908-1909) was due to increased contributions toward establishment of the League's new printing plant at Westerville, Ohio. The situation revealed both the optimism of the period 1905-1909 and the letdown after 1909. *Journal of the 26th Delegated General Conference of the Methodist Episcopal Church* (New York, 1912), pp. 660-662.

17. *ASL Proceedings, 1903*, pp. 40-41; Report of National Committee (NC) meeting, January 24-26, 1911, Chicago, "Minutes of the National Committees, Conferences and Conventions of the Prohibition Party," vol. 2, p. 14a, Michigan Historical Collections (MHC), Ann Arbor.

18. Statement of income, November 1, 1913, Cherrington Papers.

19. *American Issue*, Wisconsin edition, January 10, 1911; see also November 15, 1910.

20. Ibid., January 1912.

21. *American Advance*, November 4, 1911.

22. *American Issue*, Wisconsin edition, June 1913.

23. See *ASL Proceedings, 1911*, pp. 18-27.

24. Ibid. Italics in original.

25. See, for example, *Minutes of the General Assembly of the*

Presbyterian Church in the United States of America (Philadelphia, 1907), p. 138, and (1911), p. 110.

26. For claims of single-mindedness, see *American Issue,* Wisconsin edition, August, October, 1912.

27. Ostrander, *Prohibition Movement in California,* p. 103; *ASL Proceedings, 1913,* p. 324.

28. *ASL Proceedings, 1911,* p. 69.

29. *American Issue,* Wisconsin edition, May 16, 1911. Larry D. Engelmann finds hostility toward organized labor among Michigan Anti-Saloon League leaders. Engelmann, "O Whiskey: The History of Prohibition in Michigan" (Ph.D. dissertation, University of Michigan, 1971), p. 283.

30. *American Issue,* Wisconsin edition, March 7, 1911.

31. Ibid., December 27, 1910, February 21, 1911, July 1912; *National Prohibitionist,* February 23, 1911; *ASL Proceedings, 1911,* pp. 28, 43-44.

32. *American Issue,* Wisconsin edition, May 1910.

33. Ernest H. Cherrington et al., eds., *Standard Encyclopedia of the Alcohol Problem,* 6 vols. (Westerville, Ohio, 1924-30), vol. 2, pp. 806-809.

34. *American Issue,* Wisconsin edition, December 13, 1910.

35. *Minutes of the General Assembly of the Presbyterian Church . . .* (1907), p. 137; William H. Anderson, "The National Inter-Church Temperance Federation," undated typescript in Cherrington Papers; P. A. Baker to S. E. Nicholson, October 13, 1908, C. R. Mabee to Dear Sir, October 15, 1908, Cherrington Papers.

36. *Minutes of the General Assembly of the Presbyterian Church . . .* (1912), p. 441.

37. *American Advance,* July 8, 1911.

38. *Journal of the 26th Delegated General Conference of the Methodist Episcopal Church,* pp. 266, 660-662; *American Advance,* June 1, 1912; *Union Signal,* June 6, 1912; *American Issue,* Wisconsin edition, June 1912.

39. *American Issue,* Wisconsin edition, October 1911. See also Weisensel, "Wisconsin Temperance Crusade," p. 62.

40. *American Issue,* Wisconsin edition, April 1913.

41. Earl C. Kaylor, Jr., "The Prohibition Movement in Pennsylvania, 1865-1920," 2 vols. (Ph.D. dissertation, Pennsylvania State University, 1963), vol. 2, p. 338; *ASL Proceedings, 1911,* pp. 124, 129, 140; *American Issue,* Wisconsin edition, February 1909.

42. *American Issue,* Wisconsin edition, September, October, November, December 1911. See also *National Prohibitionist,* August 5, 1909, June 9, 1910.

43. *American Issue,* Wisconsin edition, March, April, May, June, September, 1910, March 7, 1911, February 1912, July, October, 1913.

Most of these items appeared in the national portion of the paper, the remainder in the Wisconsin section. See also Frank P. Stockbridge, "The Church Militant against the Saloon," *World's Work* 26 (October 1913): 703, 704.

44. *ASL Proceedings, 1913*, pp. 56-57, 60-61.

45. *American Issue,* January 29, 1904; *American Issue,* Wisconsin edition, September 1909.

46. *National Prohibitionist,* July 14, August 18, 1910.

47. Ibid., July 20, 1911-August 24, 1911.

48. *American Issue,* Wisconsin edition, August, October, 1909; *National Prohibitionist,* December 29, 1910; Minutes of NC meeting, January 24-26, 1911, Chicago, "Minutes," vol. 2, pp. 15-18.

49. *National Prohibitionist,* February 23, 1911; *American Advance,* July 1, 1911.

50. *American Advance,* April 29, 1911, April 20, 1912.

51. Ibid., July 1, 1911.

52. Ibid., April 6, December 7, 1912.

53. Svend Petersen, *A Statistical History of the American Presidential Elections* (New York, 1963), p. 195.

54. *National Prohibitionist,* January 26, April 6, June 29, 1911; *American Advance,* January 6, 1912, June 14, 1913, January 24, 1914.

55. *National Prohibitionist,* 1907-1911; *American Advance,* December 14, 1912.

56. *National Prohibitionist,* April 29, May 27, 1909.

57. Ibid., June 16, 1910.

58. See, for example, *National Prohibitionist,* July 7, November 24, 1910.

59. Ibid., July 28, 1910.

60. Ibid., December 29, 1910.

61. Ibid., February 2, 1911.

62. Ibid., March 2, 1911.

63. *American Advance,* April 1, 15, June 17, July 8, 1911.

64. Ibid., October 7, November 25, 1911.

65. Ibid., December 16, 1911, January 20, 1912.

66. Ibid., April 1, 15, May 13, 20, June 17, September 30, October 21, November 25, 1911.

67. Ibid., February 17, March 9, May 25, June 1, October 5, 1912.

68. Ibid., April 27, June 22, November 23, 1912.

69. Ibid., July 20, 1912.

70. Ferguson's use of the Civil War—and especially his selection of one of its bloodiest battles, Cold Harbor—was reminiscent of the League's concern with virility and violence. *National Prohibitionist,* November 12, 190? February 11, 1909, May 25, August 17, 1911.

71. Some made the same demand implicitly, as did the national platform of 1912, by asking "suffrage for women on the same terms as for men."

David L. Colvin, *Prohibition in the United States: A History of the Prohibition Party and of the Prohibition Movement* (New York, 1926), p. 350; *National Prohibitionist,* October 1, 1908, October 21, 1909, May 12, 19, July 7, 28, 1910.

72. *National Prohibitionist,* January 28, December 16, 1909.

73. Ibid., September 29, 1910; *American Advance,* December 2, 1911, January 20, March 23, October 19, November 2, 9, 1912, April 12, 1913; Chicago *Record-Herald,* July 9, 13, 1912; *New York Times,* July 13, 1912; "The Handwriting on the Wall," Speech of Temporary Chairman C. N. Howard at the Prohibition National Convention, Atlantic City, N. J., July 10, 1912, NC Papers, MHC; Frederick W. Adrian, "The Political Significance of the Prohibition Party" (Ph.D. dissertation, Ohio State University, 1942), p. 127.

74. *National Prohibitionist,* May 4, 1911; *American Advance,* April 8, August 19, 1911, and all issues in 1912, especially May 25, August 31.

75. *National Prohibitionist,* December 10, 1908.

76. *American Advance,* December 2, 1911.

77. *National Prohibitionist,* October 28, 1909, February 9, 1911; *American Advance,* November 25, December 2, 1911.

78. For frustration, see *National Prohibitionist,* February 9, March 23, 1911; *American Advance,* January 13, 1912.

79. Minutes of NXC meeting, December 28, 1908, Chicago, "Minutes," vol. 2, p. 1; *National Prohibitionist,* January 21, 1909, April 13, 1911; Chicago *Record-Herald,* July 10, 1912.

80. *National Prohibitionist,* December 16, 1909, March 23, 1911; *American Advance,* June 10, July 15, October 28, 1911, April 19, May 10, 1913.

81. See *American Advance* throughout 1913, but especially January 25, March 22, May 17, 31, June 14, July 26, August 16; C. N. Howard, "The Handwriting on the Wall," NC Papers; *The Vindicator* (Franklin, Pa.) May 9, 1913.

82. *American Advance,* October 11, November 22, 1913.

83. Ibid., November 22, December 6, 1913.

84. See, for example, James Cannon, Jr., *Bishop Cannon's Own Story: Life as I Have Seen It,* ed. Richard L. Watson, Jr. (Durham, 1955), pp. 182-183; Norman H. Clark, *The Dry Years: Prohibition and Social Change in Washington* (Seattle, 1965), p. 138.

85. See above; P. A. Baker, "Alarming Increase of Liquor Drinking among Women," *American Issue,* Wisconsin edition, March 1912. For arguments that the forward movement was implied by success, see "Twenty Facts about the Twentieth Anniversary Convention of the Anti-Saloon League," *American Issue,* Wisconsin edition, October 1913; Superintendent's Report, *ASL Proceedings, 1913,* pp. 62-64.

86. See the folder labelled, "What the States Have Accomplished since the Last Convention," Cherrington Papers.

87. H. H. Russell to Lillian D. Russell, November 20, 1912, Russell Papers; Wayne B. Wheeler, "The Inside Story of Prohibition's Adoption," *New York Times,* March 28, 1926. See also Julia Reed, "Fifty Years of Anti-Saloon," typescript dated 1943, Russell Papers.

88. For another opinion that the drive for national prohibition was prematurely launched, see Virginius Dabney, *Dry Messiah: The Life of Bishop Cannon* (New York, 1949), pp. 132-133.

89. *ASL Proceedings, 1909,* pp. 36-37; Dabney, *Dry Messiah,* p. 57.

90. Enclosure, E. H. Cherrington to H. H. Russell, April 10, 1940, p. 15, Cherrington Papers.

91. *American Issue,* Wisconsin edition, June 1913.

92. *ASL Proceedings, 1913,* pp. 25-29, 58; *American Issue,* Wisconsin edition, December 1913.

93. Steuart, *Wheeler,* p. 168; Kaylor, "Prohibition Movement in Pennsylvania," vol. 1, p. 5.

Epilogue: the eighteenth and twenty-first amendments

The years from 1913 to 1920 were exciting and happy times for prohibitionists. The years from 1920 to 1933 were equally as exciting but less happy. Ratification of the Eighteenth Amendment in 1919 made prohibition one of the most successful reform movements in American history. Repeal in 1933 brought the prohibition movement to an ignominious end, transforming it into a temperance crusade once again. By 1948 the remnants of the Anti-Saloon League had split into two fragments, the National Temperance League and the Temperance Education Foundation.[1] The Prohibition party lives on, hampered by ballot restrictions, but can find few to take up its challenge that prohibition with a party to enforce it has never been tried.

The questions of why prohibition succeeded and why it failed remain. Monographic studies of particular states and topics are insufficient in number and too uneven in quality and coverage for firm answers.[2] Nevertheless, several models have been advanced. A brief examination of the major issues will both clarify the relationship of this study to existing theory and identify the points on which further research is required

It is possible that the prohibition movement—if by that one means the Anti-Saloon League, Prohibition party, WCTU, and their followers—played little, if any, part in the decision to adopt the Eighteenth Amendment. John J. Rumbarger has argued that the most important actors were instead representatives of eastern corporate capital. National prohibition, then, functioned as "the political remedy offered primarily by corporate capital for its own failure to rationalize the labor supply, whose maldistribution and transient nature had become a structural feature of the national life by 1915."[3] Rumbarger has clearly shown that some large capitalists supported prohibition for this reason and that their goals were quite consistent with those of middle-class prohibitionists by 1915. His argument depends upon the assumption that these men did engineer congressional approval of the Eighteenth Amendment, an assumption which is plausible but unproven. On the other hand, there is considerable evidence that even opponents of the Anti-Saloon League perceived it as the key force behind the Amendment.[4]

If Rumbarger's argument is to be accepted, it must be supported by the kind of intensive analysis of the legislative process through which Gabriel Kolko has discovered corporate influence behind other Progressive reforms.[5] Until then, we must continue to regard the pressure politics of the Anti-Saloon League as decisive. After all, the League's methods were best suited to influencing the Congressmen and state legislators who submitted and ratified the Amendment. By 1917 even Woodrow Wilson, no mean political strategist, had to negotiate with League lobbyists for the postponement of a wartime prohibition act which had been inserted into the Lever Food Control Bill by overzealous drys.[6] The League seems to have been effective in dealing with state legislatures as well as Congress: of the first thirty-six states to ratify, eight had no statewide prohibition law of their own.[7]

Both the 65th Congress, which submitted the Amendment, and the state legislatures which ratified it had probably been elected for reasons which most of their constituents thought had nothing to do with prohibition. Therefore, while submission and ratification indicate the ability of the League to manipulate legislators, they do not necessarily reflect a popular majority in favor of prohibition. Nor does the number of states (31) which had adopted statewide prohibition by the time of their legislatures' ratification. Eight of those states had gone dry by legislative enactment, and most of the others contained large wet minorities. The wet states also contained dry minorities, to be sure, but since there were few elections to reveal their size, no conclusion is possible. Nor does the League's claimed percentage of the population living in dry territory at the coming of national prohibition (68.3 percent) necessarily reveal a dry majority, for the same reasons.[8]

The best indicators of prohibition's popular support are the forty-nine statewide prohibition referenda held between 1900 and ratification in 1919. In these, prohibition was uncomplicated by other issues and, since they were normally held in conjunction with general elections,

TABLE 8: STATEWIDE PROHIBITION REFERENDA, 1900-1918

Year	State	Result
1903	Vermont	Wet
1907	Oklahoma	Dry
1908	North Carolina	Dry
1909	Alabama	Wet
1910	Florida	Wet
	Oregon	Wet
	Missouri	Wet
	Oklahoma	Dry
1911	Maine	Dry
	Texas	Wet
1912	Ohio	Wet
	Arkansas	Wet
	Colorado	Wet
	West Virginia	Dry
1914	Arizona	Dry
	Colorado	Dry
	Oregon	Dry
	Virginia	Dry
	Washington	Dry
	California	Wet
	Ohio	Wet
1915	South Carolina	Dry
	Ohio	Wet
1916	Oregon*	Dry
	Washington*	Dry
	Alaska	Dry
	Colorado	Dry
	Arkansas	Dry
	California	Wet
	Idaho	Dry
	Michigan	Dry
	Missouri	Wet
	Montana	Dry

TABLE 8 (*continued*)

Year	State	Result
	Nebraska	Dry
	South Dakota	Dry
	Vermont	Wet
1917	Puerto Rico	Dry
	Iowa	Wet
	New Mexico	Dry
	Ohio	Wet
1918	Washington	Dry
	California	Wet
	Florida	Dry
	Minnesota	Dry**
	Missouri	Wet
	Utah	Dry
	Wyoming	Dry
	Nevada	Dry
	Ohio	Dry

*Two simultaneous referenda were considered as one.
**Prohibition was approved, but turnout was insufficient for adoption.

Sources: *New York Times*, February 4, 1903; Jimmie L. Franklin,
Born Sober: Prohibition in Oklahoma, 1907-1959 (Norman, Okla.,
1971); *Anti-Saloon League Yearbook, 1913, 1917, 1920*; E.H.
Cherrington, *The Evolution of Prohibition in the United States of
America* (Westerville, Ohio, 1920); Cherrington et al., eds., *Standard
Encyclopedia of the Alcohol Problem*, 6 vols. (Westerville, Ohio,
1924-30); Larry D. Engelmann, "O Whiskey: The History of Prohibition
in Michigan" (Ph.D. dissertation, University of Michigan, 1971); Charles
Merz, *The Dry Decade* (New York, 1931), p. 308; G. K. Renner,
"Prohibition Comes to Missouri, 1910-1919," *Missouri Historical Review*
62 (July 1968): 387.

turnout should have been large. On the surface, prohibition's record was
quite impressive (Table 8). During the years 1900-1912, only five out of
fourteen referenda resulted in approval of prohibition. But in the years
between the Webb-Kenyon Act and 1919, prohibitionists won twenty-
five out of thirty-five statewide referenda. Obviously, something more

than League pressure changed the minds of Congressmen and state legislators.

Prohibition victories in statewide referenda, impressive as they were, however, did not necessarily add up to a popular majority for national prohibition. For one thing, the measure for which people voted in their state was not always the same measure which they got from Congress and their state legislature. In many states, the people voted only for an anti-saloon law, one that would outlaw the liquor traffic while leaving private importation and possession of liquor untouched. Yet, with the Reed Bone-Dry Amendment in 1917, that loophole was closed by congressional fiat.[9] The Eighteenth Amendment and Volstead Act nailed it shut.

Furthermore, because of the varying sizes of the states, even victory in thirty of forty-nine state referenda does not imply a majority for prohibition in those referenda. Figures are currently available for only forty of the referenda: in those, despite twenty-six prohibition victories, only 49.81 percent voted for the often restricted measures proposed. And since the missing figures include five losses to four victories, the most tenable conclusion is that, in the nineteen years before ratification, prohibition did not attract majority support from those who had an opportunity to express themselves on the question.[10]

Clearly, most of the prohibition victories came in the less populous states. Of the twenty-four largest states in 1920, thirteen did not vote on prohibition during 1900-1918. Two of them got it anyway, by legislative action; one already had it, by referendum. Of the eleven which did vote, five rejected prohibition. To put it another way, the correlation for all states between population size and the holding of a prohibition referendum is -.2982;[11] the correlation between population size and approval of prohibition by referendum is -.4309.[12] The larger the state, the less likely it was to hold a referendum; if one was held, the larger the state, the less likely it was to approve.[13] It seems unlikely, therefore, that prohibition enjoyed majority support before ratification made the question academic.

Despite the lack of a popular majority, the increasing support for prohibition revealed by the referendum victories after 1913 requires explanation. One factor often cited, the flood of Americanism stimulated by World War I, can easily be relegated to a subordinate position. Sixteen of the twenty-five victories in referenda held during 1914-1918 came before American entry into the war. Of the remaining nine, three reiterated approval of prohibition already given; five others were the first

referenda held in those states. Only in Ohio in 1918 did voters reverse
their previous rejection of prohibition. In three of the four unsuccessful
referenda of 1917-1918, the result was the same as in prewar referenda;
in the fourth, no vote had previously been taken. In its centralizing
thrust and stimulus to food conservation, the war may have affected
Congress—but only to turn a 1914 majority for prohibition into overwhelming support by 1917. It does not seem to have had much effect
on the voters.

Nor can popular support for prohibition be explained as the
result of rural America's attack upon its cities. If we define a rural
state as one with more than 50 percent of its population living in
areas of less than 2,500 inhabitants, we find that in the statewide
referenda of 1900-1918 ruralism correlates with approval of prohibition at an insignificant +.1218.[14] For the referenda of 1914-1918, the
correlation is higher, +.2830, but is still not significant at the .05
level. During 1900-1918, twenty-one referenda in rural states approved
prohibition, but so did ten referenda in urban states; meanwhile, ten
referenda in rural states rejected prohibition, but only eight referenda
in urban states did so. Any argument based on groups below the
state level cuts both ways. To say, as Joseph R. Gusfield has done, that
"the political power of rural populations was essential in securing dry
supremacy at state and national levels" begs the question. The political power of the urban middle class, as James H. Timberlake has
pointed out, was also essential.[15]

This conclusion is consistent with the findings of Clark on Washington (state) and Engelmann on Michigan. Class and ethnicity acted more
powerfully than ruralism in determining support for prohibition.[16]
We must now ask why the native middle class came to support prohibition by 1918.

One theme which middle-class supporters of prohibition undoubtedly
found appealing was the old invocation of national unity through national
self-restraint. The period from 1910 to World War I has aptly been called
"the age of industrial violence." Middle-class men and women could not
help being constantly reminded of the distance between their privileged
position and that of the workers who filled the ranks of the IWW and
the meetings of the Socialist party. The existence of that gap must have
engendered both guilt and fear. Both could be assuaged by proclaiming
one's willingness to sacrifice and one's concern for the lower orders
through support of prohibition. But prohibition triumphant as a symbol
of national unity does not tell the whole story, for the prohibition move-

ment which the middle class brought to power in 1919 was far less committed to cross-class cooperation than the prohibition movement which
the middle class had rejected in the 1890s.

The middle class supported prohibition primarily because of a social
outlook which stemmed not from slipping status but rather from the
inescapable growth of the corporation and the resulting militancy of
labor. This outlook rested on the well-founded belief, dating from the
Gilded Age, that the middle class was in imminent danger of being crushed
between two millstones: capital above and labor below. Middle-class men
and women worried that their distinctive concern for the quality of
life would be shoved aside by farmers' and workers' demands for a share
in making the policy and dividing the profits of industrialism, or would
be subordinated to the corporations' need for stability. Three alternatives existed: to side with labor; to side with capital; or to create an independent position. If the prohibition movement is any guide, the middle
class by the mid-1890s had rejected the first alternative. Progressivism
represented the third. It was generally a failure, and as the Progressive
era gave way to the Jazz Age, the principal marks of its presence were
the Eighteenth and Nineteenth Amendments to the Constitution. Most
other Progressive reforms were at best tainted by the hands of the corporation, at worst the product of corporate strategists. And, as I have argued,
prohibition as proof of middle-class independence was more appearance
than reality, for, in its twentieth-century form, prohibition implicitly
accepted the hegemony of the corporation, as well as a lot else. But to
someone between millstones, any way to escape being crushed was wel-
come. And prohibition, by allowing the corporation to solidify its position at the expense of labor, did help to remove—for a time—the lower
millstone. That left only the upper millstone. But of course one millstone by itself was incapable of grinding. It could only topple. Ten
years after the Eighteenth Amendment, it did.

The middle class, then, supported prohibition in order to shore up
their damaged society and prove themselves to be caring and potent members of that society. At the same time, they kept their distance from the
object of reform—the lower class—and carefully refrained from attacking
the corporations which posed the greater threat to the middle-class dream
of a just and harmonious America. As humanitarian *and* conservative reform, rather than in the narrower sense suggested by Timberlake, prohibition was truly Progressive.

The final reason for the success of prohibition involves a shadowy
entity which has made only furtive appearances in these pages so far.

The liquor industry, it has been shown, made a good target for Progressive reformers because of its concentration, participation in political corruption, and indifference to the suffering it caused.[17] But in these res-
pects it differed only in degree from other industries which escaped prohibition as well as any other effective attack upon their antisocial practices.
The liquor industry did differ from others in only one important respect:
its product was taxed by the federal government. Between 1870 and 1915,
that tax provided a substantial portion of the United States internal revenue.[18] During the Civil War the liquor industry had been forced into a
partnership with the national government which other industries would
not achieve until the Progressive era. Liquor men, believing that the
federal government would never move against such a lucrative source of
revenue, thus failed to follow the lead of other industries in creating an
industry-dominated regulatory body which might protect it from the
fruits of its greed. In this understandable failure it was un-Progressive.
And as such it was vulnerable, after the coming of the income tax, to a
powerful lobby supported by a middle class on the prowl for easy targets.

By 1933, prohibition had failed in the very important sense that the
measure which the prohibition movement had presented as the ultimate
solution to the problem of liquor abuse had been overwhelmingly repudiated by the American people. The achievements of prohibition (some
of which have been pointed out by J. C. Burnham) are dwarfed by this
single fact.[19] If that failure were not so resounding, America would to-
day have a healthy prohibition movement instead of senile, isolated temperance groups.

Repeal was all the more painful to prohibitionists because of the way
in which it was accomplished. State conventions, chosen in elections
which constituted the only national referendum ever held on prohibition
(as well as being the only national referendum on any single issue since
the adoption of the Constitution), rushed through ratification of the
Twenty-first Amendment in less time than it had taken state legislatures
to ratify the Eighteenth. The process of democracy, it appeared, need not
be cumbersome.

Why did this happen? It may be that we need no more complex explanation than that the majority which had always opposed prohibition finally
got a chance to have its way. Perhaps nothing really changed.

When we lower our gaze from the national to the state level, however,
we find some evidence of change. In Michigan, majorities for prohibition
of 68,600 in 1916 and 207,500 in 1919 became a 547,200 majority against
prohibition in 1932. The change was general across the state: the county-

by-county wet votes in 1916 and 1919 correlate with the repeal vote of
1932 at +.6091 and +.6743, respectively.[20]

In the state of Washington, a dry majority of 17,600 in 1914 became
a wet majority of 80,600 by 1932. Again, the change was general: the
1914 and 1932 county-by-county wet votes correlate at +.6317.[21]
Nevertheless, Washington offers some support for Gusfield's claim that
urban and rural prohibitionists split apart during the 1920s: in 1914
ruralism and prohibitionism had correlated at only +.1881; in 1932 they
correlated at +.3646.[22] Still, support for prohibition declined in all but
two of Washington's thirty-nine counties.

Part of the reason for the general repudiation of prohibition must
lie in the various scandals, inefficiencies, and harassments resulting from
prohibition enforcement by state and federal administrations which had
little interest in effective enforcement. More important, it seems to me,
was a long-term change in drinking patterns caused by the increasing
encouragement of consumption in all goods which was required by an
advanced capitalist society. This change must be extrapolated from drinking surveys which began only in 1946. From 1946 to 1963, the proportion
of drinkers increased in all but one age, sex, educational, residence, and
religious category.[23] Most interesting for this study is the fact that today,
the proportion of drinkers rises fairly regularly from the lowest to the
highest categories of income, education, and status.[24] If the widening
use of alcohol since 1946 and today's class differences in drinking are not
merely post-World War II or post-Repeal phenomena, then it becomes
apparent that the prohibition movement, in its appeal to the middle class,
was leaning upon a weak reed. And the least-paid, least-educated, and
least prestigious Americans, over whose fate Progressives and prohibitionists shed such copious tears, have turned out after all to be the least likely
drinkers.

Despite these changes, the Anti-Saloon League might have managed
to maintain prohibition if it had been a different kind of organization with
a different method. For, although the League did win a constitutional
amendment, although it had considerable say in manning the under-
staffed and underpaid Prohibition Bureau, and although Wayne Wheeler
had the ear of two Presidents, the League never did have the power to
rule. It had never asked for it because to do so would have meant transforming itself into either a political party subject to the popular will or a
government agency whose existence would have belied the effectiveness
of the law it had fought so hard to secure. Without the power to rule, the
League could not maintain its law, and whatever symbolic value the law

held disappeared with it, leaving the League sitting amidst the ashes of
a century-long movement.

But the League's failure to maintain prohibition meant more than
the defeat of a particular method. It meant the failure of the prohibition
movement to achieve its larger goal of a society unified in pursuit of
the general welfare. In an important sense, John G. Woolley and the
other Prohibitionists who redefined the party's purpose at the turn of
the century had possessed the keenest insight of anyone in the movement
during the period under discussion. Freed by failure from the need to
secure immediate triumph, they realized that the victory of their movement would necessarily entail the conversion of a whole society to self-
restraint in the interests of all. Prohibition by itself, they knew, could
never achieve this. The League ignored this fact at its peril and, as Repeal
showed, at considerable cost to the cause of temperance as well.

One might argue that the League simply recognized the requirements
of political action in a pluralistic society and acted effectively upon that
recognition. But to say this is to ignore the fact that planned social change
can succeed only when it rests upon a consensus of values, no matter
how pluralistic the society, a lesson which subsequent generations of
reformers have had to learn again and again. The League realized this
but refused to act upon it, because the penalty for doing so was a long
campaign of persuasion on top of the century of effort behind it and
the foregoing of immediate political gains which lay within its grasp.
Instead, the League accepted, even used, the divisions within American
society and slipped through a crack in the democratic process to win a
battle which it hoped would be decisive. In the process, it lost the war.
That it did is less a cause for blame than a poignant commentary upon
the prospects for change in twentieth-century America.

NOTES

1. Norman H. Dohn, "The History of the Anti-Saloon League"
(Ph.D. dissertation, Ohio State University, 1959), p. 264.

2. Fourteen monographs have analyzed the prohibition issue in
twelve states. Among the best are: Gilman M. Ostrander, *The Prohibi-
tion Movement in California, 1848-1933* (Berkeley, 1957); Norman
H. Clark, *The Dry Years: Prohibition and Social Change in Washington*
(Seattle, 1965); and Larry D. Engelmann, "O Whiskey: The History of
Prohibition in Michigan" (Ph.D. dissertation, University of Michigan, 1971).

3. John J. Rumbarger, "The Social Origins and Function of the Political Temperance Movement in the Reconstruction of American Society, 1825-1917" (Ph.D. dissertation, University of Pennsylvania, 1968), pp. 9-10.

4. James H. Timberlake, *Prohibition and the Progressive Movement, 1900-1920* (Cambridge, Mass., 1963), chs. 5 and 6; Andrew Sinclair, *Era of Excess*, Harper Colophon edn. (New York, 1964), chs. 5-8; Peter H. Odegard, *Pressure Politics* (New York, 1928).

5. Gabriel Kolko, *The Triumph of Conservatism* (Glencoe, 1963).

6. Odegard, *Pressure Politics*, pp. 166-71.

7. *The Anti-Saloon League Year Book, 1921* (Westerville, Ohio, 1921), pp. 14, 136-320.

8. Ibid., p. 325.

9. Charles Merz, *The Dry Decade* (New York, 1931), pp. 20-23; Norman H. Clark, *The Dry Years*, p. 108; Larry D. Engelmann, "O Whiskey," pp. 227-28.

10. Figures are missing for: Alabama (1909); Oregon (1910, 1916); Colorado (1912, 1916); Arkansas (1916); Vermont (1916); California (1918); Minnesota (1918).

11. The correlation coefficient ϕ was computed from a 2x2 table using the procedure from Charles M. Dollar and Richard J. Jensen, *Historian's Guide to Statistics* (New York, 1971), pp. 71-72. This correlation is significant at the .05 level.

12. ϕ calculated as in note 11. This correlation is significant at the 01 level.

13. Charles Merz (*Dry Decade*, p. 19) has made the misleading claim that "all of the state prohibition laws which were enacted in this country prior to the war were enacted by the affirmative vote of less than 4 per cent of the adult population of the country." Merz has apparently used as his basis for comparison the adult population as of 1920. By this method, it is easy to show that Woodrow Wilson in 1916 enjoyed the support of only 15 percent of the adult population.

14. ϕ calculated as in note 11. This correlation is not significant even at the .10 level. Defining "rural" as "greater than 40 percent rural population" yields $\phi = +.1215$, likewise not significant even at the .10 level.

15. Joseph R. Gusfield, "Prohibition: The Impact of Political Utopianism," in John Braeman, Robert H. Bremner, and David Brody, eds., *Change and Continuity in Twentieth-Century America: The 1920's* (Columbus, 1968), p. 262; James H. Timberlake, *Prohibition and The Progressive Movement*, p. 152.

16. Clark, *Dry Years*, pp. 121-122; Engelmann, "O Whiskey," pp. 102-103, 110, 119-124.

17. Timberlake, *Prohibition and the Progressive Movement*, pp. 100-118.

18. Sinclair, *Era of Excess*, p. 101.

19. J. C. Burnham, "New Perspectives on the Prohibition 'Experiment' of the 1920's," *Journal of Social History* 2 (Fall 1968): 51-68.

20. Engelmann, "O Whiskey," pp. 369, 645, 646-651.

21. Pearson's r computed from data in Clark, *Dry Years*, pp. 233-234. This correlation is significant at the .01 level.

22. Spearman's r computed from Clark, *Dry Years*, pp. 233-234. Gusfield, "Prohibition: The Impact of Political Utopianism," p. 262.

23. Harold A. Mulford, "Drinking and Alcoholism: A Study of Socio-Cultural Patterns and Attitudes," paper presented at the Midwest Institute of Alcohol Studies, Madison, Wisconsin, June 16, 1969, p. 5. According to Mulford's Table 1, the incidence of drinkers declined slightly among residents of cities under one million population.

24. Ibid., Table 3; Don Cahalan, Ira H. Cisin, and Helen M. Crossley, *American Drinking Practices: A National Study of Drinking Behavior and Attitudes* (New Brunswick, N.J., 1969), pp. 24-29.

Selected sources

PRIMARY SOURCES

Manuscript Collections

In 1968, the WCTU refused access to the Frances E. Willard Papers, WCTU Archives, Evanston, Illinois, because of the papers' poor condition. The Willard Papers, together with many other important published and unpublished sources relating to the temperance movement, are now being microfilmed as a joint project of the Michigan Historical Collections, the Ohio Historical Society, and the WCTU Archives. The microfilming project is tentatively scheduled for completion in 1977.

Ernest Hurst Cherrington Papers. Temperance Education Foundation, Westerville, Ohio. Now in the possession of the Ohio Historical Society, Columbus.

Colman Family Papers. Wisconsin State Historical Society.

Samuel Dickie Papers. Michigan Historical Collections.

Isaac K. Funk Papers. Library of Congress.

Henry Demarest Lloyd Papers. Wisconsin State Historical Society.

Henry A. Miner Papers. Wisconsin State Historical Society.

Minutes of the National Committees, Conferences and Conventions of the Prohibition Party. Michigan Historical Collections.

Prohibition National Committee Papers. Michigan Historical Collections.

Thomas C. Richmond Papers. Wisconsin State Historical Society.

Howard Hyde Russell Diary. Temperance Education Foundation.

Now in the possession of the Ohio Historical Society.
    Howard Hyde Russell Papers. Michigan Historical Collections.
    John P. St. John Papers. Kansas State Historical Society.

Interview

    Warner, Dr. Harry S. Columbus, Ohio. August 29, 1970.

Prohibition Party and Anti-Saloon League Newspapers

    American Advance. Chicago, 1912-1914.
    American Issue. Columbus, Ohio, 1899-1905.
    American Issue. Wisconsin edition. Milwaukee, 1908-1913.
    The Citizen. Harriman, Tenn., 1903-1905.
    Facts and Figures. Menomonee Falls, Wis., 1900-1902.
    The Hatchet. Guthrie, Okla., July-August 1906.
    The Lever. Chicago, 1892, 1896.
    The National Prohibitionist. Chicago and New York, 1907-1911.
    The New Voice. New York and Chicago, 1889-1906.
    The Northwestern Mail. Madison and Milwaukee, Wis., 1890-1905.
    Union Signal. Chicago, 1890-1896, 1912-1913.
    The Vindicator. Franklin, Penn., 1913.
    The Wisconsin Agitator. Menomonee Falls, 1899-1900.
    The Wisconsin Issue. Madison, 1905-1907.

Non-Prohibitionist Newspapers

    Advocate (Topeka, Kansas), 1891-1892, 1895-1896.
    Chicago Times 1892.
    Chicago Tribune. 1892, 1900, 1904, 1908, 1912.
    Commercial Gazette (Cincinnati), 1891.
    Herald (Boston), 1896.
    Inter-Ocean (Chicago), 1896.
    Journal of the Knights of Labor 1891-1892.
    Kansas City Star 1891-1892.
    New York Times 1896, 1900, 1904, 1908, 1912.

People's Party Paper, (Atlanta, Ga.), 1892, 1894.

Record-Herald, (Chicago), 1908, 1912.

Republic (St. Louis), 1892.

Times-Herald (Chicago), 1896, 1900.

Articles

"Abolitionists and Prohibitionists; or Moral Reform Embarrassed by Ultraism," *New Englander and Yale Review* 262 (January 1892): 1-25.

Chafin, Eugene W. "The Prohibition Party's Appeal," *The Independent* 65 (October 15, 1908): 880-882.

_____ "The Prohibition Party's Appeal," *The Independent* 73 (October 24, 1912): 953-954.

"Decline in Methodism," *The Outlook* 64 (March 17, 1900): 610-611.

Dickie, Samuel. "The Prohibitionists and Their Cause," *American Monthly Review of Reviews* 38 (September 1908): 300-303.

Gougar, Helen M. "Christ and the Liquor Seller," *Arena* 7 (March 1893): 461-470.

_____. "Is Liquor Selling a Sin?" *Arena* 8 (November 1893): 710-716.

Ireland, John (Archbishop of St. Paul). "The Catholic Church and the Saloon," *North American Review* 159 (October 1894): 498-505.

Jackson, J. C. "The Work of the Anti-Saloon League," *Annals of the American Academy of Political and Social Science* 32 (November 1908): 482-496.

Johnson, William E. ("Pussyfoot"). "I Had to Lie, Bribe and Drink to Put Over Prohibition in America," *Hearst's International-Cosmopolitan* 80 (May 1926): 34-35, 162-164.

Martyn, Carlos. "Churchianity vs. Christianity," *Arena* 2 (July 1890): 149-158.

Miner, A. A. et al, "How to Deal with the Liquor Traffic: A Symposium," *Arena* 9 (May 1894): 827-844.

A Party Prohibitionist. "The Prohibition Party in the United States: Its Failure and the Reasons," *Anglo-American Magazine* 5 (April 1901): 307-316.

Pierce, Edwin C. "The True Politics for Prohibition and Labor," *Arena* 4 (November 1891): 723-729.

"The Prohibition Balance of Power," *The Nation* 42 (June 10, 1886): 483.

"The Prohibition Party's Vote," *The Nation* 43 (November 18, 1886): 407.

Roberts, W. H. "The Church and Men," *The Independent* 47 (February 7, 1895): 177.

Stewart, Oliver W. "Why Prohibitionists Are Undiscouraged," *The Outlook* 73 (April 11, 1903): 864-868.

Swallow, Silas C. "The Prohibition Party's Appeal," *The Independent* 57 (October 13, 1904): 832-835.

Tracy, J. V. "Prohibition and Catholics," *Catholic World* 51 (August 1890): 669-674.

Washington, Booker T. "Prohibition and the Negro," *The Outlook* 88 (March 14, 1908): 587-589.

Wheeler, Edward J. "The National Prohibition Party and Its Candidates," *Review of Reviews* 22 (September 1900): 327-332.

Wheeler, Wayne B. "The Inside Story of Prohibition's Adoption," *New York Times*, March 28-April 4, 1926.

Woolley, John G. "Has the Prohibition Party Outlived Its Usefulness?" *Leslie's Weekly* 110 (May 19, 1910): 488, 495.

_____. "The Prohibition Party," *The Independent* 52 (September 27, 1900): 2325-2327.

_____. "The Prohibition Party's Convention," *Collier's* 33 (July 16, 1904): 9.

_____. "Why I Support the Prohibition Ticket," *Arena* 32 (October 1904): 398-400.

Miscellaneous

Anti-Saloon League of America. *Proceedings of the National Conventions.* 1895-1913.

Bascom, John. *Things Learned by Living.* New York: G. P. Putnam's Sons, 1913.

Cannon, James, Jr. *Bishop Cannon's Own Story: Life as I Have Seen It,* ed. Richard L. Watson, Jr. Durham: Duke University Press, 1955.

Carhart, Albert Elijah. *A Partial Life Story, How Booze Was Beaten in a Mid-Western State.* n.p., 1931.

Cranfill, James B. *Dr. J. B. Cranfill's Chronicle: A Story of Life in Texas.* New York: Fleming H. Revell Co., 1916.

————. *From Memory: Reminiscences, Recitals, and Gleanings from a Bustling and Busy Life.* Nashville: Broadman Press, 1937.

Kearney, Belle. *A Slave-Holder's Daughter.* New York: Abbey Press, 1900.

Minutes of the National Women's Christian Temperance Union. Chicago: Woman's Temperance Publishing Association, 1888-1896.

Mulvihill, William F. *The Official Campaign Text Book of the Prohibition Party, 1904.* Chicago: Prohibition National Committee, 1904.

Nation, Carry A. *The Use and Need of the Life of Carry A. Nation.* Topeka: F. M. Steves & Sons, 1909.

Prohibition Party Campaign Text-Book, 1892. New York: Prohibition National Committee, 1892.

Prohibition Party Campaign Text-Book, 1896. Albion, Mich.: Prohibition National Committee, 1896.

Prosser, Anna W. *From Death to Life,* 2d ed. Chicago: Evangel Publishing House, 1911.

Sharpe, Mrs. H. A. Terwilligar. *Reminiscences of a Minister's Daughter, Wife and Widow.* Seymour, Conn., 1911.

Sheldon, Charles M. *His Life Story.* New York: George H. Doran Company, 1925.

Sobieski, John. *The Life-Story and Personal Reminiscences of Col. John Sobieski.* Shelbyville, Ill.: J. L. Douthit & Son, 1900.

Stewart, Gideon T. *The Prohibition Party against the Rum Power with Its Crime Ruled Political Parties and Crime Consenting Churches.* n.p., n.d.

Stewart, Jane Agnes. *I Have Recalled.* Toledo: Chittenden Press, 1938.

Swallow, Silas Comfort. *III Score & X, or Selections, Collections, Recollections of Seventy Busy Years.* Harrisburg, Pa: United Evangelical Publishing House, n.d.

Wheeler, Edward J. *Prohibition: The Principle, the Policy, and the Party.* New York: Funk & Wagnalls Company, 1889.

Willard, Frances E. *Glimpses of Fifty Years: The Autobiography of an American Woman.* Chicago: Woman's Temperance Publishing Association, 1889.

DISSERTATIONS

Adrian, Frederick Wayne. "The Political Significance of the Prohibition Party." Ph.D. dissertation, Ohio State University, 1942.

Boocks, G. Clifford. "Experiment in Municipal Reform: The

Prohibition Party in Norfolk Politics, 1892-1896." M.A. thesis, Old Dominion College, 1967.

Dohn, Norman H. "The History of the Anti-Saloon League." Ph.D. dissertation, Ohio State University, 1959.

Engelmann, Larry D. "O Whiskey: The History of Prohibition in Michigan." Ph.D. dissertation, University of Michigan, 1971.

Frederickson, Edna Tutt. "John P. St. John, The Father of Constitutional Prohibition." Ph.D. dissertation, University of Kansas, 1930.

Gemmer, H. Robert. "The Contribution of the Prohibition Party." B.D. dissertation, Chicago Theological Seminary, 1947.

Hohner, Robert A. "Prohibition and Virginia Politics, 1901-1916." Ph.D. dissertation, Duke University, 1965.

Kaylor, Earl C., Jr. "The Prohibition Movement in Pennsylvania, 1865-1920." 2 vols. Ph.D. dissertation, Pennsylvania State University,1963.

Mezvinsky, Norton. "The White-Ribbon Reform, 1874-1920." Ph.D. dissertation, University of Wisconsin, 1959.

Murrell, Daniel R. "Prelude to Prohibition: The Anti-Saloon League and the Webb-Kenyon Act of 1913." M.A. thesis, University of Western Ontario, 1974.

Otis, Delos S. "The Rise of National Prohibition, 1865-1919." Ph.D. dissertation, University of Wisconsin, 1919.

Rumbarger, John J. "The Social Origins and Function of the Political Temperance Movement in the Reconstruction of American Society, 1825-1917." Ph.D. dissertation, University of Pennsylvania, 1968.

Silverman, Henry J. "American Social Reformers in the Late Nineteenth and Early Twentieth Century." Ph.D. dissertation, University of Pennsylvania, 1963.

Silveus, Marian. "The Antecedents of the Campaign of 1896." Ph.D. dissertation, University of Wisconsin, 1932.

Small, Milton W. "The Biography of Robert Schilling." M.A. thesis, University of Wisconsin, 1953.

Turner, James R. "The American Prohibition Movement, 1865-1897." Ph.D. dissertation, University of Wisconsin, 1972.

Unger, Samuel. "A History of the National Woman's Christian Temperance Union." Ph.D. dissertation, Ohio State University, 1933.

Weisensel, Peter R. "The Wisconsin Temperance Crusade to 1919." M.S. thesis, University of Wisconsin, 1965.

Index

About the Author

Jack S. Blocker Jr. is associate professor of History at Huron College, London, Ontario, Canada. He has specialized in late nineteenth-century American political and social history. His articles have appeared in such journals as *The Historian* and the *Canadian Review of American Studies.*